FLUENCY

THROUGH

TPR
STORYTELLING

FLUENCY
THROUGH
TPR
STORYTELLING

Achieving Real Language Acquisition in School

Blaine Ray & Contee Seely

Fifth Edition

Material added in the third printing:
"Steps to Asking a Story" (pp. 69-70) and "Extended Readings" (pp. 76-77)

Blaine Ray Workshops
8411 Nairn Road
Eagle Mountain, UT 84005
Local phone: (801) 789-7743
Tollfree phone: (888) 373-1920
Tollfree fax: (888) RAY-TPRS (729-8777)
E-mail: BlaineRay@aol.com
www.BlainerayTPRS.com

&

Command Performance Language Institute
28 Hopkins Court
Berkeley, CA 94706-2512
U.S.A.
Tel: 510-524-1191
Fax: 510-527-9880
E-mail: info@cpli.net
www.cpli.net

Fluency Through TPR Storytelling
is published by

the
Command Performance Language Institute,
which features
Total Physical Response products
and other fine products
related to language acquisition
and teaching,

and by

Blaine Ray Workshops,
which features TPR Storytelling® products
and related materials.

To obtain copies of *Fluency Through TPR Storytelling*, contact one of the distributors listed on the final page, Blaine Ray Workshops or the Command Performance Language Institute (see title page).

Cover illustration by Pol (Pablo Ortega López). See www.polanimation.com. The teacher in the drawing is a likeness of Blaine Ray.

First edition published August, 1997
Second edition published October, 1998 — second printing: January, 2000
                                       — third printing: May, 2001
Third edition published June, 2002 — second printing: June, 2003
Fourth edition published November, 2004 — second printing: July, 2005
Fifth edition published April, 2008 — second printing: June, 2009
                                    — third printing: October, 2010

Printed in the U.S.A. on 50% recycled, acid-free paper with soy-based ink.

ISBN-10: 0-929724-21-6
ISBN-13: 978-0-929724-21-8

To Christy, my beautiful, loving wife of 35 years, and the greatest kids on earth — Tami, Von, Shelli and Jana.

Blaine

To Maggie, Michael and Christina — the most important people in my life.

Contee

We have ways of making you talk.

Anonymous, based on a line in
the film *Lives of a Bengal Lancer*

Contents

Acknowledgments   ix

Evolving and Spreading TPRS (Preface to the Fifth Edition)   xi
Evolving TPRS (Preface to the Fourth Edition)   xiv
Improving TPRS (Preface to the Third Edition)   xvi
What's New in This Edition and in TPRS
  (Preface to the Second Edition)   xxi
Preface to the First Edition   xxvii

Introduction   1
1   The Keys to Fluency in the Language Classroom   7
2   TPRS Essential Concepts and Practices   13
3   The Three Steps of TPRS   31
4   Developing a Mini-story through Questioning   47
5   Storytelling in the First Year   65
6   The Second Year   93
7   The Third and Fourth Years   111
8   TPRS Teaching Skills   125
9   How to Maintain High Interest and an Optimal Pace   157
10   Reading   167
11   Improved Five-Day Lesson Plan   179
12   Teaching Grammar as Meaning   183
13   Student Rapport   195
14   Adapting a Textbook for TPRS   199
15   The More TPRS List   213
16   Frequently Asked Questions about TPR Storytelling   233
17   Advantages of TPR Storytelling   247

Glossary   251

Appendix A: TPR Storytelling Presenters   263
Appendix B: Where To Find It   268
Appendix C: Research on TPR Storytelling   270
Appendix D: Vocabulary Lists: TPR and Most Frequent Words   272
Appendix E: The Grammar Covered in Three Years in
               the Look, I Can Talk! Series   276
Appendix F: Letters from Teachers   282
Appendix G: Beginning with TPR   291
Appendix H: Gestures and Kindergarten Day   306
Appendix I: Classroom Management   309
Appendix J: Multi-level Classes, Raising Enrollment and
               Teaching Present & Past Together   319
Appendix K: TPR Storytelling Materials and Other Helpful Resources
               for the TPRS Classroom   334
Bibliography   341
Chart: The Three Steps of TPR Storytelling   just before final page

Acknowledgments

We wish to thank the following people for their fine work and feedback that have figured in the development of TPR Storytelling and/or for their help in spreading the word about it in various ways:

Joe Neilson, Susan Gross and Karen Rowan have done a great deal in the development of TPR Storytelling.

Blaine's former colleagues at Stockdale High School: Gale Mackey, Dave Cline and Carole Stevens.

Melinda Forward, Shirley Ogle, Valeri Marsh, Christine Anderson, Carol Gaab, Greg Buchan, Dale Crum, Beth Skelton, Jan Kittock, Donna Tatum-Johns and Jason Fritze.

We also wish to acknowledge James Asher and Stephen Krashen, whose insights into second language acquisition have influenced our teaching, our ideas and our lives tremendously. Without their contributions to the field, TPR Storytelling would not exist.

We would like to thank especially Stephen Krashen for his detailed assistance with Chapter 12. Also Karen Rowan and Susan Gross receive our thanks for their help in writing Chapter 14 and influencing parts of Chapter 12. The chart entitled "The Three Steps of TPR Storytelling" on the next-to-last page was adapted from one devised by Pat Verano. We are grateful to her for this idea. We thank Susan Gross yet again for her own adaptation of this chart, on which we drew in revising the chart. We appreciate the advice of Helen Small, Mike Miller and Andrea Kistler about German readers.

Monique Gregory and Julie Baird contributed significant French and German material and insights. We are grateful to Susan Gross and Frank McNulty for their assistance with French details and Elisabeth Siekhaus and Helen Small for theirs with German ones.

We deeply appreciate the assistance in a variety of ways of Karen Rowan. For the fifth edition she undertook an extensive revision of Chapter 14. Nearly all of that chapter reflects her expert opinions on adapting textbooks for TPRS. We thank Scott Benedict and Tawanna Billingsley for allowing us to reproduce in Appendix I their ideas about classroom management in TPRS high school classes. Likewise, we appreciate Ben Slavic's permission to print his essay about dealing with one of his students. We also appreciate the contributions of Joe Neilson, Diana Noonan, Mark Webster and Von Ray in Appendix J. Our thanks to Amy Catania for most of the material in Appendix K. And we are most grateful to Stephen Krashen for his letter at the end of Appendix F about his experience as a student in a TPRS Mandarin course.

Last, but far from least, we thank the myriad teachers who continue to contribute their ideas to strengthen TPRS through their comments on the MoreTPRS listserv and in other fora.

Evolving and Spreading TPRS (Preface to the Fifth Edition)

As TPR Storytelling® continues to evolve and improve, it keeps spreading both in the United States and abroad. More and more students are gaining fluency because of TPRS™. We don't know how many, but very likely somewhere in the tens of thousands. I (Blaine) have given workshops in all 50 of the United States and in 15 other countries — India, Singapore, Japan, Mexico, Costa Rica, Argentina, Austria, Spain, Canada, Egypt, Senegal, the United Arab Emirates, the Bahamas, Malaysia, and the Philippines. Numerous other teachers also give workshops on TPRS and specialties within it (see Appendix A). The National TPRS Conference is becoming more and more international. We even considered changing the name to the International TPRS Conference. (We decided against it because of tradition.) The 2007 conference in Denver was attended by teachers from 20 countries. Growth is also seen on the MoreTPRS listserv, which now is subscribed to by nearly 5,000 teachers. It has been just over 20 years since I began to develop TPR Storytelling, and we now have, in a sense, second-generation TPRS teachers, teachers who acquired the language they're teaching largely in TPRS classes.

Among the most important ideas that have emerged in recent years are multi-level classes. We have seen surprising success from teachers who have eliminated levels and instead put mixed levels in one class. (See my article "Multi-Level Classes with TPRS: Unexpected Gains" in Appendix J.) I believe we will see more success with this in the future.

We continue to give the greatest emphasis to the key concepts (1) that all classes should be completely comprehensible to all students, (2) that students must hear over and over the grammatical features and basic vocabulary that are essential for fluent expression of ideas and (3) that every moment of every class should be interesting or even captivating to every student. Our ever-increasing success gives testament to the validity of these concepts, which are in general agreement with the hypotheses of Stephen Krashen. Krashen attended the most recent National TPRS Conference and, like nearly all of the other participants, took a Fluency Fast® course. At our request, he wrote us a letter about his experience in the course and about his subsequent use of the target language in Taiwan. His letter is at the end of Appendix F, "Letters from Teachers."

I (Contee) first came across TPR Storytelling in late April of 1992 at the annual conference of the California Foreign Language Teachers' Association (CFLTA, now known as the California Language Teachers' Association (CLTA)) in Modesto, where Blaine was giving a workshop. I was impressed as never before, most especially by the performance of "Princesa," one of the two first-year high school students Blaine had brought along. He asked her if she knew the story "Little Red Riding Hood." She said she did. Had she ever heard it in Spanish? No. Blaine said, "OK, I'll give you five minutes to get ready. You can draw some pictures as cues if you want to. In five minutes you can tell the story in Spanish. OK?" She said OK and remained seated facing the audience while Blaine went on addressing us teachers.

Five minutes later he said to her, "OK, ready?" She stood up and told the story in Spanish with some pauses and *uh*'s and *um*'s. She didn't know the word for *wolf*, so she substituted the word for *dog*. She told the story quite well with little preparation. She didn't use any pictures as cues. She had had about seven full months of 55-minute Spanish classes for a total (taking time out for vacations and holidays) of about 140-150 55-minute hours. Ray said that both she and "Guapo" (handsome), the young man with her, were two of his best students. He also said that even his "F students," the ones who didn't do a lot of the work that is required of them, were also able to tell stories without much trouble, although they made more mistakes.

I must have asked 50 questions, so many that even the most seasoned presenter would have felt bugged. Blaine never showed any irritation and has never mentioned this to me. He just kept giving clear, honest answers. One of the things that concerned me the most was how to get the less-talented students to acquire grammatical features of the target language correctly. At that time Blaine didn't seem to have a satisfactory answer for this question. Then and for some years afterwards, he thought that some students just couldn't acquire much of the grammar.

Now, 18 years later, as things have developed (with no influence from me about this matter), with the techniques now in common use by TPRS teachers, it turns out that even students who are on the lower end are able to acquire grammatical features and use them in their own speech. It just takes them longer than most other students.

I used to think of language teaching methods as one thing and a teacher's ways of dealing with students as another, although I knew they were both important in helping students to succeed. "Student Rapport," Chapter 13 in this edition, has not changed since the first edition was published in 1997. However, emphasis on the way students are regarded and treated has grown immensely, to the point where in recent years it is clearly an integral part of TPRS. Many key techniques are now in common use that make students and their lives central to the method and that help teachers to be truly caring about students' succeeding in school and in life. These two separate elements are both extremely effective. Integrated together they constitute a remarkably powerful package.

> Blaine Ray and Contee Seely
> Arroyo Grande and Berkeley, CA, respectively
> February, 2008

Please note:
  Some of the information given in earlier prefaces is no longer valid.

Evolving TPRS
(Preface to the Fourth Edition)

In the last two years, since the third edition of this book was first published, numerous significant developments have occurred. One major change is the name. While it is still TPRS™, we refer now to it as "Teaching Proficiency through Reading and Storytelling." We believe this describes what we are currently doing much more accurately, especially in high schools and middle schools.

We now use three steps — vocabulary, story and reading — instead of seven, as you can see on the chart on the next-to-last page of this book. Clearly the three steps are not only more effective but also much easier for teachers to follow.

Our approaches to comprehension and grammar are significantly different from before. The result is that students — the lower ones as well as the top ones — are gaining fluency faster and producing more correct spoken and written language. We are now teaching beginning classes with both the past and the present tenses from day one. Von Ray taught his level one students in both the past and the present and compared them to his level two students at the end of the year. Even though the level two students had had twice as much time in the language, the sixth-graders were much more accurate in their use of the tenses.

Our TPRS workshops for teachers have changed considerably. We have been able to identify several specific skills that help teachers to help their students get excellent results. There is more coaching and more practice in our workshops than ever before, better preparing teachers to put TPRS into practice. Chapter 5 describes these skills as well as what we have found to be the most effective use of class time. As the new name reflects, we are using more of our precious class time for storytelling and reading activities.

In 2001 Jody Klopp organized the first NTPRS, the annual National TPRS conference. Thus far we have met in Oklahoma City, Atlanta, Chicago and Las Vegas. The conferences have been hugely successful, attracting over 200 teachers each year from all over the U.S. and from many foreign countries. The 2004 conference was attended by teachers from seven countries outside the U.S. Future conferences are planned for Kansas City and Buffalo, Hartford or New Jersey.

In the summer of 2003, Associate Professor Shelley Thomas organized a summer language institute at Middle Tennessee State University. Participants were trained in Spanish for 27 hours. The results were outstanding. Sarah Moran, a French teacher, tested into fourth-year college Spanish even though she could not produce even a single sentence of Spanish before the week-long session. This year another teacher who knew no Spanish took the week-long class. The following week she attended an immersion dinner for Spanish teachers and spoke Spanish the whole evening. When she told the Spanish teachers after three hours that she only had had one week of Spanish, they didn't believe her. Every summer we are expanding the language classes, which we call Fluency Fast (see www.fluencyfast.com).

We are launching a new online quarterly publication for foreign language teaching research. It is called The International Journal of Foreign Language Teaching. See www.tprstories.com to find a link to it.

> Blaine Ray and Contee Seely
> Bakersfield and Berkeley, respectively
> September, 2004

Improving TPRS
(Preface to the Third Edition)

Five years have passed since the first edition of this book appeared. We thought and we still think that TPR Storytelling is the best way yet devised to teach and learn a second or foreign language in classrooms. Could it be even better? We (including hundreds of teachers) keep finding little ways to improve it. The major thrust in the last two or three years has been finding ways to make it more efficient. The central question in this quest is: How can we best use class time? We believe that some activities are essential for all students, that some are useful to most, and that some are of little or no use. Some activities that we had earlier considered useful, now — after closer examination and consideration — we deem to be a poor use of time in comparison to alternative uses of the time.

All language teachers know that it takes time to learn a language, more time than anyone would like. There are no Spanish or French or German or Chinese pills that will instantly allow a human being to speak, understand, read or write a language. And yet most teachers underestimate the difficulty of learning a second language. They already know the language and have a feeling of ease about it. Many don't realize just how much practice it takes to be able to speak a second language with such ease. The great majority of teachers who are teaching a language which they themselves learned as a second language learned/acquired most of it outside of the classroom.

Proficiency in a new language is achieved through human learning and living. We all know that only so much can be accomplished in a single class session. Circumstances severely limit the time we have with our students. We feel we must make the best use we can of this time.

Our main goal is to help our students become proficient in speaking and understanding their new language. We believe that the main factor in the development of proficiency is *contextualized, repetitive and varied comprehensible input that keeps learners' interest*. It follows that the great majority of class time should be devoted to providing interesting comprehensible input. So we need to (1) find ways to provide it constantly and (2) limit greatly the time used for other, less productive activities.

We ask two questions then:

1. What are the best ways to provide contextualized interesting comprehensible input?

2. What activities should we eliminate or minimize the use of?

The answers we have found to the first question are the arsenal of TPRS™ activities that we describe in this edition.

What activities should be eliminated because they are not good use of class time? One we suggested in previous editions that teachers use is games. Games are usually fun, but then so are most of the things we do in TPR Storytelling. Fun alone is not a good reason to use an activity. Theoretically, there could be games which provide contextualized interesting comprehensible input without wasting time on other things. We don't know of any yet. (Games were one of the techniques in "Techniques, Testing and Checking Comprehension" which was Chapter 2 of the first and second editions of this book. That chapter is not in this edition. Most of the techniques are now in other chapters, described in the situations in which they are used.)

There are many activities we did not mention in earlier editions but which are commonly used by some teachers and which steal valuable class time that could and should be used for efficient development of proficiency. Many so-called cultural activities are among these, such as doing reports on cultural customs, watching videos about other countries and eating foods of other cultures. The "five C's" which constitute the national standards (see www.acftl.org) of the American Council of the Teaching of Foreign Languages (ACTFL) and ten other national language teachers' associations are communication, cultures, connections, comparisons and communities. We believe that communication is the important one, that nearly all of class time should in some way be devoted to this one. This is what language classes are for. It is fine to include the other four within communication, but it is counterproductive to work on any of them in class time without at the same time mainly focusing on the development of communicative proficiency.

Always Trying to Improve

We keep learning more about how to improve our teaching. We want to know what works and what doesn't work. It is worth the effort to occasionally or even frequently test the limits of what our students can achieve. In this process we necessarily find that they reach points that are a bit beyond what they can accomplish. When we hit these "breaking points", we can always drop back to a point where they can function. For example, we have been experimenting to try to determine how early in our classes it is useful to have students read material that they can understand from what they have been exposed to orally/aurally. By challenging students in this way, often they and we find that they can do better or more than they and we thought they could. We and many other TPRS teachers would like to hear from teachers who try to test the limits. If you are one of these, please let us know the results via the More TPRS List (see below and Chapter 13).

Always Looking for Trouble

In a more limited way we are always trying to find out what details students have not yet mastered. This is most important. We must help them to master them before moving on. If we don't, they don't comprehend and then get discouraged and drop out mentally and later drop the language. We do what have been called "enabling activities" so that they do master them. This usually is a matter mostly of providing more comprehensible input through a variety of oral/aural repetitions. We look for and find students' "breaking points" and provide the necessary practice so that they don't break down at these points.

Reading

In addition to many significant changes in revised chapters, you will find two new chapters in this edition: Chapter 13, on the More TPRS List, which is described just below, and Chapter 6, on reading. More and more we have come to realize the importance of reading as a means of consolidating language that has been acquired through aural comprehension and as a way to expand vocabulary.

The More TPRS List

A major source of improvement of TPRS has been the More TPRS List, which was started in August, 1999, by Michael Kundrat, of Central Lake High School in Central Lake, Michigan, and Kristy Placido of Fowlerville High School in Fowlerville, Michigan. The ideas and opinions expressed by hundreds of teachers who are using TPRS in the classroom have profoundly affected our thinking. An important factor in this is that Blaine reads every posting on the list (see samples in Chapter 13) and takes seriously teachers' opinions. Blaine sometimes puts a new suggestion on the list and then waits for teachers to try it out and give their reactions to it. In most cases teachers find the suggestions work; they are improvements. In some cases they don't work, and so Blaine revises his thinking to fit the realities of the classroom. The Internet and the very possibility of the existence of highly interactive communication through such lists have provided an opportunity to improve more quickly and thoroughly than ever before. This phenomenon is an informal kind of research which allows, on a comparatively large scale, relatively quick testing in classrooms of hypotheses about how to teach and then revision of them, followed by subsequent testing of the revised hypotheses. To our knowledge (which is admittedly limited), this sort of interactive educational research has never been done before. It could serve as a model for educational research in other disciplines besides language teaching.

The fact that Blaine and so many users of TPRS take advantage of this opportunity is a reflection of their keen interest in a language-teaching method that has met with unparalleled enthusiasm and success.

The kinds of unsolicited comments that you can read on and inside the back cover and in Chapters 13 ("The More TPRS List") and 12 ("Adapting a Textbook for TPRS") and Appendix F are among the most favorable comments we have seen about TPRS. But they are also typical of the way TPRS teachers feel about TPRS. We have seen and heard negative comments. These have come almost exclusively from teachers who have not used TPRS. There are of course a few who find it difficult to change or even to attempt to change.

We are not aware of any phenomenon in language teaching that has ever received such widespread and enthusiastic reactions as TPRS. If it's new to you, we hope you'll give it a try. As you can see from the comments, it can make a tremendous difference in how a teacher feels about teaching and how students feel about learning and about what both achieve. If you are currently a user, we hope that this book helps you to be an even better teacher than before.

We would like to point out that we still believe that TPRS as we described it in the first two editions of this book can help teachers to help their students learn a language far better than most any other way. We of course believe that this edition can help teachers do an even better job.

Contee Seely
Berkeley
June, 2002

What's New
in This Edition and in TPRS
(Preface to the Second Edition)

In the year between the appearance of the first and second editions of this book, TPR Storytelling has gained considerable ground in the language teaching world of North America. Blaine Ray, Melinda Forward, Shirley Ogle, Valeri Marsh, Carol Gaab, Gale Mackey, Dale Crum, Michael Miller, Joe Neilson, Lynn Rogers, Susan Gross and Karen Rowan have given scores of workshops all over the continent. Articles have appeared in a leading ESL journal (see below) and in foreign language teachers' newsletters (Marsh, 1997; reprinted in three or four others). FLTeach, on the Internet, has been alive with commentary about TPRS — mostly extremely positive. (Ah, yes, it is now often called "TPRS.") Students of TPRS teachers have been actually acquiring and speaking lots of language and having fun doing it.

Stephen Krashen has given several presentations along with Blaine, has learned a lot about TPRS and has declared: "TPR Storytelling is much better than anything else out there." In his many conversations with Krashen, Blaine has come to better understand Krashen's theories of second language acquisition and learning. He now better appreciates the role of comprehensible input in acquisition. As a result, he now believes that students should receive even more comprehensible input than he thought before. In Chapter 8 there is now a thorough and accurate description of Krashen's ideas and a discussion of their relationship to the success of TPRS.

While you will find signs of this shift in Blaine's thinking in various parts of the second edition, Blaine and I do not agree with Krashen about every aspect of what to do in the second language classroom. A couple of significant areas of disagreement are the preteaching of vocabulary and frequent comprehension checking. In Chapters 1 and 2, respectively, these two important matters are discussed more thoroughly than they were in the first edition.

With all of the commotion about the successes of TPRS have come calls for research into what it accomplishes and what aspects of it account for its accomplishments. James Asher has proposed several specific research topics. As the first printing of the second edition of this book went to press, Ronald Sheen, of the University of Quebec at Trois Rivieres, was attempting to get a research project underway. Unfortunately, as of April, 2001, the project has not materialized. Still there is a great need for solid research to back up the results that so many teachers have observed. (See Appendix C for a list of Asher's proposed projects and for details about Sheen's [the latter has been left out of the third edition].)

Not every teacher who is attracted to TPRS is using it. Usually the reason is that they are tied to a textbook. A new chapter, Chapter 12, written largely by Karen Rowan and Susan Gross, is filled with practical suggestions about how to adapt a textbook to use TPR Storytelling.

At this time we are aware of several significant varieties of TPRS, and there is in addition an approach which is in large part derived from it.

Materials by Valeri Marsh, Christine Anderson and Carol Gaab of the Phoenix area are aimed at children from (1) kindergarten through third grade, (2) third grade through fifth and (3) sixth through eighth. The target languages are Spanish, French, ESL and Japanese (see bibliography for levels available in each language). Their books are very thorough and clear, both the students' books and the teacher's guides, with every step for every story spelled out for the teacher. Everything is in the present tense. One rather minor thing they do that we don't is TPR "partner vocabulary practice." It is done in two ways:

1. One partner says the vocabulary word and the other performs the action.

2. One partner performs the action and the other says the word.

Then the students switch roles, of course.

Melinda Forward, who teaches French at Springtown High School in the Dallas-Fort Worth area [but no longer does (May, 2002)], and Shirley Ogle, who teaches Spanish at Rio Rancho High School in Rio Rancho, New Mexico, are developing well-organized high school materials for Spanish, French and English. As this edition goes to press, they are available on a chapter-by-chapter basis. The first-year book is theme-based with chapters on such topics as the supermarket, the cafe and seasonal activities. The teacher's guide is extremely thorough and teacher-friendly. As part of the process of teaching the vocabulary, they have their students draw their own pictures of each new item. They often have them draw the mini-stories as well. They find that drawing enables many students to internalize the vocabulary more quickly and that it helps them to remember the story line. It particularly helps slower students. For retelling purposes, they use only mini-stories that are generally no longer than 10 to 12 sentences. They use longer stories for reading comprehension purposes. In teaching vocabulary and the mini-stories, they use oral activities — based on Berty Segal's levels of questioning (Segal, 1992) — as a "transition to speaking." They include "extension activities" to allow students to apply what they have acquired in a variety of situations. And they also give suggestions for including culture within the thematic units.

Michael Miller, of Cheyenne Mountain Junior High School in Colorado Springs, Colorado, has published two years of effective German materials which bear the title *Sabine und Michael* (1999, 2000 and 2002), based on the names of a girl and a boy who are the main characters of the mini-stories. They are useable not only at the middle school level but also in the first two years of high school and in fifth and sixth grades. Lots of cultural content is included in the stories, which are all mini-stories. The teacher material is very detailed, with quite a few suggestions for TPRS tricks, pacing, homework, etc. The materials generally function on a three-day plan. Day One the vocabulary is taught, the story is told, and the students retell the story. Day Two there is a variety of creative activities, the main one being skits made up by groups of four students. Drawing and writing are featured in others. Day Three is writing day, when students write the main vocabulary words, cognates, notes and the mini-story. Sometimes they play vocabulary games as well.

Laurie May of St. Paul's Middle School in Brooklandville, Maryland, and Kaoru Kimura of Osaka, Japan, have published three effective one-year Japanese student books called *Japanese in Action* (1998). They have been used in grades 5 through 8 and are also suitable, with minor adaptations by the teacher, for high school and fourth grade. The stories are all mini-stories. In addition to regular TPRS activities, a variety of games are included. The comprehensive teacher's manuals have explanations for the teacher in English. Illustrated by Kimura, the series has a very Japanese look to it and includes reading and writing lessons in hiragana, katakana and kanji, depending on the level of the book.

To obtain copies of any of the materials mentioned above, see Appendix B, "Where To Find It."

All of the above variations contain elements that we do not use, and yet all of them seem to be bringing about unusual success in terms of students' acquiring a new language and in terms of students' and teachers' enthusiasm. One conclusion to be drawn from this evidence, anecdotal though it may be, is that TPR Storytelling is such a powerful method that it brings impressive practical results even though some elements of it may be altered and others may be added. Despite this fact, of course some elements of it are essential to success. Obviously it is not a cure-all but it does achieve much that usually is not achieved in language classrooms.

Just as this edition was about to go to press, an article appeared in the *TESOL Journal* by Jeff McQuillan and Lucy Tse (1998) on "the narrative approach," which is based primarily on TPR Storytelling. It has much in common with TPRS but differs in certain significant respects:

1. There is no classical TPR period (five or six weeks in TPRS) or even any use of TPR.

2. The vocabulary of a story is not taught in advance. Rather, vocabulary is made "comprehensible within the context of the story." (p. 19)

3. Apparently students do not act out the stories, although the teacher does "dramatize" it.

4. After the teacher tells a story for the first time, s/he tells it again in slightly expanded form, adding a little vocabulary. Then s/he tells it a third time, expanding it further.

5. Students do not retell stories.

6. Students only tell stories that they have created themselves, individually, and they only do so on a voluntary basis. And "since students at the lowest levels are not yet able to tell stories independently, they are not asked or required to do so. They are, however, given opportunities to work in conjunction with more proficient students or the teacher to present the story, participating in whatever way they feel comfortable, including non-verbally, in such ways as role playing. Students are encouraged to narrate their stories when they themselves feel ready and are given many opportunities to do so." (personal communication from Tse, August 14, 1998)

7. Comprehension checks are thought to be largely unnecessary and even to be a hindrance since "the opportunity for students to lose themselves in a meaningful, content-focused activity is interrupted and often lost." (p. 21; this quoted clause is based on a personal communication to the authors of the article from Krashen on July 15, 1997)

As of this writing, as far as I could determine, the narrative approach has been used very little for as long as an entire semester, so there is little to judge its success on, although reportedly students enjoyed it and accuracy in speech was relatively good (personal communication from Béatrice C. Dupuy, Assistant Professor of French and Director of Basic Language Instruction at Louisiana State University, August 20, 1998).

It will come as no surprise that we prefer to do things as we describe them in this book. We feel that it is particularly important both to preteach the vocabulary of a story and to do frequent comprehension checks. Blaine's experience with not doing these two things has convinced both of us that there are serious consequences to omitting them. For discussions of these two questions, see number 1 in Chapter 1 and "Continual Aural Comprehension Checking" Appendix G.

We wish you and your students every success with TPRS.

Contee Seely
Berkeley
August, 1998

Preface to the First Edition

> They say you can't do it, but some-
> times that doesn't always work.
>> Casey Stengel

I have been a language teacher for 36 years. About five years into my career I started looking for better ways to teach. I have experimented with many. Discovering TPR was a big breakthrough for me. While it continues to be exciting for both my students and me, it alone never brought the full results my students and I wanted. I always wanted to see my students actually express their own needs, desires and ideas in the target language with considerable fluency and accuracy. While this happened with some students, I knew they were far too few.

Sometime in the '80s I found a book by the British drama teacher Keith Johnstone called *Impro: Improvisation and the Theatre* in which there is a section about his own art teacher Anthony Stirling, who inspired him to conclude that "the teacher's skill [lies] in presenting experiences in such a way that the student [is] bound to succeed" (1981: 20). I thought this was a noble goal, but unattainable to the degree that I wished in language teaching. After I discovered Blaine Ray and TPR Storytelling, I changed my mind. He has found a way, or rather a combination of ways, to accomplish this goal to a degree I had not thought possible. I want to do what I can to spread the word about this most significant breakthrough. This is why I am helping to write this book.

I would really like to have developed a method myself that achieves what TPR Storytelling does, but I think I never had the clear and broad vision about what was required to do so. For many years Blaine didn't either. But he knew what some of the missing ingredients were. And after he had done some work with TPR and a little with stories, he thought he was finding some of the answers. It is obvious in hindsight that real language acquisition in the classroom is an immense and complex puzzle.

During these last ten years Blaine has developed an expansive view of what must take place at each stage of acquisition. He has found ways to apply efficiently in the classroom much of the most insightful theory of acquisition. He is especially perspicacious in regard to what a particular technique actually accomplishes, what it doesn't and where it fits into the big puzzle. He is willing *and* able to try most anything and to replace a technique which had seemed to be the best with another that has proven to be better. By this time he appears to have nearly all the pieces in place.

I think it had to be a language teacher who would do this. A theorist, a linguist or a psychologist who is not a language teacher would not be likely to find the kinds of practical answers that Blaine has.

He has been developing TPR Storytelling for about ten years. He has had help along the way from various sources, but in the main TPR Storytelling is his achievement. It is a comprehensive method that makes use of numerous techniques. The method is founded on the language acquisition hypotheses of Stephen Krashen, tempered in some cases by realities.

Krashen has argued for some 20 years that second and foreign language acquisition — the development of real language skills — occurs through comprehensible input, not through "learning," which is exemplified by the traditional kinds of activities that occur in second and foreign language classes. He particularly opposes the use of repetition, the learning of grammar rules (with few exceptions), extreme correction of students and forced speech beyond the acquisition level of the student. He says, "Real language production happens only after the acquirer has built up competence via input." (1983: 298) Krashen's ideas are laid out quite fully in *The Natural Approach* (Krashen and Terrell, 1983: 5-62), a book which advocates the use of a method of the same name which was developed chiefly by Tracy Terrell (1977).

Where TPR Storytelling differs from the Natural Approach, broadly speaking, is in the use of techniques that foster efficient acquisition. More specifically, the major differences are in the deep ingraining of vocabulary aurally through Total Physical Response (TPR) and other techniques and in the use of stories as a means of both instilling comprehensible input and eliciting expression at the acquisition level of the student. These are very important differences that bring far different results in most students. Despite the fact that Krashen co-authored *The Natural Approach*, TPR Storytelling seems to adhere more closely to Krashen's guidelines for acquiring a language in school courses than does the Natural Approach, at least as it is prac-ticed in most circumstances.

TPR Storytelling changes the whole picture of the effect of lan-guage courses. The usual picture, in North America certainly, is one of study without the development of communication skills to a practical degree. With TPR Storytelling it is the reverse. There is very little study but considerable development of practical skills.

The number one interest of almost every student of language is to be able to speak and understand. Learning about the language is, at best, a peripheral interest for most. When students actually accomplish in courses what they want to accomplish — something they perceive as valuable to them — their attitude about the subject matter is entirely different. We have seen generations of students who are, in general, sour on or, at the very least, disillusioned with language classes. We would like to see current and future generations look on language classes positively.

There may be other methods, now or in the future, that allow large numbers of students to achieve proficiency in a second language by the end of high school. If in time any or various of these become widely used, there are sure to be significant effects on the study of languages in higher education and on society in general. In college this might allow many more students to pursue language study much further. It could affect the variety of course offerings. There might, for example, be more content courses other than literature offered in foreign languages, e.g., history or political science courses. It would also be likely to affect society in general. More people might be inclined to study, travel and work abroad; engage in international business; marry foreigners; etc. There might also be greater understanding and tolerance of native speakers of other languages and their customs. These are speculations, of course, but if they should occur only partially, they would certainly have an important influence on the lives of hundred of thousands of individuals, perhaps millions.

At the time this book goes to press, in the middle of 1997, several TPR Storytelling books and a few other materials are available for teaching. First, there are Blaine's own works which were written for high school and some of which he co-authored (most often with Joe Neilson). Gale Mackey has two Spanish song cassettes (one with lyrics and exercise book by him and Seely) based on stories in Blaine's first two textbooks. Valeri Marsh and Christine Anderson, the 1995 Arizona Foreign Language Association Teachers of the Year, have published excellent books directed at third- to sixth-graders and other books especially for seventh- and eighth-graders. Melinda Forward and Shirley Ogle have published two very helpful books for TPR Storytelling teachers and expect to have their own first-year high school French and Spanish texts out soon. See the bibliography for details on all of these.

The great majority of the ideas in this book are Blaine's. Some are mine. I filled in gaps, added opinions and removed repetitions. We both contributed in writing and in research. There is purposely still a lot of repetition of procedures used in TPR Storytelling and also of some details, so that the reader won't have to go searching so much. Our intent is to offer a variety of examples and to show how the same techniques can be applied at different levels. The book may be read straight through or piecemeal. You will find numerous cross-references. After this paragraph, any place you see the words *I, me, my* and *mine* they refer to Blaine. We welcome your suggestions and corrections. We hope you find this book useful.

Contee Seely

Berkeley

July, 1997

Introduction

For about 45 years teachers all over the world have been discovering the magic of TPR (Total Physical Response). During this time James J. Asher, Professor of Psychology at San José State University in San José, California, has presented this striking approach to hundreds of audiences of language teachers. Asher himself conducted numerous experiments in the '60s and '70s which demonstrated the effectiveness of TPR, and he has published many articles about it.

Noted language acquisition expert Stephen Krashen, Professor of Education at the University of Southern California, has stated in hundreds of presentations to language teachers and in print for at least the past 28 years that, in empirical studies which compare TPR to grammar-based approaches, TPR has always come out ahead.[1]

I first experienced the power of this technique in 1980. I ordered the first edition of James Asher's book *Learning Another Language Through Actions* (1977) and could not put it down. I read each page with intense interest as I contemplated the power of this teaching strategy. I longed for school to start so that I could try TPR for myself and find out whether language could be learned in a classroom situation much the same way that a baby learns her/his first language.

When August arrived, I started my class just the way Asher had suggested. I had my students stand up and sit down. We progressed to walking, jumping and running. After about three months my students had internalized hundreds of words. At that point, a former student of mine had just returned from six months in Costa Rica. She was the first to admit that my Spanish class (with a traditional book approach) had done nothing to prepare her to speak the language. When she arrived in Costa Rica, she said, she remembered about three words from my class.

I invited Tammy to come to my class. I was excited for her to see my students. I turned the class over to them and let them give her commands. They had her do many different crazy, zany things. They had her take off my shoe and throw it out the window — which she did to the delight of the class. One student stood up and walked to the window and looked at my shoe lying on the ground outside. He said in very understandable Spanish, "A dog runs, grabs the shoe, runs away with the shoe." I ran to the window, expecting to see that my shoe had disappeared. I was relieved when I looked out the window and saw my shoe still there. After the class I asked Tammy what she thought about it. She said, "That is the most amazing thing I have ever seen. They have learned more Spanish in this short amount of time than I learned in my first three months in Costa Rica."

As I continued to use the TPR approach with this class and others, I realized that the students were not always eager to stand up and sit down. They showed me with their faces that they had had enough. It distressed me to stop teaching through commands, but I just did not know how to keep it going and to make it interesting. I started handing out worksheets and the class became less and less productive. As the emphasis switched from TPR to learning grammar, more students started tuning out.

Over a period of five years, I tried using various, perhaps all, of the TPR books available at the time and kept running into the same roadblock. No matter what I did, if I stuck to just using commands followed by actions, before long most of my students would lose interest. This is a phenomenon which Asher, who is a psychology pro-fessor at San José State University in California, has recognized and calls *adaptation*, a term borrowed from biology which indicates that a living being which initially had been responding to a stimulus has stop-ped doing so.

A few years later I read *The Natural Approach* by Krashen and Tracy Terrell (1983). They explained that language is best acquired through comprehensible input. Therefore, I thought that if I just spoke the language in class in a comprehensible way, my students would internalize it and would over time acquire grammatically accurate fluency.

Krashen in a 1998 article said:

> TPR is not a complete method. It cannot do the entire job of language teaching, nor was it designed to do this. For beginners there are several other powerful means of supplying comprehensible input, means that utilize other ways of making input comprehensible (e.g. the use of background knowledge and pictures, as in story telling). At the intermediate level, extensive pleasure reading (Krashen, 1993a) and sheltered subject matter teaching, a form of content-based language teaching (Krashen, 1991), have produced very good results.

Part IV of the third, fourth and fifth editions (Part III in the first and second) of *Learning Another Language Through Actions* consists of a description edited by Asher of 53 three-hour lesson plans written and used by Carol Adamski with an ESL class in San José, California, in about 1974 or 1975. On page 4-32 there is a story about Mr. Smith not being able to find his umbrella. This was the first story that I taught (to a first-year Spanish class in the third month) using a procedure which I gradually developed into the method that I now call TPR Storytelling. Since this seemed to work, I decided to try teaching some other stories. I used stories from various books (including many Clifford the Big Red Dog[2] stories and others in the same vein), and I wrote some myself. Some of the latter were driven by vocabulary. My colleague Greg Buchan, a French teacher, and I took the vocabulary from a chapter in the Natural Approach college textbooks *Dos mundos* (Terrell et al., 1986) and *Deux mondes* (Terrell et al., 1988) and wrote a long story that included all of the vocabulary from the chapter.

Three years later my first-year text *Look, I Can Talk!* was published by Sky Oaks Productions, Asher's publishing company. When I was using the above-mentioned stories in the period just previous to the publication of *Look, I Can Talk!*, I found that kids hated doing long stories and mentally dropped out. So I made the stories in *Look, I Can Talk!* quite short. Actually, I had written a few of the stories in *Look, I Can Talk!* earlier and used them many times. I had already developed the basic method of TPR Storytelling in class, and I had had mixed results. It was only after writing all the relatively short stories for *Look, I Can Talk!* that almost all of my students enjoyed the process of learning Spanish through stories. In writing it, I came up with a few new activities which enhanced the process. If I had not written the book, I would probably still be using many of the stories I was using before and probably wouldn't have developed the method so quickly. Writing it helped to get everything organized into a more coherent and effective program. This was a major step in the development of TPR Storytelling, a powerful new language teaching method that combines the best of TPR and the Natural Approach and adds to them.

Notes

1. Krashen's address at the Teachers of English to Speakers of Other Languages (TESOL) conference in 1980 in San Francisco. See, too, Krashen's article "TPR: Still a Very Good Idea" (1998). Also, Marianne Nikolov and he wrote:

> Studies with adults show that students in comprehensible input-based methods are as accurate as students in grammatically based methods and are sometimes more accurate. In addition, students in comprehensible input-based methods are always superior in tests involving communication. ... Acquisition may happen most efficiently when the acquirer forgets that he is listening to or reading another language. This theory implies that second language classes should be filled with comprehensible input presented in a low-anxiety situation. This is precisely what newer and more successful methods do, such as Terrell's Natural Approach, Asher's Total Physical Response method and Lozanov's Suggestopedia. (1997)

2. There are numerous Clifford the Big Red Dog books by Norman Bridwell. Originally published in English, many of the titles are also

available in at least Spanish and French. See the bibliography for examples.

Chapter 1

The Keys to Fluency[1]
in the Language Classroom

"Current language acquisition theory claims that we acquire language in only one way, when we understand messages, that is, when we obtain 'comprehensible input.' Thus, we acquire when we understand what people tell us or what we read, when we are absorbed in the message. More precisely, we acquire when we understand messages containing aspects of language that we are developmentally ready to acquire but have not yet acquired." (Krashen, 1997: 3)

Language acquisition is not a conscious process. It is something that happens to a person. It happens when one understands messages. If a person understands messages in the target language, s/he cannot prevent the acquisition of that language. Learning to speak a language comes from hearing it. Reading helps a person advance in learning the language and structures, but generally fluency comes from hearing. Since we only learn to speak by listening and comprehension, we can assume there are no gains from listening unless there is comprehension.

First language research has studied how babies and toddlers pick up language. Parents limit vocabulary that they use with small children and often talk slowly. They don't always care if the child doesn't understand. These same things have been tried in the classroom. Teachers have tried to teach using only the target language, not translating and not worrying about comprehension, with the idea students would eventually get it.

This works with small children but it doesn't work with older humans in the classroom. The main reason is that children have over 20,000 hours in the first six years to learn a language if they hear it ten hours a day for six years. A student might only have 400 to 600 hours in the classroom to learn to speak. Since time is the main difference in how small children pick up a language compared to how students learn to speak, we have to use a different model in the classroom.

The Keys to Fluency

1. A language class must be comprehensible.

2. Students must receive sufficient aural comprehensible input of basic structures and vocabulary to be able to truly acquire them. This enables students to use them orally to say what they want to say in their new language. This is the *golden key to fluency*.

3. The aural input must continually maintain the interest of students.

4. There must be at least one vehicle for developing fluent oral expression — a way for students to express themselves orally in their own words, not memorized lines. This must include a way for them to develop an often ignored aspect of fluency — connected speech in which they say one sentence after another.

5. The class must be conducted almost completely in the target language.

6. The process must involve relatively little stress. Preferably, it should be easy and enjoyable and/or interesting.

7. Teacher expectations must be high.

The TPRS Classroom Fluency Model

The TPRS™ model for fluency consists of four main elements:

1. Making the class 100% comprehensible.
2. Frequent aural repetition of the targeted material in the development of stories.
3. Keeping the class interesting.
4. Oral interaction about students themselves, topics of interest to them and stories that they hear and that they read.

How to accomplish all of this and how to do so efficiently are what this book is about. The results achieved by applying this model consistently are extraordinary by any measure.

We target limited vocabulary in early stages, focusing on the most common words in the target language, many of which are function words — such as pronouns, conjunctions and the most common prepositions — which are some of the words necessary for the acquisition of the most common grammatical features. We do not limit grammatical features very much, mainly taking care not to deal with longer, more complex structures until later. In the first week of teaching a language we often use the past tense and some more advanced features, like noun-verb agreement and adjective-noun order and agreement.

Some grammatical features are better acquired when they are provided in contrast to other features. This is the case with the past tense. If it is delayed until the present tense is rather well acquired, the present tends to become ingrained and seems to get in the way of the acquisition of the past (see Appendix J). Overcoming this obstruction then requires much more time than simultaneous frequent comprehensible input of both tenses. (Still, one tense may indeed be acquired a bit earlier than the other in the natural order of acquisition.) If we resort to conscious learning instead of acquisition through comprehensible input, the learning is likely to be short-term and the acquirer is less likely to produce the correct tense without consciously choosing. This would slow the development of fluency. It is the repetition of the basic grammatical features of the language that causes students to acquire them and to develop fluency from early on.

Carefully limiting the vocabulary, frequent repetition of it, and quick translation (when needed) are the principal ways we use to keep a class totally comprehensible. In order to provide sufficient repetition of targeted grammatical features while simultaneously maintaining interest, we have all students respond appropriately to varying and repetitive questions about a developing story. We are ever vigilant as to how quickly students are processing what we are saying. When they are not understanding, we slow down our oral delivery and/or we clarify, usually by translating quickly; and then we move on. Keeping everything comprehensible is most essential, since students who are not following what the teacher is saying cannot be interested (they are likely to be confused or lost), nor can they acquire language that they don't understand.

We use a variety of other devices to keep the class interesting, among them humor, material about the students themselves, input from students (especially creative input), dramatization of stories with student actors, and story lines that involve problems to be solved. We are always alert to the level of student interest, always ready to shift gears when interest wanes or appears it might.

We interact with students orally about their own lives and topics of interest to them, and we read and discuss stories and how they relate to our students' own lives.

Our goals are realistic. We don't expect students to be able to speak and write their new language fluently and flawlessly as a result only of learning in a classroom. A realistic goal is for students to be able to produce the language confidently with some errors. Of course, the degree of perfection varies from student to student. In many approaches to language teaching, the goal is for students to produce with confidence and no errors. Many teachers find that they actually come much closer to this goal with TPRS than with any other way of teaching. Their students can speak with considerable confidence and can understand the spoken word better than students they had taught before they taught with TPRS.

TPRS is used to teach fluency in the classroom. One important goal is for teachers to use the class time in the most effective way possible. We believe that the best way to do this is to consistently provide repetitive, interesting comprehensible input.

Note

1. The following applies nearly always to this book as well as to the book from which it is quoted:

> The term *fluency* is used in many ways. In this book the word *fluency* alone refers to the ability to express intelligibly in speech (without reading) what one wants or needs to without undue hesitancy or difficulty. The concept includes the ability to produce one sentence after another in "connected discourse." It does not refer to grammatical correctness or native-like pronunciation. (This is not to say that correctness and good pronunciation are not important or that they should never be worked on, just that they are not part of the concept of *fluency* as we use the word in this book.) What we might call "full fluency" is quite a different concept and is more or less equivalent to *full proficiency* in a language, indicating that a person who has achieved this is able to function at about the same level as most native speakers of the language. This is what is often meant when people say in English, "S/he is fluent in Navajo" or some other language.
>
> Seely and Romijn, 1998: 35

Chapter 2

TPRS Essential
Concepts and Practices

Three pillars of TPRS are comprehension, interest and repetition.

Class must be 100% comprehensible.

There is a common saying that "repetition is the mother of retention." We agree, but we also know that in order to be effective the repeated material must be comprehensible and interesting to students. So how do we consistently provide repetitive, interesting comprehensible input? In the ten years since the publication of the first edition of this book, we have gradually developed more and more effective and efficient ways of accomplishing this. It is important to use class time efficiently since there is so little of it available for the purpose of developing proficiency in a foreign or second language. An important part of how we consistently provide repetitive, interesting comprehensible input to our students is avoiding certain common unproductive practices.

The Main Techniques of TPRS

Below we mention not only the principal techniques we use but also a few things we believe it is essential not to do. Later in the book we elaborate on these techniques and give examples of how they are used.

To keep a class fully comprehensible, our main techniques are:

1. Conscientious limitation of the input, specifically the grammatical features and the vocabulary. This means that (a) when a new item is introduced, it is clarified immediately and (b) care is taken not to introduce extraneous items.

2. Regular checking on the comprehension of a few selected students, usually by having them orally translate particular sentences, phrases and words.

3. Quick clarification whenever there appears to be lack of understanding or even a hint of doubt about meaning. The most effective means of doing this usually is (a) translating or (b) quickly asking and answering about previously introduced material.

4. Using the first language also to quickly explain grammatical elements in context. We explain them by saying what they mean, not by using grammatical terminology. We do not explain grammar when it is not in context, so we do not explain it before students meet it in context.

5. Explaining TPRS™ class procedures in the first language.

6. Using cognates and translating them whenever their meaning is not obvious to students.

7. Taking care to speak at a speed that is comprehensible to all students at any given time.

8. Making sure at all times that the pace of the class is not too fast for any of the students.

9. Having one or more students orally translate almost all readings.

10. Not directly correcting students when they make mistakes orally. Instead, we notice what element has not been acquired so that we might provide more repetitions of it. Sometimes we also restate correctly what they intended to say.

To provide oral repetitions in sufficient quantity, the techniques we utilize the most are:

1. "Asking a story," rather than telling a story. In asking a story, we are involving students in the creation of the story. Students are able to provide part of the content in the story while the teacher maintains control of the content, deciding whether or not specifics suggested by students should be included.

2. "Circling," asking a series of different types of questions about a particular fact (a phrase or a word) in a story.

3. Using different levels of questions, such as yes/no, either/or and *why* questions.

4. Making sure we keep orally providing interesting repetitions until students are able to understand the material instantly, i.e., without translating mentally. Their processing speed develops gradually as they keep hearing and understanding the repetitions.

5. Adding new details to a sentence to allow for further questioning about the same sentence.

6. Using "vertical questioning," asking students to provide more and more specific details.

To keep interest high, we do a variety of things, the principal ones being:

1. Establishing and sticking to TPRS class procedures.

2. Having students participate in the development of stories.

3. Making students the stars of stories.

4. Dramatizing stories with students often playing themselves.

5. Asking students about their lives.

6. Having discussions about how readings relate to students' own lives.

7. Using unexpected (and bizarre) content in stories and encouraging students to do the same.

8. Paying attention to signs of lagging interest and, when they appear, introducing new details, changing pace or changing activity.

Below and in the following chapters you will find many examples of these techniques and detailed explanations of how we generally proceed at the various levels.

How Early Fluency Develops in the Classroom

We get early fluency in TPR Storytelling® classes because our students hear the basic structures of the target language repeatedly while they understand the content. (Examples of basic structures are on pp. 150-152 in Chapter 8.)

We make sure they hear the structures over and over again so that they get a feeling for how words fit together in the target language. A constant goal in our TPRS classes is to have students hear a sentence enough times so that they don't have to mentally translate. This may happen rather quickly specific sentences for a particular student. But in TPRS, the teacher wants the students to go beyond just fast processing.

At first a student is a slow processor. Later, the student is a fast processor but can't produce or at least feels like s/he can't produce. With more practice, the student can produce the language without confidence. In other words, s/he can produce but is not sure s/he is saying it right. After more practice the student can produce the language with confidence and some errors. In a final stage, s/he produces with ease of expression and with very few, if any, errors.

The Fluency Circle

In TPRS we refer to the basic structures and vocabulary as the fluency circle (or the small circle). We limit vocabulary to a few hundred words. The fluency circle is a concept. It starts out very small and expands as students understand more and more language. We spend class time practicing the fluency circle. When language learners speak, they nearly always use the easiest way they know to say things. For lower-level learners, trying to use more advanced words or structures requires editing and therefore hesitancy. So they use the easiest structures and vocabulary possible. That's why we generally teach just one way to say things. We could teach the word *wants* or the phrase *would like to*. Both mean basically the same thing. But in lower-level classes we always teach *wants*, since we are teaching fluency. We would rather practice a high-frequency word or structure than one that students wouldn't really need or would likely never use.

In the series preface of the book *A Frequency Dictionary of Spanish*, editors Anthony McEnery and Paul Rayson say: "60 percent of speech in English is composed of a mere 50 function words" (Davies, 2006: vii). A look at the first 100 words in the Spanish list — and the frequency of each — shows a similar proportion. The implication is that this is the case in all languages. If we are going to teach for fluency, then much of our teaching time needs to be devoted to working with high frequency vocabulary.

The Reading Circle

The reading circle (or the big circle) includes the fluency circle but also refers to the vocabulary and structures not needed for fluency. This concept is important for teachers so they will only practice vocabulary and structures needed for fluency during class. We use our class time to work on fluency. Reading circle words do turn up in class, in readings and in speech. When they do, the teacher quickly translates them and then doesn't deal with them further.

As students read numerous novellas and other readings and discuss these month after month and year after year, their passive (comprehension) vocabulary keeps expanding and so, to a lesser extent, does their active (production) vocabulary. In discussions they inevitably use and acquire words and phrases that are outside the fluency circle. Meanwhile, the structures that they use when they speak, for the most part, are more basic (fluency circle) ones, although they are gradually acquiring more advanced structures as they progress.

The Steps of TPRS

1. Establish meaning:

   We establish meaning mainly through translation because it is clear and fast. We also use gestures, pictures, and props along with translation because they help students process the language faster. We always err on the side of clarity.

2. Ask a story:

   We ask a story because asking a question requires a response. When our students answer a question, we have evidence of comprehension. We also ask a story because we can use repetitive questions. We can use the same structure as we ask the question in many different ways. This allows the students to hear the structure many times, without adding a lot of vocabulary words, which would make it much more difficult to make the lesson comprehensible. Adding details allows us to be even more repetitive without adding more words. Often the details are proper nouns which add to the interest of the story without adding new words.

   When we ask a story (step 2), we also have the story take place in three locations. In the first location we introduce a problem. The problem is something that can be resolved like a boy needing or wanting something. In the second location we make an unsuccessful attempt to solve the problem. We either change the problem or add information about why the problem can't be solved in that location. Finally, we solve the problem in the third location. Each location allows us to look at the same problem from a new perspective. In other words, it is like starting over with the problem. This allows us to make our lessons even more repetitive, and it helps students remember the plot and the details of the story. [See also "Steps to Asking a Story" on pp. 69-70.]

3. Read and discuss:

   We (a) translate a paragraph, (b) ask the facts of the paragraph, (c) add additional details to the story and (d) create a parallel story.

a.   To ensure complete understanding we (i) choose a student to read the paragraph in English (the students' first language) or (ii) do a choral translation in which we read a line in the target language and the students chorally say the line in English. Students also write down the meaning of any word they don't understand.

b.   We simply ask the facts of the paragraph sentence by sentence.

c.   To enhance interest, we add additional details to the written story. We can add a detail by asking the students a question and having them guess or we can just tell them the detail.

d.   To make the discussion more interesting and repetitive, we also create a parallel story about a student in class. As we discuss and add details about the written story, we also add details about the student in the class.

Chapter 3 deals with the three steps in detail. There is also a reproducible chart at on the next-to-last page of the book which can serve as a reminder of the details of the steps.

TPRS Procedures

When teaching with TPRS, a teacher will do one of the following:

1.   Ask a question which the students know the answer to. Students will all answer the question. For example, the boy's duck is red. Class what color is the boy's duck? Here the class will respond chorally with the word *red*.

2.   Ask a question that the students don't know how to answer. In this case, the students guess. Class, what color is the boy's shirt? This is a fact that hasn't been established, so now the class members know they should guess the answer. Students are encouraged to guess the most interesting or creative answer. When students guess, the teacher must (1) verify the detail, (2) modify it or (3) say no and tell the class what the detail is.

3.   Make a statement of fact about the story. When s/he does, the students will respond with an expression of interest. An expression of interest would be something like "Ohhhhhhh" or "Wow."

It is important for the teacher to establish these procedures and to follow them throughout the year. If the procedures are ever not followed, the teacher stops the class and explains the procedures in English. For example, "Class, what is the name of the duck?" A student says, "I don't know." The class stops and the teacher explains, "I know you don't know. That's why I asked the question. Remember that whenever I ask a question you don't know the answer to, you have to guess. Let's try that again." Then the teacher asks the original question again.

Sometimes the teacher can have the students follow the procedures with a pat answer. A pat answer would be "I'll try that again," or "You must not have understood," or "That was weak; I'll do that again," or "That was interesting." For example, the teacher says, "The boy has a big duck." No one responds. The teacher says, "Class, that was interesting. You must not have understood. I will try that again." The teacher goes right back and repeats the sentence. This time the students respond with an expression of interest. Following through with these procedures will yield great results by the end of the year.

Don'ts and Dos

In the beginning of the first year, there is a silent period when students hear the language and don't produce it. The silent period could be very brief or it could be a longer period of time. We don't force students them to produce language. The goal of the class is comprehension. We also know that repetition is the key and that students will be able to speak when they have received enough comprehensible input.

We also don't correct errors. Instead, we notice them and soon thereafter provide more repetitions of the correct structure or form in meaningful contexts. Also, sometimes we restate just the way a parent would to a child. If the child says, "Me go store," the parent says, "Yes, honey, we are going to the store." The child self-corrects over time. We do the same thing in class. We don't point out student errors. We just restate their statements correctly.

We also don't teach grammar rules or teach about language in general. But we do teach grammar. What we want to achieve in regard to grammar is not knowledge of rules but, rather, correct production of language by students to express what they want to say in speech and in writing. In the past we have focused on the acquisition of vocabulary. But acquiring structure or how words fit together in a sentence so they sound right to a native speaker is actually the most difficult part of language learning.

We don't teach grammar out of context. All of our teaching of grammar could be described as teaching meaning, limiting the explanations to the sentence we are working on, and pointing out patterns and features that students have seen and heard before. We explain the meaning of grammatical features rather than discussing them in grammatical terminology. For example, we point out that *–aron* at the end of the word *hablaron* in Spanish indicates that they spoke in the past instead of saying that it is the third person plural preterite of the verb *hablar*. We don't teach grammar going forward. In other words, we don't explain grammar points before they come up in the stories we are teaching. We teach grammatical elements a piece at a time as they emerge in context. For instance, we teach the phrase *the cat* and the past tense form *went* separately.

Use of Translation

A prime element of this way of teaching is the frequent use of translation to make meaning clear. Teaching methods that establish meaning by gestures or pictures often leave students wondering exactly what the teacher is trying to say. Even though the teacher gestures the meaning or uses pictures, students often don't understand since the picture or gestures can have multiple interpretations. The class becomes more difficult over time because students often tune out when they don't understand.

As long as we translate and speak slowly enough, students will understand. After initially translating and speaking slowly, we generally can stop translating and can gradually increase the speed of our speech, always paying attention to students' comprehension and going back to translating and/or slowing down whenever necessary.

In Bounds versus *Out of Bounds*

If we are *in bounds*, we are taking care to be sure that our class is comprehensible to the slowest-processing student. It is always our goal to be in bounds 100% of the time.

The term *out of bounds* means someone in class doesn't understand. A teacher goes out of bounds two ways:

1. *Whenever you use a word or phrase the students don't know*, they will not understand. When this happens, just write the word on the board with the English translation. Leave it there. Students might forget the word if you erase it. Once you introduce a new word, you must practice the word. You practice the word by using it over and over. At first you ask repetitive questions using the word. Later you consciously go back and use the word. Learning the word is a function of them hearing the word enough times in meaningful contexts.

2. The other comprehension problem occurs *when the teacher speaks faster than the students can process*. If that is the case, the teacher must speak slower. It is easy to learn how to use only vocabulary words students know or to translate any time a new word is used that they don't understand. But it is very difficult for many teachers to speak at a pace at which the slowest-processing students can understand. The reason is that the teacher has a feeling of ease in the language. If the teacher feels the students know all of the words of a sentence, s/he also feels they should be able to process meaning regardless of how fast the teacher talks. For many teachers, speaking slowly is the biggest challenge in learning how to make the class 100% comprehensible to all students. One

way to speak slower is to point to a word in the front of the class and say it. Pointing to words automatically slows you down. A laser pointer is a good tool for this purpose.

Barometer Students

In order to make the class totally comprehensible, we focus on a limited number of students. I personally like to focus on no more than four. These students can be slower processors but they don't have to be. We just need some feedback from students when they don't understand. We need students who are comfortable stopping us when we are out of bounds. We coach them to give a signaled response when they don't understand. The signaled response might be hitting their hand with a fist or a time-out sign. Some teachers make signs for their students to say "slow down." Other teachers give their students red, yellow and green cards to let the teacher know how his/her speed is. We want to know whenever there are comprehension problems.

Comprehension Checks

It is important to check from time to time to be sure that comprehension is total. The main ways that we regularly check comprehension are the following:

1. When students chorally respond they are giving evidence of comprehension.

2. Ask for a show of percentage of comprehension. Ask: "How much of class have you understood?" Have them hold up fingers to represent a percentage of comprehension. Ten fingers represents a 100% while five fingers represents 50%.

3. If you say a sentence in the target language, you can then ask a student, "What did I say?" Her/his answer in the first language lets you know if that individual understood the sentence. If s/he didn't, then you would practice it through repetitive questions.

4. Say a word and ask them what you said. For example, say "cuando" and ask, "What does this word mean?"

Use of English (the First Language)

We use English in the classroom for several reasons.

1. We use it for translation. The alternative is for the students to not understand. Teachers that don't translate can only guess that their students understand.

2. We use English to explain classroom procedures. These procedures are crucial to the running of the class. The procedures have nothing to do with language comprehension.

3. We use English to explain about the language. We only explain language we have already taught or that we are currently teaching.

While the ideal would seem to be to not use English at all, we find that doing so creates huge classroom problems. Students would not understand the language or your expectations of how the class is run.

Cognates that the Students Can Hear

We want to use as many words as possible that the students understand without demonstration or translation. For example, if you say the word *elefante* in Spanish and they understand it, you don't have to do anything to teach it. You can just go ahead and use it in any context you want to. Such words are freebies for the teacher.

Easily-Taught Words

An easily-taught word is a cognate that can be taught for recognition with just a single exposure to the word. Sometimes students know a word but can't hear it. You have to be sure they can hear the word. An example of a word in Spanish that most students can't hear is *idea*. The pronunciation is so different that most students can't hear it. But it is easily learned. A word like *comunidad* in Spanish is easily taught. Once students know that *-dad* words in Spanish are *-ty* words in English, they can usually hear similar sounding words. Don't assume students can hear these words the first time you use them. Be sure to tell them the meaning unless you are absolutely sure they understand.

Another type of easily-taught word is a TPR (Total Physical Response) word — a word the meaning of which can be easily demonstrated with a bodily action. We start off with some of these with true beginners, but we limit the number of them because we want to keep adding words that are needed for fluency. See Chapter 5 and Appendix G regarding the use and limitations of TPR.

In all stories you want to use as many easily-taught words as possible. A significant percentage of vocabulary is already known by English-speaking students learning Spanish, French or German, largely because there are so many cognates. These words are a great help in speeding up the process of acquiring language.

High-Frequency Words and Grammatical Features (TPRS Words and Structures)

Since we are focusing more on grammatical features (sentence and phrase structures, verb endings, other grammatical elements, usage of them, etc.; when we use the word *structures*, we mean all of these things) than vocabulary, we want both our words and our structures to be high-frequency. And because we can teach fluency by only teaching a few hundred words, we need to be sure the structures we teach are necessary for fluency. Since you are focusing on structure, you will find it is easy to use easily-taught words and previously-taught words in the structures you are teaching. You will find a list of high-frequency words in Appendix D.

Special Word Lists

It is useful to put up lists of selected words on posters in the front of the class with the equivalent first language words. For example, to do TPRS the students need to understand the question words. So we put these words up in front of the class where students can refer to them at any time.

English	español	français	Deutsch
what	qué	que	was
who	quién	qui	wer
when	cuándo	quand	wann
why	por qué	pourquoi	warum
how	cómo	comment	wie
how much	cuánto	combien	wie viel
where	dónde	où	wo
to where	adónde	jusqu'où	wohin

We also suggest you make two other charts. These list of words with their translations stay up all year long. One is a *positive rejoinder* chart. It has words and expressions like:

> fantastic, great, wonderful, I like it, wow, marvelous, incredible, etc.

The other one is a *negative rejoinder* list:

> Oh no!, how terrible, too bad, What a pity!, How sad!, I can't believe it!, etc.

There are positive and negative rejoinder lists in English, Spanish, French and German on p. 145 in Chapter 8.

Interest

We must make the class interesting. Interest begins with comprehension. There can't be any interest without comprehension. We make class interesting by adding details to the story. There are two ways we add a detail to the story:

1. We just tell them the detail.

2. We ask a question the students don't know and have them guess. We prefer having students guess because it makes the class more interesting.

The teacher needs to firmly establish the concept of "It's my story." This allows any detail to be believable to the students since it is the teacher's story. The students have no right to question a story that isn't theirs.

Our bias is to have unexpected details in the story. Storytelling works without the unexpected details, but it is more interesting with unexpected details. Unexpected details require explanations. If a duck can fly to Hawaii in 3.5 seconds, an explanation might make the class more interesting. Possible explanations:

1. He is the fastest duck in the world.

2. He is a super duck.

3. He is a slow duck. A normal duck can fly to Hawaii in 2.2 seconds.

4. He is an electronic duck.

Here the explanation of the unusual detail can be as interesting as the detail itself.

Details also need to be specific. A book is general. We generally keep asking questions so that we end up with "Johnny's green book he bought at the 3rd Avenue Barnes and Noble in Lubbock. The book cost 33 cents and is called *Gone in 3.5 Seconds.*"

Personalization

We need to personalize our stories as much as possible for high student interest.

1. Each story has one or more student actors. The story is about the student. It uses the student's name. We verify details of the story with the student actor.

2. We use details from the student's life in the story. If the student plays football, the story is about someone who wants to play in the Super Bowl. If a student is a dancer, the story can be about someone who dances on Broadway.

3. Student actors dramatize certain parts of the story. A story might have the line *Jill taught Steve how to dance the moon-*

walk. The story stops and Jill teaches Steve how to do the moonwalk.

4. Students also have dialogue. Steve wanted to learn the moonwalk, so he went to Jill and said, "Jill, I want to learn the moonwalk." At this point, the story stops until John says to Jill, "Jill, I want to learn the moonwalk."

5. Details of the stories always make the students look good. We use famous people so we can compare the famous people to our students. Our students always are better looking or more intelligent than the famous people.

6. PQA (Personalized Questions and Answers): We ask the students personalized questions to practice vocabulary. We ask, "Who knows how to swim?" A student raises her hand. We then make the story about a girl who could swim 23 miles in just ten minutes.

Repetition

We must make our teaching repetitive in order for the students to acquire the language in the limited number of hours we have in class. We use repetitive questions to make language repetitive.

1. Circling — a basic skill of TPRS is asking repetitive questions.

    a. Start with a positive statement.

    b. Ask a question that demands a "yes" answer.

    c. Ask an either/or question.

    d. Ask a question that requires a "no" answer.

    e. Restate the negative and then restate the positive.

    f. Ask questions with who, what, where, when, etc.

    g. Make the positive statement again.

2. Add a detail to your sentence. This creates a new sentence. You can then circle the new sentence.

3. With two characters you can compare and contrast them. We do this with parallel stories and characters.

4. Go back in the story and ask previously established details.

We teach by feel. We need to feel when there is a need for more repetition. We circle to help slow processors become fast processors. If students are already processing fast (not translating), then we don't need to circle. We also circle when we practice advanced structures. Chapter 4 deals with circling in detail.

The keys to TPRS are comprehension, interest and repetitions. Most of what we do in workshops is help teachers perfect their skills. Their skills are all related to higher levels of comprehension as well as to greater interest and more repetition. There is much more about TPRS teaching skills in Chapter 8.

Chapter 3

The Three Steps of TPRS

"Asking" a story is the centerpiece of TPRS™ as it is currently practiced. It is a set of techniques that allows us to efficiently accomplish our main goal of helping students to achieve fluency in the classroom. There are three basic steps to asking a story:

1. Establish Meaning

2. Ask the Story

3. Reading

This chapter details how to accomplish each step effectively so that you can consistently provide comprehensible input while maintaining a high level of interest. We do a lot of asking. We have found that doing so is a very effective means of sustaining high interest with full comprehension and adequate input.

Step One: Establish Meaning

We establish meaning through translation. We generally practice two or three phrases in a mini-story. These phrases are written on the board and translated.

Before starting the story, you can also ask personal questions, using the words. You are practicing the words you will use in the story and also looking for personalized information you can use in the story.

We have found that there are two effective ways to start establishing meaning:

1. The teacher begins to ask the story. When s/he comes to a target phrase, s/he says it slowly and immediately gives the translation orally in the first language and also makes a gesture that represents the phrase. As s/he continues asking the story, s/he uses the gestures for the first little while whenever s/he says the target phrases. S/he also interjects the translation whenever it appears any student might not understand. S/he uses both the gestures and the translations because they help students process the language faster. The teacher is constantly aware of (a) using, as much as possible, only vocabulary students know, (b) translating words they don't know and (c) speaking slowly enough for students to be able to process the language.

2. Before beginning to ask the story, the teacher pre-teaches the vocabulary with gestures. The class practices the vocabulary by making the appropriate gesture when the teacher says a target phrase or word.

Notice that in the first option, you do not actually pre-teach the new vocabulary. You start right in with the story. We think this is probably more efficient than pre-teaching the phrases through student gestures. We are always interested in making the best use of class time to help students become more and more proficient as quickly as we can.

In any case, it is essential to have all new words translated on the board.

Step Two: Ask a Story

A mini-story is a brief story that focuses on three phrases or fewer. These phrases generally incorporate the structures to be practiced in a class session. Basic structures are used in most stories. These structures include:

there is, there are	hay
has, doesn't have	(no) tiene
wants to + VERB	quiere + INFINITIVO
prefers to + VERB	prefiere + INFINITIVO
needs to + VERB	necesita + INFINITIVO
is going to + VERB	va a + INFINITIVO
has to + VERB	tiene que + INFINITIVO
likes to + VERB	le gusta + INFINITIVO
there is, there are	es gibt
has, doesn't have	hat, hat nicht + VERB, hat kein + NOUN
wants to + VERB	will + INFINITIV
prefers to + VERB	VERB + lieber
needs to + VERB	braucht + zu + INFINITIV
is going to + VERB	VERB + *später oder* wird + INFINITIV
has to + VERB	muss + INFINITIV
likes to + VERB	VERB + gern
there is, there are	il y a
has, doesn't have	a / il n'a pas
wants to + VERB	veut + INFINITIF
prefers to + VERB	préfère + INFINITIF
needs to + VERB	a besoin de + INFINITIF
is going to + VERB	va + INFINITIF
has to + VERB	doit + INFINITIF
likes to + VERB	aime + INFINITIF
goes to the house of ...	va chez ...

As the year progresses, each story will practice a new structure or two. Your goal is to always practice the basics of communication.

Before starting your first story, make sure all of the question words are posted in the class with their English equivalents. They will be on a chart or on the board. Also, be sure the two or three phrases of the story, with their translations, are visible to everyone.

Preparing a Mini-story

1. Establish a problem. Look in the teacher's guide and see the suggested problem. A problem is something that can be resolved. For example, a boy/girl needs or wants something.

2. Write down two or three structures and translate them. Your goal is to practice these structures, but you needn't worry about it if you don't.

3. In a TPRS student book there are two stories. The first story is a shorter story. The second story is the extended reading. The shorter story is a skeleton story. To prepare, look at the story in the student book and make a list of the facts of the story. Each sentence can be a fact but it doesn't have to be. You might write down 20 or 30 facts or statements.

4. Review the facts of the story. Find the things in the sentence that can change. Underline them. These are your variables. For example, a boy has a red horse. In this sentence, *boy*, *has*, *red* and *horse* are all variables. Each one can change.

5. After you have identified the variable, write down an alternative variable. You could have 20 or 30 variables with an alternative variable for each one in each story.

6. Add additional variables. In the teacher's guide you will see the story has been scripted for you with suggested answers. Many of these suggested answers were not a part of the story. Add any of these details with variables. You will also add any other details and variables.

7. Add a parallel character. This character will not be a part of the story. He will actually be part of another story. The parallel character is there so that you can compare and contrast the main character with the parallel character.

[See also "Steps to Asking a Story" on pp. 69-70.]

Creating a Story for Class

The first story of *Mini-stories for **Look, I Can Talk!**: with an Extended Reading for Each Mini-story* (Ray, 2004) is about a boy who wants cats. The first step to plan the story would be to establish a problem. Your story might be about a boy who wants cats, lots of cats, five cats, blue cats or orange cats. The problem is actually a fact of the story. The teacher's guide suggests the problem is: "A boy wanted to have two blue cats."

Now that you have the problem established, you will also want to write down some phrases that you will practice. For the first story you will need at least five phrases. These phrases will be used in most mini-stories throughout the year, so this is the only time you will start out with five phrases. They are:

> There was a boy
>
> He wanted to have two blue cats
>
> He was
>
> He had
>
> He went
>
> He liked them

You are now ready to write down the facts of the story. Look in the student book and write any facts of the story you want. Even though the story is written in the present tense, you write your facts in the past. (See Appendix J.) Below are the facts of the story with the variables in italics. In parenthesis are the alternative variables.

1. There was a *boy*. (elephant)

2. He wanted to have *two blue cats*. (four green gorillas)

3. He lived in *California*. (Hong Kong)

4. He went to Wyoming because he wanted to talk to the *president of the cats*. (an elephant from India who was visiting Wyoming)

5. He wanted to have *blue cats*. (green gorillas)

6. The president didn't have any *blue cats*. (green gorillas)

7. The president had *red cats and green cats*, but he didn't have any *blue cats*. (black horses and red elephants) (green gorillas)

8. The boy went to *Australia*. (Cairo)

9. He wanted to talk with the *vice-president of the cats of Australia*. (an elephant in Cairo)

10. The *vice-president of Australia had two blue cats*. (an elephant in Cairo had green gorillas)

11. The boy liked *the cats*. (the gorillas)

12. He grabbed *the cats*. (the gorillas)

13. He went to *California with the cats*. (Kalamazoo with the gorillas)

14. Additional details as questions with sample answers:

15. What was the boy's name? (David)

16. Did he have cats? (Yes, he had cats.)

17. How many cats did he have? (He had two cats.)

18. What color were his cats? (White)

You have written down the facts, identified the variables, listed alternative variables, and added other possible facts and variables. So now you are ready to plan the parallel story. The following are suggested facts of a parallel story. These sentences are also subject to change.

1. There was a girl.

2. She had a mouse.

3. She wanted to have a horse.

Now you can add this information to the story. The only reason you are adding a parallel character is for help in circling (repetitive questioning). With two characters it is much easier for you to ask repetitive questions about two characters instead of one. The parallel story doesn't go anywhere. It only serves the dual purposes of making your questioning more interesting to the students and providing more repetitions.

Choose Student Actors

You are now ready to choose (an) actor(s) or (an) actress(es) for your story. Since the action is really more between you and the class, these actors are more props than real actors. Some of them are truly props, such as a rock, a tree or a door that can be opened and closed with a fist as a doorknob. They don't really do anything until you say something that can be dramatized. At that point, wait until the actor actually carries out what you said. Then go back to asking questions.

Student actors also verify details of the story. If you say there was a boy who wanted to have blue cats, you would turn to your actor and ask, "Did you want to have blue cats?" The boy would verify that fact since the story is about him. We would like a complete sentence from our student actor. Naturally, as the students improve in the target language, the actor answers with a complete sentence when s/he verifies the information in the story. (If the student doesn't know the "I" form of the verb, you tell him.) This allows students to hear dialogue and acquire appropriate correct verb forms in a realistic context.

Three Locations

A mini-story has three locations. We have found it useful to have three locations in mini-stories, because at each location it is easy to come up with more repetitions while asking questions related to the problem in the story.

1. In the first location you introduce a problem.

2. In the second location you try to solve it but, for some reason, the problem is either changed by adding more information or the problem isn't solved.

3. In the third location you solve the problem.

Asking a Story

Before starting the first story, you explain the procedures to the class. You say, "Class, I am only going to do three things."

1. I will ask a question that you know the answer to, and you will all answer the question.

2. I will also ask a question that you don't know the answer to. In that case, you will guess the answer. Since the story is a (target language) story, I will only allow answers in (the target language), or you may also answer with proper nouns.

Proper nouns are names of people, places or things that begin with a capital letter, like McDonald's.

3. I will also make a statement. When I make a statement you will respond with an expression of interest. An expression of interest sounds like this. "OHHHHHH." (You can also point to your chart of positive rejoinders and suggest they say one of them also.)

Remember to use gestures for the target phrases of the story and to translate anytime any student seems unclear on meaning. Both of these techniques will accelerate students' processing time.

When you ask a story, you can add information in two ways:

1. You can just say the detail.

2. You can ask a question that the students don't know how to answer, and they will guess. (We prefer letting them guess because it is more interesting for the students and for the teacher.) When the students guess, the teacher listens for the most creative answer. If students don't give a creative answer, the teacher says, "No." S/he then tells the students the answer. For example, "Class, was there a boy?" The students say, "Yes." The teacher says, "No, there was a girl." Now you have established the first detail. You will now add another detail to the story. You can either tell them or ask. You prefer to ask, so you say, "Class, where did the boy live?" The students suggest Atlanta, New York, or Chicago. Each of these answers was an expected response. You would say, "No." The boy lived in Council Bluff, Iowa." Since you just made a statement, students would then respond by saying, "OHHH." You have now added a statement to the story. Whenever you have the students guess, you can (a) accept one of their answers, (b) modify one of their answers, or (c) say "no" and give your own answer. You must always do one of these three things. This is a conversation with the class. You can't ask a question and not establish an answer.

Since you have added two details, you now have a choice of (1) going back in the story and asking a previous established detail, (2) circling or (3) adding another detail. You can circle if you feel the students are translating (processing slowly) or need more practice with the structure of the sentence. Otherwise, you can go back in the story and ask any established detail in any question form.

You might ask, "Was there a boy? Was there a girl? What was there? Where did the boy live? Did the boy live in Chicago? Who lived in Council Bluff? Where did the boy live?"

After asking several questions of facts that have already been established, you are now ready to add another detail to the story. You can only add a detail in two ways: You can tell them, or you can ask a question the students don't know the answer to and have them guess. You decide to add the problem to the story. (The problem now has changed. It is now that there was a girl from Council Bluffs who wanted a big elephant.)

"Class, did the girl want cats?" If you class responds with yes, you would say, "No, the girl wanted a big elephant." Now you have added another detail to the story. Whenever you add a detail to the story, you have three options:

While asking a story, you only have three options:

| Go back | Circle | Go forward |

1. Go back and ask previously established details. (After you have more than two or three details in the story, you always go back.)

2. Circle. (See below) There are only two reasons to circle.

   a. You circle to practice a new structure.

   b. You circle to reduce processing time. (As students' processing time gets faster, your need to circle decreases unless you are practicing a new or advanced structure.)

3. Go forward. (You go forward only by adding a detail. You want to be careful to not add details too fast.)

As you continue to add details, you always have the option of adding your parallel character at any time. The purpose of the parallel character is to compare and contrast as you ask repetitive questions about the story.

Continue adding details after you have gone back and asked previously established details. When you don't know where to go, have your student go to another location. Going to location two is adding more information to the story.

You can only add a detail in two ways. You can tell the class or you can ask them a question they don't know how to answer and have them guess. You can say, "The girl went to Medicine Hat, Canada." Or you can ask, "Class, where did the girl go?" Students then guess where she went. If a student makes a creative response, you agree with the student and that location will be a part of the story. Any time you add a detail to the story, you can circle, go back in the story or go forward by adding another detail. Usually you go back and ask about previously established details.

When you have students guess, you must establish the detail (answer the question) before going on. You can accept an answer by saying yes and restating the answer. You also can say "yes" and restate the answer with some modification, or you can say "no". If you say "no," you must follow up with a statement that tells the class the detail.

The story continues like this until you eventually solve the problem. You don't care how long the story lasts. You only care about whether the story is interesting and engaging. Comprehension will keep your students engaged. The details will add interest to the story.

Types of Questions

You can ask binary-type questions (*yes/no*, *either/or*), or you can ask questions with question words (*who*, *what*, *when*, *where*, *why*, etc). We have observed that beginning TPRS teachers tend to ask binary-type questions. Teachers should ask more challenging questions even with beginning classes. In a recent class I asked over 180 questions in 25 minutes. One-third of the questions were binary-type questions. Two-thirds of the questions were more advanced types of questions. In the same 25 minutes, I added nine details to the story. That means I went forward only nine times while going back 175 times. These numbers give a fairly good indication of what should happen in a beginning class.

Step Three: Reading

An important part of TPRS is reading. All TPRS books have readings or extended readings. It doesn't matter which story you read and discuss. There are four steps:

1. Translate by paragraph. The reason you translate a paragraph at a time is to keep the discussion focused. You might have a student translate the entire paragraph. During the translation, other students will write in the translation of any unknown words. Another option is to read a sentence in the target language and let the students chorally translate the sentence. Be sure that students write in the translation of words they don't know so they will be able to fully understand the discussion.

2. Ask the facts of the story. The facts of the story are written and can't change. You just look at the sentences in order and ask students about them one by one with different types of questions. It is easy for students to answer the facts.

3. Explain to the class that the readings don't include all of the information about the story. Remind the class that it is "your story" as you add information to the story. Plan the details by reading the teacher's guide for ideas that will make the discussion more interesting. As always, add a detail by making a statement or asking a question that the students don't know how to answer and having them guess. When they guess, either (a) verify the detail, (b) agree with the students but modify it, or (c) say no and tell them the detail. Adding details heightens interest.

41

4. Develop a parallel story. The parallel story is about a student in the class. It is a key part of the discussion of the written story. The original story is about a boy named John, but the parallel story is about Jane from your class. As you discuss and add details about the written story, also add details about Jane and compare what happens in the two stories. When you do this, you are both making the discussion much more interesting and providing more opportunity for repetitions of targeted content.

[In "Extended Readings" on pp. 76-77, we recommend a fifth step.]

For example:

There is a boy named John. He wants to buy a piano. He goes to Pianomart. They have a little piano but John wants a big piano. He goes to Pianos are Us and they have a big piano. John is very happy. He buys the piano and goes home.

1. Students translate this paragraph aloud, as mentioned above, and they write in translations of words they don't know.

2. After the translation, you ask the facts of the story:

Is there a boy? What is his name? Is John a boy or a girl? What does he want? Who wants a piano? Does he want a big piano or a little piano? What does John want? Where does he go? Who goes to Pianos are Us? Why does he go to Pianos are Us? What do they have at Pianos are Us? Do they have a big piano or a little piano? Who has a little piano? Where does John go? Why does he go to Pianos are Us? What does he want to buy? Does he buy a big piano or a little piano? Who buys the little piano? Where does he go with the piano? (All of these questions are about the facts of the story.)

3. Next you ask about facts that aren't in the story. These are questions the students don't know the answers to, so they guess. You are trying to get a thread going, where one detail will lead to a more specific detail:

Where does John live? (Hawaii — students guess and you choose the most creative response.) Where does he live in Hawaii? (Maui) What part of Maui? (Lahaina) Where does he live in Lahaina? (On the beach) Why does he live on the beach? (He has a friend who lives on the beach.)

4. Parallel story:

What is the name of the girl? (Jane, a student in our class) Is Jane a boy or a girl? What does she want? (A cat) Who wants a cat? (Jane) What kind of cat does she want? (A cat from Peru) Who wants a cat from Peru? (Jane) Where does Jane go to get the cat? (Bolivia) Who goes to Bolivia? (Jane) Why does she go to Bolivia? (She wants a cat from Peru.) Is there a cat from Peru in Bolivia? (Yes, she finds a cat from Peru and is happy.)

Notice the wide variety of possibilities in the discussion. Your own creativity is the only limitation.

Pop-ups

We frequently use "pop-ups." Pop-ups are questions about meaning, very often about the meaning of grammatical elements. *Quiere* in Spanish means *he wants* (or *she wants*). We want our students to feel *he wants* and not just *wants*. If they just feel *quiere* means *wants,* then they will be more likely to make statements like "Yo quiere" ("I he wants"). Therefore, we always point out exact meanings of words. We want our students to know the difference between *quiere* and *quieren.* We also want them to know the difference between *quiere* (present tense) and *quería* (a past tense). We ask repetitive questions all year long about the differences in meaning between the same words with different endings. We want our students to *focus* on the exact meanings of the different endings. Asking pop-up meaning questions is an important part of TPRS and it never goes away.

Vertical versus Horizontal Questions

We want to make the discussion of the reading as interesting as possible. We do this by adding details. We add details by doing both vertical and horizontal questioning.

We think of a sentence and ask the question, "What don't we know about this sentence?" If the sentence is "The boy has a book," then we can think of some vertical questions about the boy. What don't we know about the boy? *A vertical question has an answer that leads you to ask another question about the same topic, often a more specific question.* You generally want to develop a thread of several questions. For example:

Boy:

What is the name of the boy?	John.
Where does he live?	Hong Kong.
Where does he live in Hong Kong?	In a house.
Where is the house?	Kowloon Blvd.
Why does the boy live in a house in Hong Kong?	He likes Hong Kong.
Why does he like Hong Kong?	His favorite duck lives there.
What is the name of the duck?	Afflack.
Why does the Afflack duck live there?	He is a friend of John.

You ask horizontal questions with the idea of starting a new thread of vertical questions. In relation to the thread of vertical questions above about the boy, asking about the book would be a horizontal-type question because it isn't about the boy. But you could start a new vertical thread about the book by asking, "What don't we know about the book?"

Book:

What was the name of the book?	*Heidi*
Where did he buy the book?	Borders in Hong Kong.
How much did he pay for the book?	Thirteen cents.
How did he pay for it?	MasterCard.

| What did he do with the book? | He gave it to the Afflack duck. |

Another example of horizontal questioning is going off on a tangent from the original statement. You start with "The boy has a book," but you also want to know about the boy's mother, so you ask a horizontal question about her to lead to a thread of vertical questions:

Mother:

What is the name of the boy's mother?	Shirley.
Where does Shirley live?	Tokyo.
Why does she live in Tokyo?	She has an apartment there.
Why does she have an apartment there?	She likes to visit Hong Kong.
Why doesn't she live in Hong Kong?	She doesn't speak Chinese.

These stories and readings are infinitely expandable. Details are the key to interest.

On the page that precedes the final page of this book, you will find a summary of the three steps of TPRS in the form of a chart. You have our permission to copy the chart for classroom use.

Chapter 4

Developing a Mini-story through Questioning

A very effective and efficient way we have found to develop fluency is to create mini-stories in collaboration with our students by repeatedly making statements and repeatedly asking questions based on those statements. On the face of it, this sounds very boring. However, we have ways of actually making it very interesting and entertaining. Some of these ways are illustrated in this chapter.

Three Locations

A very useful device that is having mini-stories take place in three successive locations:

1. In the first location, a problem is introduced.

2. In the second location, there is an attempt to solve the problem, but it fails.

3. In the third location, the problem is usually solved in some way.

Using three locations helps student remember the details of the story, since they can identify certain language content with each location. It also allows for more repetition of aural comprehensible input.

Circling

Circling is a basic technique or skill of TPRS™. Circling is a way to make a statement repetitive by asking repetitive questions. Circling involves just one statement. Circling always starts with a statement:

> The boy wants to have a cat.

We then ask a question that gets a yes answer:

> Does the boy want to have a cat?   Yes.

(Generally such a simple question would seem silly, but to a beginning language learner it feels good.)

We follow up with an either/or question:

> Does the boy want to have a cat or a dog?   A cat.

We then follow up with a question that gets a negative answer:

> Does the boy want to have a dog?   No.

We then state the negative and restate the positive:

> No, the boy doesn't want to have a dog. The boy wants to have a cat.

We then ask any *who*, *what* and *where* questions that make sense:

> Who wants to have a cat?   The boy.
>
> What does the boy want to have?   A cat.

And we restate the positive again:

> Yes, the boy wants to have a cat.

Now we have completed the circle.

In circling we have to learn some other skills:

1. Whenever possible, we say back the entire answer. We get used to repeating the statements to the students so they can hear them again.

2. We gesture negatives. When we say he doesn't want to have a dog, we gesture the negative.

3. We don't follow the predictable order. We don't want anything in TPRS to be predictable. Therefore we do the questioning out of order. We suggest teachers make a poster of the circling steps and put it on the wall. It is always there for reference and will help teachers ask the questions out of order.

4. You can create a parallel sentence about a student. The boy wants to have a cat. Shirley wants to have an elephant. Now you have two positive statements. You can circle both statements at the same time. In fact, we have found it is much easier for beginning TPRS teachers to get lots of repetitions by circling two sentences.

Circling Different Parts of the Sentence

1. The variable can be the subject of the sentence. In the statement *The boy wants to have a cat*, the boy can be a variable. In your either/or statement you can ask whether the boy or Shirley wants to have a cat.

2. You can also make the verb a variable. You can ask, "Does the boy want to have a cat, or does the boy have a cat?"

3. You can also make *cat* the variable: "Does the boy want to have a cat or a dog?"

Expanding the Statement

Now you are ready to make the first sentence of your story longer. Remember you can only add one detail at a time. There are lots of possibilities for more details. For example, we don't know anything about the cat. You can add details about the cat one at a time. The cat might end up being a small, blue plastic cat. Each detail is added and circled before adding another detail. For instance:

Class, does the boy want to have a big cat?

If the class all says yes, you will disagree and say:

No, the boy wants to have a small cat.

Now you have established new information, so you circle the new information:

Does the boy have a big cat?

No, the boy doesn't have a big cat, but he wants to have a small cat.

Does he have a small cat?

No, he doesn't have a small cat. He wants to have a small cat.

Does he want to have a small cat or a big cat?

Who wants to have a small cat?

What kind of cat does he want to have?

Yes, he wants to have a small cat.

You have circled the one new piece of information. At any time, you can also recycle information. For example, you can go back and also ask questions about your student:

Does the girl want to have a small cat?

No, the girl doesn't want to have a small cat. Shirley wants to have an elephant.

What does Shirley want to have?

What does the boy want to have?

Who wants to have an elephant?

Who wants to have a small cat?

Does the boy want to have a small cat?

What does the boy want to have?

Yes, the boy wants to have a small cat.

You have now recycled old information and circled the new detail. Now you are ready to add another detail. For instance: "Class, what kind of cat does the boy want to have?" They suggest possibilities. You listen for unexpected responses. One student suggests a white cat, another one says a black cat, and another one says an orange cat. These were all expected responses, so you say, "Ridiculous. Class, it is obvious. The boy wants to have a purple cat."

Now we know the boy wants to have a small purple cat. Now the possibilities for repetitions grow geometrically. You are now able to compare and contrast a big purple cat with a small purple cat. You continue to circle and recycle. You will notice that you have spent 15 to 20 minutes and you have only been working on *one* sentence. You might be tempted to go on through the story, but don't. Keep working on the one sentence. Your students need the repetitions. Continue to add a detail and circle and recycle even more.

After 20 or 30 minutes working on the first sentence, you are now ready to go to the second location. For example, you say:

Class, where is the boy?

Listen for responses. You will only accept an unexpected response. If only expected responses are suggested, you say:

Class, it is obvious. The boy is in Cairo, Egypt.

You have established where the boy is. So now you can attempt to solve the problem. For example:

Class, who is in Cairo?

Is the boy in New York or Cairo?

Where is the boy?

Does he want to have a cat in Cairo? (The class says yes. You say no.)

Class, there is a problem. There are *no* cats in Cairo. There are 13 elephants and two gorillas, but there are *no* cats.

Where does the boy go? (Someone in the class suggests Alaska.)

You say:

Yes, he goes to Alaska.

You have now made a new statement that needs to be circled:

Class, does the boy go to Alaska or California?

Does the boy go to California?

No, he doesn't go to California. He goes to Alaska.

Who goes to Alaska?

Why does he go to Alaska?

This is the first time you have asked why. You can ask why here because you spent 30 minutes on the phrase *wants to have*. Since you spent so much time on that phrase, your students should be able to produce it. So the class will say, "He wants to have a small, purple cat." You say:

Correct, he wants to have a small purple cat. Class, is there a small purple cat in Alaska? (Someone says no and someone else says yes.)

No, there isn't a small purple cat in Alaska. There is a small blue cat, but not a small purple cat.

You have made a new statement, so it must be circled:

Is there a cat in Alaska?

Is there a blue cat?

Is there a purple cat?

Is there a big cat?

Is there a small purple cat?

What kind of cat does the boy want to have?

Yes, he wants to have a small purple cat.

Is there a small purple cat in Alaska?

No, there isn't a small purple cat in Alaska. There is a small blue cat.

At this point you can add more details or have the boy go to the third location. In the third location there will be a small purple cat. The boy will have the cat and be happy.

Key Points in Developing a Mini-story Through Questioning

1. Start with a small sentence.

2. Circle every part of the sentence that can be circled (when you have slow processors in your class).

3. Recycle often by going back to the beginning of the story and asking previously established information.

4. Never make a statement without circling it (when you have slow processors).

5. Introduce the problem in location one. Attempt to solve it in location two. And solve it in location three.

6. Remember that your students don't know the language and need all the repetitions you can give them. You know the language and feel it is easy. You will likely have a desire to not give them the repetitions they need. To get to be a good TPRS teacher you will learn to thrive on repetitions by following the above model.

Another Example of Developing a Mini-story Through Questioning

To get the repetitions of the words, you have to ask questions. Try to use one of the vocabulary words in each question. You aren't trying to get the students to say the new word. You are only trying to get them to *hear the new word in context. The best use of class time is comprehensible input.* This is what brings about real acquisition and long-term remembering.

In TPRS we make a statement and then we mirror the statement in a question. We say there is a boy and then we ask, "Is there a boy?" Asking questions using the same word feels repetitive to teachers. Since teachers already know the target language, they have a feeling of ease in the language. They don't feel the need for repetitions because they already know the language. It is hard for a teacher to see how important these repetitions are. Yet in the end, it is crucial in teaching language to give the students as many repetitions of the word as possible. We want all the students to be successful.

When you ask a question, wait for a response from your class. You can have students shout out the answer, or you can have them raise their hands. When they give an answer, you answer with *yes*, *no* or *almost*. You are listening for the most interesting response. For example, if you ask for the gorilla's name:

TEACHER	INDIVIDUAL STUDENTS
What is the gorilla's name?	Bubba Smoothie.
Yes, correct. His name is Bubba Smoothie. (You say "yes" because the answer was bizarre. You must verify the answer, modify it, or tell them the answer. For example, "No, his name isn't Bubba Smoothie. His name is Fred.")	
Where does Bubba Smoothie live?	The zoo.
No. (Once again you verify the answer, modify it, or say "no.")	New York.
No.	Africa.
Yes. What part of Africa?	Big Creek, Egypt.
Correct. How long does it take to go to Big Creek, Egypt? (Again, you verify the answer, modify it, or tell them the answer. In this case you modify the student's answer.)	13 years.
Almost. Actually it takes 13 years and 3.2 seconds.	(New plot information, so the class says:) Ohhh!

The interaction that takes place in this questioning process is where most of the interest is generated in the mini-story.

It is helpful to have details of the story in mind already. If you have taught a mini-story earlier in the day or have planned it before the class, you have lots of possible details already in your mind. When you know you want the boy to go to Dripping Springs, Texas, you ask the question, "Where does the boy go?" Someone replies, "New York." You must verify the answer, modify it, or tell the class the answer. You say no. You say no to any answer and then you tell them the correct spot is Dripping Springs, Texas.

Start the story with your actors in front of the class. Whenever you are speaking to the class, you make eye contact with the entire class. You always look at them when you ask questions. When you give plot information, you look away from the class to your actors. You make sure they carry out the plot. If you say the boy is sad, you look at the boy to make sure he is acting sad. If he isn't acting sad, you repeat, "The boy is sad." If he still doesn't act sad, you repeat the same sentence and model it exactly the way you want the student to present it.

You present the story like this:

TEACHER	CLASS
There is a girl.	(This is plot information, so the class responds with:) Ohhhhhhh!
Is there a girl?	Yes.
Is there a girl or a boy?	A girl.
Is there a boy?	No.
What is the name of the girl?	Princesa de la clase de español. (This is the girl's actual nick-name in class. She keeps her same name because she is playing herself in the mini-story.)
Is her name Princesa?	Yes.
Is her name Princesa de la clase de español?	Yes.
Is her name Bubba?	No.
What is her name?	Princesa de la clase de español.
Princesa thinks she is a gorilla. (Princesa acts like she is thinking.)	(Plot information so the class says:) Wow!
Does Princesa think she is a gorilla?	Yes.

TEACHER	CLASS
Does she think she is a gorilla or an elephant?	A gorilla.
Does she think she is an elephant?	No.
Does she like gorillas?	Yes.
Does she think she is a big gorilla or a little gorilla?	Little.
No, she thinks she is a big gorilla.	Ohhhhhhhh!
Why does she think she is a gorilla?	(Any possible answer would be accepted here.)
What does Princesa think?	She is a gorilla.
Is this a problem?	Yes.
Why?	She is a girl.
Is she a girl or a gorilla?	A girl.
Princesa goes to the doctor. (The teacher moves Princesa to doctor number one.)	Ohhhhhhh!
Does she go to the doctor?	Yes.
Does she go to the moon?	No.
Where does she go?	To the doctor.
Who goes to the doctor?	Princesa.
Why does she go to the doctor?	She thinks she is a gorilla.

TEACHER	CLASS
Does she think she is a gorilla?	Yes.
Who thinks she is a gorilla?	Princesa.
Where is the doctor?	In Bliss, Idaho.
Yes, that is right. The doctor is in Bliss.	
What is the name of the doctor?	Bud.
Yes, his name is Bud.	
Does Bud like gorillas?	No.
But you say, "Yes, Bud really likes gorillas. Bud has five gorillas at his house in Bliss. Bud wants 13 more gorillas."	Ohhhhh!
The doctor says, "You aren't a gorilla. You are a girl."	Ohhhh!
Does the doctor say, "You are a girl"?	Yes.
Who says, "You are a girl"?	The doctor.
What does the doctor say?	You are a girl.
The next day Princesa goes to another doctor.	Ohhhh!
Does Princesa go to another doctor the next day?	Yes.
Who goes to another doctor the next day?	Princesa.
Does Princesa go to another doctor the same day or the next day?	The next day.

TEACHER	CLASS
When does Princesa go to another doctor?	The next day.
The doctor thinks for 23 years.	Ohhhh!
Does the doctor think?	Yes.
Does the doctor think a lot or a little?	A lot.
But you answer back, "Not a lot, only 23 years."	Ohhhh!
Who thinks for 23 years?	The doctor.
Does the doctor think exactly 23 years?	Yes.
No.	Ohhhh!
The doctor thinks for 23 years and 13 seconds.	Ohhhh!
Finally he says, "You are a girl but you need gorilla hair."	Ohhhh!
Finally, does the girl need gorilla hair?	Yes.
Who finally needs gorilla hair?	The girl.
Who finally says the girl needs gorilla hair?	The doctor.
The next day she goes to the hospital and receives gorilla hair.	Ohhhh!
Does she go to the hospital the next day?	Yes.
Who goes to the hospital the next day?	The girl.

TEACHER	CLASS
Why does she go to the hospital the next day?	She needs gorilla hair.
Where is the hospital?	Florida.
No. The hospital is in Celeryville, Ohio.	Ohhhh!
What is the name of the hospital?	The Celeryville Medical Center.
That is correct. Does she need gorilla hair or cat hair?	Gorilla hair.
What does the girl receive the next day?	Gorilla hair.
Who receives gorilla hair the next day?	The girl.
When does the girl receive her gorilla hair?	The next day.
Where does she receive the gorilla hair the next day?	At the hospital.
She is happy because she finally has gorilla hair. She likes gorillas.	Ohhhh!
Is the girl happy?	Yes.
Does she finally have gorilla hair?	Yes.
Who finally has gorilla hair?	The girl.
What does the girl finally have?	Gorilla hair.
Does the girl like gorillas?	Yes.
Who likes gorillas?	The girl.

The above questions are a sample. Each time you ask a question, you have three ways to respond to the student answer. You can say "yes," thereby verifying the student answer. You can say "no," but when you do, you must then have your own detail in mind and then tell the students the detail. You also can modify their answer.

Preparing a Story

Unless you are very experienced, it is important to prepare your story.

Make a list of the facts of the story. Underline the variables or details that can change. List alternative details for the story. Be sure to have a problem and a resolution of the problem planned out. See "Creating a Story for Class" in Chapter 3.

It is not necessary to plan out all of your questions. Just list the details of the story and the alternative details, knowing that any or all of the details can change during the presentation of the story.

Levels of Questions

It is important to be aware of the levels of questions that your students can handle. Notice the following levels of questions[1]:

1. Yes/no and either/or questions. Examples:

    Does Princesa think she is a gorilla?

    Does she think she is a gorilla or an elephant?

2. Easy questions which can be answered with a word or a short phrase. Example:

    Where does she go?

3. Easy questions which must be answered with a complete sentence. Example:

    What does Princesa think?

4. Open-ended questions to which students must come up with something original as an answer. The answer is usually a

complete sentence, often a few sentences. Many of these questions are *why* questions. Examples:

Why does she think she is a gorilla?

After she receives the gorilla hair, what does her boy-friend tell her?

Even the lowest-level learners of mini-stories can handle level 1 and 2 questions. You can try introducing level 3 and 4 questions at any point. If you provide students with possible obvious answers to level 3 or 4 questions, some of them will be able to answer them quite early on. I personally like to push my students and challenge them with level 3 and 4 questions. It is rare that they can't handle them. You should keep on using the lower level questions, of course, mixing the higher level ones in with them as your students progress. Just make sure you are aware of your students' level and the levels of the questions you are asking them. Use your judgment.

Creativity, Expansion and More Repetitions

When you ask open-ended questions in step 2, you give your students the opportunity to be creative. Be sure to show your excitement when they come up with great answers. And be sure to take advantage of the opportunities that many great answers give you to expand the story, to add interest to it and to provide more aural repetitions of the target vocabulary items through your questions.

For example, if you have asked, "After she receives the gorilla hair, what does her boyfriend tell her?" and someone answers, "He likes it a lot, because he is a gorilla," you can proceed with more questions and with subplot information in which you use *think*, *receive*, *next* and *finally*.

This of course requires you to think on your feet. The more you do this, the easier it becomes. It usually pays off with more spontaneity and creativity on the part of your class and increased interest, which in turn contribute to better motivation, fluency and learning.

As you are doing step 2, remember that you can always jump back to any point in the story and repeat lines of the story and questions based on them. When you do this, you are giving students more repetitions of vocabulary items and of grammatical features.

Note

1. The levels of questions presented here are similar to the ones Berty Segal Cook (a.k.a. Berty Segal) suggests for use in acquiring tenses with TPR (1992: 9; see also Seely and Romijn, 1998: 119-120).

Chapter 5

Storytelling in the First Year

Starting with TPR

We start true beginners with TPR. In 1960 James J. Asher, a psychologist at San José State University in California, began doing research on using commands with action to teach a language. He found that it was extremely effective and named this approach Total Physical Response (now widely known as TPR). Soon thereafter he discovered that the same approach had been invented by Englishman Harold E. Palmer in the 1920s.

The reason we start with TPR is that we seldom have to translate and we don't have the problem of processing time since the meaning is nearly always apparent when we model the command for the class. With TPR we can easily teach several vocabulary words and structures quickly and easily.

Words that can easily be taught with TPR are action words like *stand up*, *sit down*, *run*, *jump*, *throw*, *touch*, *hit*, *look at*, *laugh*, *cry* and *put*. Classroom objects, clothing and even colors can also be easily taught with TPR.

With TPR we teach words that students understand immediately when they see them acted out. We make sure that students correctly understand the words that we teach with TPR. Some actions may be misinterpreted. So, when necessary, we give the first-language translation. We want to be certain that there is no confusion or misunderstanding about TPR actions. For example, the action for *walk* and *go* can be the same, and a student may think the meaning is one or the other.

The miracle of TPR is that almost everything is comprehensible. When students don't understand in TPR, we model the word. We frequently check to make sure students understand. (For more on comprehension checking, see "Comprehension Checks" in Chapter 2, "Essential Skill: Comprehensibility" in Chapter 8 and "Continual Aural Comprehension Checking" in Appendix G.) Comprehension checking of some of the slower processing students is an essential part of teaching the vocabulary.

Teaching must be done in such a way that students can remember the words on a long-term basis. Anyone can learn a word if s/he hears it enough in a meaningful context. We can tell if they have learned vocabulary on a long-term basis by giving unannounced tests months after they have practiced the words.

James Asher explains why TPR produces long-term memory:

> My hypothesis is that comprehensible input with *high believability* will produce long-term memory compared with short-term memory for *low believability* input. The Total Physical Response works because it is *comprehensible input with high believability* since we create intimate, personal experiences for the students. (1996: page 3-67)

Another reason that TPR produces long-term recall, he suggests, is that "in the initial learning, there was keen activation of the kinesthetic sensory system or 'muscle learning.'" (ibid.: page 3-17) By using your muscles you can remember. A person who doesn't ride a bike for 20 years can get on and ride away. The same is true in all sports as well as other skills involving movement. The basic memory is there years later. If our students use their muscles to learn language, they will remember better what we teach.

We use TPR only for a short time at the beginning for three reasons:

1. The imperative gets ingrained if it is used exclusively for too long. Since we are trying to teach structures so that they sound (feel) right, we now use the third-person singular instead of the imperative. For example, we say, "He stands up" or "He sits down." The teacher models the phrase and has the students perform it.

2. Another problem with TPR is that very few of the words we have always taught with TPR are among the most frequent words of a language. Of the TPR words listed in Appendix D, only five are in the top 100 most frequently used words (also listed in Appendix D).

3. Asher himself has pointed out that after prolonged use of TPR, "adaptation" sets in. The novelty of moving wears off and students don't want to continue with TPR. (ibid.; pp. 3-53 to 3-56)

TPR and TPRS™ are used to teach fluency in the classroom. One important goal is for teachers to use the class time in the most effective way possible. We believe that the best way to do this is to consistently provide repetitive, interesting comprehensible input.

Mini-stories

In TPRS, for level one we use the books *Mini-stories for **Look, I Can Talk!*** (Ray, Thompson, Sanchez and Andrews, 2004; currently available in French, Spanish, English and German) and *Look, I Can Talk!* (Ray, 1990; available in Spanish, French, English and German) The mini-story book includes extended readings and is used to teach the structures and vocabulary used in the chapter stories of *Look, I Can Talk!*

In TPR Storytelling we teach a chapter of mini-stories. Mini-stories practice the basics of communication every day in class. After we teach a mini-story, we then read and discuss a story.

Notice that we teach high-frequency vocabulary in TPRS. By teaching high frequency words, we are teaching the vocabulary needed for fluency. We limit the vocabulary that we teach so that we can focus our teaching on structure. Our aim is to teach structure very well. Structure is actually a feeling of how the words fit together. It is the essence of fluency. Structure isn't learned in a lesson. It comes by frequent practice — preferably daily practice — of the language through stories, as long as the stories are interesting, repetitive and comprehensible. This does take time but it is worth it if fluency is the goal.

To accomplish this thorough ingraining of structure, you must focus on getting the students to listen to the basics of the language for hundreds of hours in a variety of circumstances that hold their interest. As you do this, be sure to use only vocabulary that is "in bounds." Use only words they know or can understand. If you do need to use a new word, write it on the board with the translation. The goal is to make the class repetitive and interesting while making it 100% comprehensible at all times. Repetition and comprehension go hand in hand.

Personalization of the Mini-stories

Mini-stories are more interesting if they center on the lives of your students. We always choose a student actor. The actor comes to the front of the class. This actor is mainly a prop since most of the class activity is between the teacher and the students. But the story is about him/her. We use his/her name. We act like all the details of the mini-story are about him/her and are true. We also dramatize anything that can be dramatized. For example, "Class, how did John react?" The class responds, "He was mad." You say, "Correct." You turn to your actor and wait for him to act mad. If he doesn't, demonstrate being mad and wait for him to act mad. These little episodes of dramatization add amazing interest to your stories. Look for ways to use the personalities of your actors by having them dramatize different parts of the stories. You can make the mini-story more interesting by using actual facts or events from your students' lives. In talking to the class you might have found out that one of your students has a cat named Garfield. You could make up a mini-story about Garfield, e.g.:

> Ashley is sad. Ashley is sad because she doesn't have Garfield. Garfield is a very large cat. Ashley sees Garfield and yells,

"Yippee!" Ashley grabs Garfield. Garfield yells, "Meow!" and looks at Ashley. Ashley is happy because she has Garfield.

Interesting and Effective Performances

Susan Gross, formerly of Cheyenne Mountain Jr. High School in Colorado Springs, Colorado, and I have noticed certain factors that help make the acting out of mini-stories more interesting and effective:

1. Personalize everything, using names of students in the class (taking care not to embarrass or insult any of them). A person needs to be a celebrity or a student or someone else all the students know unless there is a "bad guy" in the story. In such case, the character may have another name and definitely is not the student who acts the part. In addition, make any common noun a proper noun that the kids know about. If there is a park, it needs to be a local park.

2. Find and use your superstar actresses and actors.

3. Spacing. Make sure the "set" is arranged adequately and the actresses and actors are located appropriately. For example, one actress is in her house. Another actor is in Hawaii. When the part of the story involving their locations comes up, make sure the students are in the proper places.

4. Timing. When you say a line in the story, make sure your actor or actress acts out that line before going on. If you say, "The boy is sad," make sure the boy acts sad. Don't let your actors anticipate the next part of the story. Don't let them do anything unless you say it. They can exaggerate but they can't improvise.

Steps to Asking a Story
[added for 3rd printing of 5th edition]

1. Establish a problem. Someone needs or wants something. John needs a duck from Columbus, Ohio, that can sing in Spanish.

2. Creatively establish details. Add background information and additional characters. Include information about the main character and one or more parallel characters.

3. Make an unsuccessful attempt to solve the problem.

4. Solve the problem.

We are trying to not finish the story. We want to make it last as long as possible. To do this, we add multiple characters. We compare and contrast these characters and add slightly different details about each character. We also talk about the characters' mother or mouse or uncle. We then add more information about these additional characters. They allow us to create exponential repetitions of the structures we are practicing in each story.

Getting the Most Out of Mini-stories

Most effective mini-stories have two elements — unexpected details and personalized details. These details are what make the mini-stories interesting. You begin a mini-story by going to an unusual place. While you can use things that are normal, it is usually more interesting to use unexpected details. You exaggerate size, shape, quantity and quality. The boy is the best in the world. The bottle of Scope is the biggest ever made. Use gestures whenever possible to help with processing time. Show size with your hands. Move your hands far apart to show big or put them close together to show small. Time is either incredibly long or extremely short. Prices are in the millions of dollars or in pennies. They are always prices no one would ever pay. Even though you know nothing described in a mini-story actually happens, you act as if it is all real and your students play along.

In short, the students are constantly getting practice on the structures of the language by focusing on the details of the story. This is not practice as most language teachers think of it. Since comprehensible input is the major factor in bringing about fluency, it also the main means of practice. The teacher provides most of it.

Even though we don't have the students answer in complete sentences, it is valuable for the teacher to always repeat facts in complete sentences. Any time you can say a sentence that the students understand, you are giving them practice in the language. This happens as they focus on what happens in the story.

You can find out how repetitive you are by having a student keep track of the number of times you use a particular structure during the lesson. Hopefully it will be over a hundred. Having an actual count will help you become even more repetitive.

When asking a story, be firm on the procedures. Be sure to have the students respond with an expression of interest if you make a statement. If you ask a question they don't know the answer to, be sure they guess. If you ask a question they do know the answer to, be sure to have them respond chorally. Whenever the procedures aren't followed, everything stops and you explain the procedures again. Sometimes a pat answer will work, for example:

"You must not have understood."

"I will try that again."

"That was weak."

When you get a class response, there are three possibilities:

1. The class can respond with enthusiasm.
2. The class gives a weak response.
3. Silence.

   There are three possible reasons the class responds with a weak response or with silence.

   1. They didn't understand. If they didn't understand, (a) you were speaking too fast, or (b) you used a word they didn't know. If you are sure they knew all of the words in the sentence, then just repeat the sentence or question more slowly. Use your laser pointer to point to the words.
   2. The students weren't focused on the procedures. If this happens, the lesson stops and you explain the procedures again. If you think they know the procedures, then you might remind them by just saying, "I will try that again" or "You must not have understood."

3. The students weren't engaged. It must be the teacher's expectation that students are engaged at all times. If they aren't engaged, explain to the class your expectations of student engagement. If it is just one individual or two, ask the student, "Why didn't you answer my question?" If you go after individuals, you will send a strong message that you expect all students to always be engaged during your class.

About Associations

A majority of our students report that associations help them learn the meanings of words. However, it seems that associations don't work with some students. Students learn in different ways. And you might be a teacher who can't learn easily with associations. Recognize that students do have different learning styles and you need to give them every opportunity to succeed. Associations will give them one more mental hook to hang new words on.

If you are teaching ESL to students who speak several first languages, associations might be more of a hindrance than a help.

In classical TPR, there is not much need to use associations. You are dealing with real actions and concrete nouns which are very believable to the mind, since students experience them directly — seeing them, doing them and feeling them. In most other situations we find associations are useful to many students.

To help students remember vocabulary, give them any word association you can think of. A great variety of associations may be used. The Spanish word for *look* is *mira*. I tell students they can remember this word from the sentence "Look in the *mirror*." For the word for *cry* (*llora*, pronounced "yora") I tell them to think and picture "*you're a* baby." For the word *give* (*da*) I tell them they always ask their "dada" to give them something. The word *tiene* (*has* in English) sounds close to the English word *tin*: "He has a *tin* can." For *gato* I associate the word *got* with *cat*: "I *got* your *gato*." When the students hear *gato*, they will remember that they *got* a cat.

Students report that some of the associations help a great deal and they remember a word with one trial. Other times they do not work at all. In spite of this, it is still probably worth the time to give your class the extra help. It requires very little time to include them.

One key to coming up with effective associations is that students must be able to hear the sound in the association. You practice the words aurally, so the clue needs to be something they can hear. In other words, the association is for the spoken word, not the written word. The word for *foot* in Spanish is *pie* (pronounced "pyay"). Your association would be something like "Pierre has a big foot," not "pie is a dessert you eat on your foot."

Another key to their effectiveness is the image. A startling or humorous image makes a greater impact (though it must not be obscure). We tell students to picture the association. Often, if they can picture it, they are able to recall it later. Visualization ability is an important factor in various cognitive arenas; we try to encourage the development of it. (See note 1 on visualization, at the end of Appendix G.)

I have tested classes many times the day after presenting only words and associations, when the students have not studied the words at all. There were always many of the words that most of the students were able to remember just from the associations.

Personalized Questions and Answers

- Ask questions using the new words. A couple of examples: If the word is a noun, ask if a student likes it. If the word is a verb, ask if s/he does it.
- Show interest by asking follow-up questions.
- Ask the entire group about the first student.
- Invite reactions by the entire group.
- Ask similar questions of another student.
- Compare and contrast students.
- Always look for confusion (hesitation or no response) and use translation to clear it up.
- Show interest and enthusiasm. Look for information that can be used in the story.
- Compare students by inventing little stories about them.

Personalized questions and answers (PQA) are a conversation be-tween you and individuals in the class about something regarding those individuals. Before you start a story, you list two or three phrases on the board with translations into English (the students' first language). You can use these phrases for your personalized questions and ans-wers. If they are learning *eat dinner*, you ask some of the students where they eat dinner or how many times a week they eat in a restau-rant. You ask a question and a student answers you. In the earliest stage, you can't ask much about their lives, but you can still ask ques-tions that have to do with individual students themselves. In the first week of class you might say something like this:

Teacher: Who has a cat?
Brigitte: Me.
Teacher: Is it a big cat or a little cat?
Brigitte: Little.
Teacher Does it have a name?
Brigitte: Fluff.

Answers can be just a single word and they don't have to be gram-matically perfect. You are *always* trying to make first-year students feel like they are right. Feeling right builds confidence in them.

A little later in the course, when you are doing weather terms, you might be doing *it's raining* and you might say:

Teacher: Lobo, do you go to the mountains sometimes?
Lobo: Yes.
Teacher: When you go to the mountains, does it rain a lot?
Lobo: No.
Teacher: Are you sad when it rains?
Lobo: Yes.

Early in the year, all PQA will require very simple short answers, including yes/no answers. If the question is too difficult, rephrase it so that it is an either/or question or a yes/no question. As students get more advanced, your questions will be more personalized. You will ask more detailed questions about their lives in order to add interest.

Class Discussion

When you first begin class discussions in level one, you are working with a very limited vocabulary. Most students are more hesitant to respond. You must use lots of cognates with very simple questions. If you are teaching a language which does not have a lot of cognates with the students' first language, you will probably have to limit greatly what you ask or delay starting class discussions until your class has become familiar with a bit more vocabulary. Generally you have to direct questions to individual students rather than to the class. By directing questions to individual students, you will be asking repetitive questions, which will be helpful to all. They need to hear even more repetitions at this low level. Below are examples of the kinds of questions you can ask very early. These are all yes/no and either/or questions. At this stage the answers may be just *yes* or *no* or a single word that the student has heard in the question.

> Do you have a TV? Do you watch TV? Do you watch a lot of TV? Do you like TV? Do you watch TV with your family? With your dad? With your mom? With your cat? With your cat or with your dog?

As students get more fluent, you can direct questions more at the class instead of at an individual.

When the students know enough vocabulary, you can always ask them about their weekends. Ask them if they have had any experiences they want to share with the class. Often they have traveled, gone to parties or had car wrecks that they will share with the class. One year I had about seven students who had been in car accidents (some were very minor), but we always had students act out those wrecks. It was always interesting to everyone to hear exactly how the accident had taken place.

It is important for the teacher to speak a fair portion of the time to provide a good deal of comprehensible input in a truly conversational mode. Tell them what you did over the weekend. If no one speaks up, ask individual students what they did. If they don't have an answer, ask them specific questions such as:

Did you watch TV?

Did you watch football yesterday?

Did you go to the football game Friday?

Did you go alone or with a group?

How many were in the group?

What time did you get up Saturday morning?

What did you do Saturday night?

Questions like these help you get the class speaking and thinking in Spanish. They also help build good feelings in the class. You can tell them, as I do, to think of their class as family. They can talk to us, their class family, any time they want. A little practice with questioning techniques will make this part of the class easy.

Make sure you always are going from the general to the specific. If you ask a general question and don't get an answer, just ask a more specific one. If you get specific enough, they will always answer. Likewise, if a student gives a general answer, make him/her come up with something specific. They either watched TV or they didn't. There is no in-between on that question.

Keep asking questions and they will answer. Your main purpose here is to keep the discussion going. Whatever they say, challenge them to flesh out their ideas or be more specific or develop them more. Ask them questions like, "What do you mean when you say ... ?" or "Why do you think that?"

Extended Readings
[added for 3rd printing of 5th edition]

Each mini-story has an extended reading. The extended reading is a longer story with more details. It usually is similar to the mini-story. There are five steps to teaching the extended reading.

1. Translate part of the story. Read a sentence in the target language and have the students chorally say the meaning in English (the students' first language). Be sure students write in the meaning of any word they don't know. Now that you

have translated part of the reading, you go on to discuss what you just translated.

2.   Choose a student to play the part of the main character in the story. Begin the discussion by asking the facts of the story. Ask only about the part you have translated. Be repetitive. Practice new vocabulary and structures by asking about the facts that use those words or structures. Verify the facts with the student actor. Ask him/her what his/her name is. Ask him/her other information. Be sure s/he talks in first person. (Write his/her answer on the board if s/he doesn't know how to answer with accuracy.)

3.   Add background information about the first part of the story. Add details about the main character. Add details about where he lives and what he does at night. Add other information about his friends and/or family. In planning this step, you will ask the question *What don't we know about* _____*?* Be creative. Surprise your students with some unusual additions. Let them guess the details, but if they don't surprise you, then you must be prepared to surprise them. Each detail will be more and more specific. Be aware of the importance of adding proper nouns. Proper nouns help practice language without adding more vocabulary.

4.   Add a parallel character. The parallel character will be a student. Add details about the student. Let your student guess the details, but if s/he doesn't come up with good guesses, surprise her/him with your answers. Be sure to add details that make your student look good. Add details from your student's life. Add her/his favorite song or singer. Add her/his favorite football team or baseball team.

5.   Make the discussion last as long as possible and then translate the whole story, as in step one, including the rest of the extended reading. Finally, have your student act out the entire story. Ask lots of questions while the student is dramatizing the last few paragraphs. Do this last step right before the end of the class period.

Timed Writings

We use two types of timed writings:

1. Once a week the students do a "freewrite"[1] or "speedwrite." When students enter class, they start writing and are given five minutes to write as many words as they can, based on the assignment. Their goal is to continue to write without stopping. They don't edit or correct during this time. They just keep writing. If students try to edit or look something up, it slows them down. Accuracy is not the objective of this assignment. We want to know how much language they can produce in a given amount of time. Fluent writers of the language are able to write 100 words in five minutes. Even many second-semester first-year students are able to write 100 words in five minutes.

    Having them do timed writings without editing is an excellent way to assess fluency. The accuracy of their acquired language can be appraised quite well, since they don't have time to think about rules. When students have to write a certain number of words in a given time, it is easy to evaluate their abilities. And you can see how they are developing in both fluency and accuracy throughout the year.

2. "Relaxed write": Students are given 10 to 12 minutes to write a story or an essay. In a relaxed write they can ask questions about vocabulary or grammar. They can look up whatever they want. You want them to be able to write as accurately as possible while still writing the required number of words. You can walk around the class and see their writing.

Grading the timed writings is easy. Just have the students count the number of words they wrote. Their grade is totally based on the number of words they have written. Beginning students should be able to write 25 to 40 words for a B and 40 or more for an A in a five-minute period. As the year progresses, increase the number of words required for an A. Let them know the standard before they start writing so they will push themselves. Both the speedwrites and the relaxed writes are graded exactly the same way. Many teachers spend time correcting errors. Research has clearly shown this does little or nothing for lasting student achievement despite what teachers may believe. Correcting errors on student essays does not show up in gains in the language.

At the beginning of the year, students write stories. Remind them they can make up a story with different characters. Tell them to use proper nouns. As students progress in their language skills, assign topics. Below is a list of topics for first-year students:

1. their family

2. school

3. their favorite class

4. their least favorite class

5. an ideal weekend

6. their room

7. their car

8. their cat

Novel

We suggest you have your students read an easy-reader novel such as *Pobre Ana*, *Pauvre Anne*, *Arme Anna*, *Poor Ana* or *Bednaya Anya*. These easy readers are great for beginners. They expose them to comprehensible language and culture.

We do the reading in the novel in the same manner we do the read-and-discuss portion of the stories. Once again there are four steps:

1. Have a student translate a paragraph. You can also do a choral translation, where you read a sentence and have the class say the sentence in English. Remind students to write in vocabulary words they don't know. Even if you only have class sets of the novels, having translations of words won't hurt your next class. The translations will help the students understand the discussion of the paragraph.

2. Ask the facts of the paragraph. The facts are written, so they can't change. Students just read along and you ask questions about the paragraph.

3. You brainstorm additional facts or details you want to add to the story.

4. Create a parallel story to go along with the paragraph. The parallel character in this parallel story will be the same person all through the novel. You might even add another parallel character.

Here are the first two paragraphs of *Poor Ana*:

> Ana is a girl with problems. She has many problems. She has problems with her friends and her family. She's a normal girl, but she has many problems.
>
> Ana is fifteen years old. She's not very tall. She has long hair. She has brown eyes and black hair.

Questions:

What is the name of the girl?	Ana.
Does she have problems?	Yes.
Who has problems?	Ana.
Does she have a lot of problems?	Yes.
Who else has problems?	Brittney Spears.
Who doesn't have problems?	Susie from our class.
Why doesn't Susie have problems?	She is perfect.
Is Ana perfect?	No.
Is Brittney Spears perfect?	No.
Is Shelly (another student) perfect?	No, she is almost perfect.
How many problems does Ana have?	Many.
How many problems does Brittney have?	Many.

How many problems does Susie have?	Zero *or* none *or* no problems.
Why doesn't Susie have problems?	Because she's perfect. *or* Because _____.
Does Ana have problems with her elephant?	No.
Does she have an elephant?	No.
Does Susie have problems with her elephant?	No.
Why not?	Because her elephant is perfect.
Does Shelly have many problems?	No.
Why not?	Because she is almost perfect.

You continue to ask questions. Ask as many questions as you can and then go to the next paragraph and repeat the process.

As you go through the novel, it will take a long time to finish the book. The destination is not the goal. The journey is. You are trying to make the novel interesting to your students.

Chapter Story

There are no new words taught in a chapter story. Since students should already know the words in the chapter story from the mini-stories which you have been working on, you don't review or pre-teach any of the words. You teach the chapter story the same way you teach a mini-story. You start by getting student actors to come up in front of the class. You know the story line because you have read the chapter story. You give a statement and then start asking questions.

In *Look, I Can Talk!* the first chapter story is "The Cat Story." You have a girl in front of the class. She acts like she has a cat. You start out:

There is a girl.

1. Is there a girl?

2. Is there a girl or a boy?
3. Is there a boy?
4. What is the name of the girl?

The girl has a cat.
1. Does the girl have a cat?
2. Does the girl have a dog?
3. What does the girl have, a cat or a dog?
4. Who has a cat?
5. Does the girl have a cat in her hands?
6. Does she like the cat?
7. What is the name of the cat?
8. Is the cat big or little?
9. Why does the girl have a cat?
10. Does she want a dog?
11. Is the girl nice?
12. Is she bad?
13. Is the cat nice?
14. Is the cat bad?

There is a bad boy.
1. Is there a boy?
2. Is there a good boy or a bad boy?
3. Is there a good boy?
4. What is the name of the boy?
5. Does the boy have a cat?
6. Does the boy want a cat?
7. Why doesn't the boy have a cat?
8. Who doesn't have a cat?
9. Does the boy have a gorilla?

The boy sees the girl.

1. Does the boy see the girl?

2. Does the boy see the cat?

3. Does the boy like the girl?

4. Does the boy like the cat?

5. Does the boy want the cat?

The boy runs to the girl and grabs the cat.
(You stop while the boy runs to the girl and grabs the cat.)

1. Does the boy run to the girl?

2. Who runs to the girl?

3. Does the boy grab the cat?

4. What does the boy grab?

5. Who grabs the cat?

6. Does the boy grab the girl?

7. Does the boy like the cat?

8. Does the cat like the boy?

9. How does the cat react when the boy grabs the cat?

The boy throws the cat and the cat runs away.
(Stop until the action has been carried out.)

1. Does the boy throw the cat?

2. Does the cat run away?

3. Who runs away?

4. Does the boy run away?

5. Why does the cat run away?

6. Does the bad boy run away?

7. Why does the boy throw the cat?

8. Does he like the cat?

9. Is the cat a bad cat?

The boy laughs and the girl cries.
(Stop until the actions have been carried out.)

1. Who laughs?

2. Does the boy laugh?

3. Does the girl cry?

4. Why does the boy laugh?

5. Why does the girl cry?

6. Who cries?

7. Does she cry a lot or a little?

8. How long does she cry?

There is another girl who has a cat.

1. Is there another girl?

2. Does she have a cat?

3. Is it a different cat?

4. What does the girl have?

5. Who has another cat?

6. Does she like the cat?

7. Why does she like the cat?

8. Is the cat a good cat?

9. Does the girl have an elephant?

The girl sees the other girl, who is crying.
(Stop until the second girl looks at the crying first girl.)

1. Who is crying?

2. Why is she crying?

3. Who sees her?

4. Why does she see her?

5. Who has a cat?

The girl walks to the girl and gives her the cat.
(Stop until the action has taken place.)

1. Does the girl walk to the other girl?

2. Does she give her the cat?

3. Who gives her the cat?

4. Why does she give her the cat?

5. What does she give her?
6. Does she give her a cat or a dog?

The girl is happy because she has a cat.
(Make sure the girl acts like she has a cat and acts like she is happy.)

1. Is the girl happy or sad?
2. Why is she happy?
3. Does she have a cat?
4. Who has a cat?
5. What does she have?
6. Is she happy because she has a cat?
7. Is she sad because she has a cat?
8. Does she prefer the first cat or the second cat?

You can also add any details you want. Details make the story much more interesting for your students. You can also make up a parallel story about one of your students. The girl has a cat, but your student had a penguin. As you add details about the girl, you also add details about your student.

There are many details we don't know about this story. We can add information about the characters:

1. Where do they live?
2. What music do they like?
3. What sports do they play?
4. Does the boy like cats?
5. Does he like girls?
6. Why does he grab the cat?
7. What is the name of the cat?
8. Where does the cat live?
9. What kind of cat is it?
10. Does the cat play sports?
11. Which ones?

12. When the cat runs away, where does he go?

13. Who is the other girl?

14. Where does she live?

15. Where does she go to school?

16. What does she study?

17. What sports does she play?

18. Is she nice? Does she like cats?

19. Does she have a cat?

20. Does she have other animals?

21. Which ones?

22. Does she have an elephant?

23. Where does the elephant live?

24. Where does she go to find the cat?

25. Does she find the same cat, or is it another cat?

26. Does the first girl pay the second girl for the cat?

Another option is to treat the chapter story as a reading. When you read there are four steps that you use for each paragraph:

1. Have a student translate the written paragraph from *Look, I Can Talk!*, or have the class do a choral translation.

2. Ask the facts of the paragraph.

3. Ask information that isn't in the story. What do we not know about the story? Brainstorm details that can be added to the information already given in the reading. (See above for ideas on what we don't know about the story.)

4. Plan a parallel story about a student. As you ask details about the reading, also ask details about your student.

Chapter Exercises

The students now are ready to read the story. I prefer to have them translate the story out loud. They all open their books and one or several students read the story in English (their first language) to the class.

They can also read the story in English to their partners in groups of two.

Written Exercises Are First Done Orally in Class

In the book *Look, I Can Talk!*, there are written exercises. We go over them orally before they are assigned as homework. I ask them the questions and they shout out their answers. I ask for as many possibilities as they can think of on each question. I don't want them to think there is only one right answer. If a sentence calls for an adjective, encourage them to call out as many adjectives as they know. For example: "The girl has a _____ cat." The students say, "blue, big, bad, green, good, etc." Just before they turn in their homework, I allow them to ask about anything they didn't understand. I grade them by giving them points for doing the work. I only take away points for sentences not done. I do not require that they write in complete sentences.

The Class Invents a New Story

The following day, I help the class make up a new story. In the teacher's guide for *Look, I Can Talk!*, there are 40 suggested questions for each story. These questions are only a guide and aren't meant to be followed question by question. The answers from the students naturally lead to other questions. Refer to the book only when you can't think of another question based on what they have already said. I always write the story in narrative form on the overhead projector (You could write it on the chalkboard or on large pieces of paper.) The students each copy the story. They will have it for a test that will be given soon after we finish working on it. As the story goes along, I often pause and have one or two students retell the story in their own words. Sometimes I will have a student translate the story on the overhead out loud to see if s/he understands every word. Other times I have the class read the story chorally in the target language.

Below is a sample "class invention" based on "The Moon Story" in Chapter 8 of *Look, I Can Talk!* Notice that the questions are not the same as the 40 "sample discussion questions about the story" on p. 32 of the *Look, I Can Talk! Teacher's Guidebook* (Ray, 1992):

1. What is the name of the boy?
2. Where does he live?

3. What kind of car does he have?

4. What kind of space ship does he have?

5. Why does he go to the moon?

6. Why does he like Madonna?

7. Can he buy her CDs more cheaply on the moon?

8. How much does a CD cost on the moon?

9. How many rocks is a television set?

10. How many rocks does it take to buy a soda?

11. How many rocks does it cost to buy a car?

12. Does Bubba have a car on the moon?

13. What does Bubba do when he goes to Madonna's house on the moon?

14. What do they eat?

15. Madonna and Bubba rent a movie on the moon. Which one?

16. What does Bubba do after the movie?

17. Why does he go there?

18. Does Madonna go back to Earth?

19. Where do they get married?

The teacher asks the questions to the class as a whole. They will shout out answers so that the overhead story will look something like this:

> The boy is named Bubba Samuel Brinkley Smith. BSBS lives in Laja, Utah, in the country of France. He has a Ford Pinto car. He has a spaceship made by Ford. It is called Galaxy. He is going to the moon because Madonna is giving a cheap concert. It only costs 2 small rocks. He likes Madonna because she sings 3 of his favorite songs. Her CDs are cheap on the moon. They each cost one small rock. They cost over $15 at Wal-Mart. A television set on the moon costs 68 big rocks, and a soda only costs one small rock. A car like a Toyota on the moon only costs 4,000 medium rocks. BSBS has 3 cars on the moon. One is a Toyota Corolla. The second one is a Ford Ranger. The third one is a Honda Civic.

BSBS goes to Madonna's house because Madonna likes to practice her English with him. Everyone on the moon speaks Moon, but BSBS speaks English. They like pizza from Pizza Hut, but there are no Pizza Huts on the moon yet, so they order Moon Pizza from McMoon Pizza. They go to Moonbuster Video and rent movies from Earth. They rent "Star Wars" and "Return of the Jedi." After the movie, BSBS gets in his Ford Galaxy Spaceship and goes back to Earth. He goes back to Earth to see a concert by Huey Lewis and the News. Madonna goes back to Earth because she wants to marry BSBS. They go to the top of Pikes Peak and get married.

After we have finished with the story, the students take a quiz — either the next day or sometimes the same day. They read their notes as I ask simple questions about the story. I have students correct each others' papers so they can hear the right answers immediately and to save me time later on.

The Class Creates Different Versions of the Story from Pictures

We then teach Versions A and B in *Look, I Can Talk!* I discuss the pictures in Version A, which I display on the overhead.[2] (Again, you could use large posters with hand-drawn pictures or have students look at the illustrations in their books.) Versions A and B are treated like a mini-story. Students look at the pictures while you ask questions about the pictures. For example:

There is a girl.

1. Is there a girl?
2. What is her name?

The girl has a cat.

1. Does she have a cat?
2. What is the name of the cat?
3. Where does she live?
4. What is the name of her dad?
5. Why does she have a cat?
6. Does she have a dog?

7. Does the girl like the cat?

8. Who likes the cat?

There is a dog.

1. Is there a dog?

2. What is the name of the dog?

3. Does the dog look at the girl?

4. Does the dog look at the cat?

5. Why is the dog looking at the cat?

6. Who is looking at the cat?

Again, you ask what we don't know about the characters in this story:

1. What don't we know about the girl?

2. Where does she live?

3. What does she do at night?

4. Does she go to school?

5. Where does she go to school?

6. What music does she listen to?

7. What is her favorite football team?

8. Why does she have a dog?

9. What is the name of the dog?

10. Is the dog a good dog or a bad dog?

Continue with this type of questioning. At the end you will have a story line with details. Have students retell the story with all the details. Have one student retell the story to the class and then have the whole class do a partner retell.

Students Write a New Story as Homework

For homework, I also have them each make up a new story, using all the new vocabulary of the chapter, and write it in their books. This gives them a chance to write their new language and be creative by making up a new story on their own. Notice there is a difference between making up a story that they write out versus making up a story using pictures. Telling a story from pictures encourages a student to think in the target language and express what the pictures say. Writing out a story is more of an exercise to develop their writing skills. I give them a grade for doing this, not a grade for accuracy. I know that, if they keep doing the things we do in class, their Spanish will get more and more correct.

Chapter Test

After each chapter we give an unannounced vocabulary test (my colleague Gale Mackey's idea). Students see target-language words and write the English equivalents. They used to study the night before. Now they must be in class to be successful. We tell them the first day they will never know when a test is coming. In fact, we try to give it when they least expect it. This way we find out what students really know (long-term memory) instead of what they studied the night before (short-term memory). Vocabulary lists and tests for *Look, I Can Talk!* are available separately.[3]

It is easy to make your own tests. Just test words your students know. If most students get an A or a B on the test, then go on. If not, practice the words more with more stories and give the test again.

Final Exam

Our final exam in the first year is all vocabulary translation (target language to first language), but you may prefer another option. See Forward and Ogle (1997a: 36-42) for some good ideas on testing in TPR Storytelling. Michael Kundrat of Central Lake High School in Central Lake, Michigan, put the following on FL Teach on the Internet on June 6, 1997:

Subject: TPR Storytelling/final exams

I'm finishing my first "Storytelling" year, and exams are as much fun as everything else has been. The students really enjoy demonstrating what they have learned since last September. What I came up with was a 3-part test covering reading comprehension, speaking, and writing. (no listening, at least for this time around)

For reading, I wrote a story using as much of the vocab and structure as I could fit into a "reasonable" length, followed by questions for them to answer. Matching, true/false, short answer.

For speaking, I looked at all the stories we had covered, then selected about 15 photos from different ones that, collectively, made a "new" story. I glued them down onto a new grid, then sent the students one-by-one to the back of the room where I put a copy of the photos and a cassette recorder. They were given around ten minutes to tell me this new story as best they could.

For writing, I stuck with the basic format we've used all year. Choose x number of vocab words from a given list and incorporate them into an original story 125-150 words in length.

I am so pleased with the papers I have graded so far and the cassettes I have listened to, that I know things went well, certainly for the first year. I feel the students made great progress — and I know they agree...we discuss this frequently — and I can't wait to see if they can continue this spiral into next year.

Notes

1. Freewriting is a technique used in Fluency First (see "Research and Experience" in Chapter 10, "Reading"). See also MacGowan-Gilhooly (1993a: 4, 1993b and 25-26 and 1995: 13-15) and Rorschach (1991) in MacGowan-Gilhooly (1993b: 10).

2. Overhead transparencies of the main stories only in Look, I Can Talk! are available from Blaine Ray Workshops (see title page or Appendix B) and from Sky Oaks Productions (see the final page).

3. Vocabulary lists and tests are available on CD from Blaine Ray Workshops (see Appendix B).

Chapter 6

The Second Year

Storytelling in Second Year

Whether your class has finished *Look, I Can Talk!*, or not, they would now start with *Look, I Can Talk More!* (Ray et al., 1992; available in Spanish, French and English (and German, 1997)) You would also use *Mini-stories for **Look, I Can Talk More!*** (Ray, 1996a; available in English and Spanish (1998) and French and (2000) German) These books follow the same pattern as in level one. Teach all of the corresponding mini-stories in the mini-story book first to prepare the students for the chapter story in *Look, I Can Talk More!*

With TPRS™ even if your students haven't had first-year TPRS, they will learn more of the language by doing second-year stories. By following the steps you can make it comprehensible and the students will learn the material. We have found that beginning students can learn with advanced stories and advanced students can learn with beginning stories.

One teacher reported that she got good results in 2007 by using the second-year TPRS book *Look, I Can Talk More!* with her first-year students. Other schools have done this successfully.

On the other hand, if you feel you have a lower-level class in the second year, you could start with the level one book. Also, an inexperienced TPRS teacher might want to start level two students in level one material for the purpose of practicing the method. Such a teacher might use a level one book in both level one and level two classes.

In the second year, as in the first, we teach the words through mini-stories. It is in hearing the mini-stories that students develop fluency. We follow the steps each day to teach the structures and the vocabulary for long-term retention.

Teaching a Second-Year Mini-story

We start with two or three phrases and ask a story. As in the first year, the story has unexpected and personalized details. By now, your students will have had lots of practice in the past tense. In level two you continue what you have done in the past. Teach the oral story in the past tense and read and discuss it in the present. As they get more advanced and have internalized the present tense(s) in the readings, you can have them read stories in the past.

There is a big difference between a level two class and a level one class. You are still working on getting repetitions of the basic structures and responses to questions about the stories. But now the students know much more vocabulary than they did in level one. If you have been doing TPRS, you can see what fast processors they are as a class. For level two students it is somewhat easier to learn new vocabulary, because they already know so many words and because they are now used to the sounds of the language and to the forms of the words.

In short, you are focusing on getting repetitions both of the vocabulary words and of the grammar. When a student gets to the point where s/he always recognizes that a verb form is the correct one in the circumstances it is being used in (i.e., it sounds right), s/he has acquired that form and is able to produce it consistently and reliably. In order to accomplish this, students need to hear the basic structures of the language over and over.

The next part of this chapter from this point on consists of examples of how we teach a mini-story in the second year. It is similar to how we teach in the other levels in that the goals are always the same. We want to make the class interesting, repetitive and comprehensible and we want to practice the basics of language necessary for communication.

For an idea for a story line, go to *Mini-stories for* **Look, I Can Talk More!** Read the mini-story to get the facts and details of the story you are going to teach. Plan out the story with details and alternative details. Generally second-year stories will have many more details than level one stories. Below is a greatly abbreviated example of a second year mini-story.

There was a girl. She wanted 20 million dollars. She was sad.

There was a boy. He went to the girl and gave her 19 million dollars. The girl was very sad because she wanted 20 million dollars.

Choose a good actress and a good actor. Have them go stand at the places where you want them to be as the story begins.

In a level two class you don't circle as much. Faster processors don't need so many repetitions as you can produce in circling. You would only circle advanced or newer structures. Your main focus is on keeping student interest high. You accomplish this by adding interesting details to the stories. As in level one, you focus on always asking *who-*, *what-*, *when-*, *where-* and *why*-type questions more than *either/or-* and *yes/no*-type questions.

Notice that one of the target vocabulary items in this example is *he gave her*, which not only contains a past tense verb but also is a grammatical structure, subject-verb-indirect object pronoun in English. Grammatical features of various kinds are and should often be target vocabulary items. Even though you have practiced this many times in level one, it is still something you want to continue to focus on in level two. This is perhaps the most effective way that students acquire grammatical features in TPRS.

TEACHER	CLASS
There was a girl.	(This is plot information so the class says:) Ohhh.
What was the name of the girl? (Ask for the name of the girl. Usually have her use her name from our class unless her character is a negative or bad person.)	Lindísima.
She wanted 20 million dollars. (Make sure the girl is acting like she wants money.)	Ohhhh!
What did Lindísima want?	20 million dollars.
Who wanted 20 million dollars?	Lindísima.
Did she want a lot of money or not a lot?	A lot.
No, not a lot.	

In level two you give more explanations. You take every opportunity to explain why things are the way they are and why things happen in the stories. Your explanations are always in the target language. In this case you need to explain why 20 million dollars is not a lot of money. Whether the explanation really makes sense or not doesn't matter. It is "your story," so you have to explain your story to the students. The crucial thing is that the students understand the explanation. In this case you would explain that the girl is from a family where everyone has 31.5 million dollars. Twenty million dollars isn't a lot.

Fifty-five million dollars is a lot. After explaining, go back to the questioning.

TEACHER	CLASS
When did the girl want a million dollars? (Teacher says yes, no or almost. If s/he says yes, then s/he repeats the fact. If s/he says no, s/he gives the answer with an explanation. If s/he says almost, s/he says what the fact is. Listen for responses and then say, "No, she wanted the money the 3rd of June, 2001." Again, give a reason. "She wanted to buy a duck on that day. The duck was named Walter. Walter was at Wal-Mart in the Bahamas.")	(Students in the class guess.)
She was sad. (You check the girl to make sure she has a sad face.)	Ohhh. (Students react with distress.)
Who was sad?	The girl.
Why was she sad?	She wanted 20 million dollars.
Why did she want 20 million dollars?	(The answer could vary:) She was poor. She was in Tennessee and didn't have her purse.

TEACHER	CLASS
There was a boy.	Ohhh.
What was the name of the boy?	(I usually have the boy take the name he uses in class.)
He went to the girl and gave her 19 million dollars. (Make sure the boy went to the girl and acted like he gave her the money. You might have a paper that represents a 19-million dollar bill or a check for 19 million dollars. If it is a check, there might be a subplot of the girl trying to cash the check. If she is in the Bahamas, maybe she can't cash the check. Maybe the check isn't good. You will ask about these possibilities.)	Ohhhhhhh!

Class is a discussion between you and the students. You have firmly established that this is your story. But sometimes a student will suggest something interesting and you will agree. For example, you might be giving a subplot about the above statement. "Class, the girl went to the bank with her 19 million dollar check." A student then suggests that she needs the money for her sick kangaroo. Since this is such an interesting suggestion, you agree and now that fact becomes a part of your story. You are always listening for student explanations and you are always giving your students the opportunity to explain possibilities. When you get into a subplot, you go with it. You continue to ask for details and come up with reasons why this happened.

TEACHER	CLASS
The girl was very sad because she wanted 20 million dollars.	Ohhh.
Who was sad?	The girl.
Why was she sad?	She wanted 20 million dollars. (Or they could give answers that came from the subplot.)

In level one interest is created and maintained by simple details. As students get more advanced, you look for more subplots and create them with the assistance of the class. These subplots lead to more questions by you, which in turn lead to more discussion and more repetitions of the words in the past tense.

At the end of the story, the student actors sit down. Even in level two, you still try to have three locations and lots of repetitions, but your main focus will be on adding details to the story.

Read and Discuss

Just like in level one, you read and discuss the extended reading in the student book. This has four steps.

1. Have a student translate the first paragraph or have the class do a choral translation. You read a sentence and have the students translate the sentence out loud. Be sure to have all students write in the translations of the words they don't understand.

2. Ask the facts of the paragraph.

3. Create additional facts. Brainstorm ideas that you can add to the story. Ask yourself, "What do we not know about this paragraph?" Write ideas that you could add. Remember to think of expanding a sentence horizontally. Also look for details about which you can ask vertical-type questions, i.e.,

questions the answers which suggest follow-up questions. Each fact gets more specific and more interesting. (See "Vertical versus Horizontal Questions" at the end of Chapter 3.)

4.   Create a parallel story.

[In "Extended Readings" on pp. 76-77, we recommend a fifth step.]

Here is a sample paragraph from an extending reading in *Ministories for Look, I Can Talk More!*:

Rodolfo likes to play golf in various parts of the world. Now Rodolfo goes to many places to play golf. He goes to Hong Kong. He likes to play golf in Hong Kong because there are many pretty golf courses in Hong Kong. He also likes to eat American food and there is a good McDonalds in Hong Kong. He also likes to play golf in Dead Horse, Alaska. He loves playing golf when it is cold and there is a lot of snow.

This story is about Rodolfo playing golf. When you discuss it, the focus of the discussion may be totally different. Let's assume you don't like golf and want to talk about dancing. The class discussion might go something like this:

Class, Rodolfo likes to play golf.

Does Carla (your student) like to play golf? (Class says, "no.")

What does Carla like to do? (Students guess. Baseball, hockey, tennis, bowling.)

You know that Carla has taken dancing lessons for nine years and so you say, "No, Carla likes to dance. She dances day and night. She dances in the shower. She dances at the football game and she even dances when she goes to Dead Horse, Alaska."

You would then ask some facts about Carla and Rodolfo:

Where does Rodolfo like to play golf? Where does Carla like to dance? Who likes to dance in Dead Horse? Who likes to play golf in Dead Horse? What does Carla like to do in Dead Horse?

You would then want to add additional details about both Rodolfo and Carla. These details are in the reading. As always ask questions the students don't know and have them guess.

What else does Carla like to do in Dead Horse? (Students guess, play tennis, read, watch TV.) You say, "Yes, Carla likes to watch TV."

What does she watch? (She likes to watch MTV and Fox News.)

Why does she like MTV? (She likes to watch "Real World.")

Why does she like Fox News? (She likes to watch the "Fox and Friends.")

Where does she watch TV? (At the Dead Horse Marriott.)

When does she watch TV? (Before she goes out dancing.)

When does she dance? (Every morning at 4 a.m.)

Does she dance alone? (Usually she dances alone, but today she saw Rodolfo. Rodolfo was going to the golf course. She invited Rodolfo to go dancing. Rodolfo accepted the invitation.)

Since the story is infinitely expandable, you can continue asking questions forever. The above example is an example of vertical questions (see "Vertical versus Horizontal Questions" at the end of Chapter 3). Each question was part of a thread about Carla in Dead Horse, Alaska. You could also go onto a different thread about Rodolfo. You also have the option of talking about either one of them in Hong Kong or in any other city in the world. Seeing where these discussions go is highly interesting. You are leading the discussion but you are listening to student input. As you all try to come up with new interesting details about each thread, the class becomes more engaged. They are learning the target language without realizing it.

Timed Writings

We still do timed writings one day a week. We still have students write about topics. The topics become more challenging as their ability to express themselves improves. You still just have them count their words for a grade. Hopefully, most students will be able to write nearly

101

100 words in the five-minute period. If not, push them. Challenge them to get more words in their timed writings.

Second-year topics:

1. Compare Tyler, Texas, to Dallas. (A smaller city to a larger one.)
2. Describe what you did last summer.
3. Describe an ideal day.
4. What would you do on a perfect vacation?
5. Describe your favorite book.
6. Describe a day in the life of a student in Mexico.
7. Describe your favorite activity.
8. Talk about a trip to Europe.
9. Describe your favorite Christmas.
10. Is it important to be happy?

Novels

We continue to read and discuss a novel. A second-year novel might be *Pobre Ana bailó tango* or *Mi propio auto*; or *Ma voiture, à moi*; or *Die Reise seines Lebens*.

There are four parts to the discussion of a novel:

1. Translate by paragraph — choral translation or a student translation. Have students write in translations of the words that they don't know.
2. Discuss the facts of the paragraph.
3. Add other details to the paragraph.
4. Do a parallel story.

Here is an example from *Mi propio auto:*

1. Translate from Spanish to English:

Today is Ben Carmeno's birthday. He is 17. He knows what he wants for his birthday. He wants a car. He wants to have his own car.

Ben doesn't have a car. He has a lot of things, but he doesn't have his own car. He wants to have his own car.

2. After translating, ask the facts:

    What is today? How old is Ben? Who is Ben? What does he want for his birthday? Does he have a car?

3. You now want to ask questions that aren't in the story:

    Why does Ben want to have a car? What kind of car does he want? How much does that kind of car cost? Is that a lot of money? Is it normal to get a car for your 17th birthday? Why?

4. Your parallel story would be about a student who also wants a car:

    Class, does Diane want a car? What kind of car? When will she get her car? How much will the car cost?

As you go through the paragraphs, you continue adding details to Ben and Diane. You can even add another student who wants or gets another type of car or a third student who gets a bike or a horse. Three characters make what you are doing more interesting and much easier to get repetitions of what you are practicing.

A Typical Week

I like to do a mini-story a week. You do step two (ask a story) on Monday and Tuesday and step three (read and discuss the extended reading) on Wednesday and Thursday. On Friday do a timed writing and read and discuss the novel.

Teachers starting out in TPRS might have a hard time expanding the stories and readings to make them last four days. If that is the case, then just do a story more often or do other activities. As your skills improve, it will be easy for you to do an oral story for two days and to read and discuss a story for two days.

After you do a chapter of mini-stories from *Mini-stories for Look, I Can Talk More!*, you are ready to do a chapter story from *Look, I Can Talk More!*

**The remaining sections of this chapter deal with content
in the student book *Look, I Can Talk More!***

Story Strips

Every story strip consists of four cartoon panels without words. To make the strip stories more interesting, you will want to embellish them. You will want to make the stories come alive by adding to them and also having students act them out. In Story 1, Strip 1, the story is like this:

a.   There is a woman who has a suitcase because she is going to travel. She is going to the counter to purchase a ticket.

b.   The woman gets on the plane.

c.   The plane takes off and flies to another city.

d.   Finally the plane lands and the woman gets out of the plane.

Joe Neilson, co-author of *Look, I Can Talk More!*, suggests the following:

a.   There is a woman that has a suitcase because she is going to take a trip. Therefore, she is packing her suitcase and putting in _____ (the class will suggest things she will pack). She goes to the airport in Denver and buys a ticket on United Airlines for Hawaii. The ticket costs $2,000. She puts it on her Visa card. The travel agent gives her the ticket.

b.   She gets on the plane and sits down. She sits in seat 12A, which is a window seat. She puts her suitcase on the floor of the plane.

c.   The plane takes off. The lady reads *Time* magazine while the flight attendant offers her orange juice. While she is flying, she gets sick and throws up on her suitcase. Afterwards she feels better.

d.   Finally she arrives in Hawaii. There is a gorgeous guy waiting for her. She doesn't know him, but he gives her a big hug, puts a lei around her neck and offers to pay for her taxi. She goes to her hotel, takes off her clothes and puts on her swimming suit. She goes to the beach and has lots of fun, but she is sad because she never sees the good-looking guy again.

The main thing to remember is to add *surprises*. If a person goes to a counter in the airport, have him/her meet a famous person (e.g., Madonna) or a gorilla or some other surprise animal or person. If s/he is taking a trip, have her/him go to Paris or some other exotic location for the evening. Creatively using size can create surprises. Have a student be a 200-pound bird.

Here is another example of how to embellish a strip story. On page 25 of *Look, I Can Talk More!* (Ray et al., 1992), the third story is about a boy who goes to a girl's house to serenade her:

a. A boy named Bubba has been practicing the guitar for two hours every night for ten years. The reason he has been spending so much time practicing is that he wants to impress the girl of his dreams, the sweet Mary Ann. Bubba takes the bus to Mary Ann's house. He is so excited to play her favorite song. He is sure that once she hears it she will want to marry him, and all his years of practice will be worth it. As he climbs the wall in front of her house, thoughts of love run through his head.

b. Bubba sings Mary Ann's favorite song. Mary Ann is sitting in her room listening to the radio. She hears a person singing but thinks it is on the radio, so she stays in her room.

c. Bubba continues to sing. He knows all ten of Mary Ann's favorite songs. He sings each one in a very romantic voice. Finally Mary Ann realizes that Bubba is not singing on the radio. She runs to the window and opens it. Much to her surprise, she sees Bubba with his guitar singing her ten favorite songs. Mary Ann quickly grabs a flower and throws it to Bubba. Bubba catches it. It is the happiest moment of his life.

d. Bubba doesn't know that Mary Ann's father doesn't like boys to serenade her. He thinks she should be 21 years old before any boy can visit her. She is only 19. When her father sees Bubba singing Mary Ann's ten favorite songs, he goes into a mad rage. He runs to the balcony and pushes Bubba. Bubba escapes and never goes back to sing to Mary Ann.

The Chapter Story

Once all the mini-stories and the strip stories have been taught, it is time to teach the main story of the chapter.[1] Always tell the story in your own words as some of your students act it out. Notice how some students make the stories come alive more than others. Choose them to act out the story.

Teach the Chapter Story

Teach the main story just as you would a mini-story. Be sure to add lots of details to the story. Be creative. Add a parallel character. Identify the variables and list alternative variables for the facts of the story. Remember the chapter story is just a skeleton story.

These stories are longer and they have lots of details. Each one of these details can be changed. There are also songs that go along with these chapter stories. Many times the story line is told in the song. Students will enjoy learning these chapter stories. If you have taught the vocabulary and structures well, the story will be easy for your students.

Have Students Retell the Story

Choose two or three students to retell it to the class. As a variation you might time each student for 15 seconds and let her/him tell as much as s/he can in that time period. That gives each student a chance to retell part of the story to the class. Afterwards have the class sit in groups of two and retell the story to each other. As they retell, they may look at the pictures projected on the screen[3] or drawn on the board or a large poster, or they may look at the illustrations in the book.

Translate the Main Story as a Class

The class has learned the story and acted it out. Now they are ready to read and discuss it. Since you changed many of the details of the story when you acted it out, this story will seem somewhat new, yet recognizable to your students. Go through the four steps of reading and discussing the story. Translate the first paragraph. Ask the facts. Create additional facts and create a parallel story.

The story is a longer story with more details. There will be a lot to discuss. If you add a parallel story, you will be able to keep the class engaged for a long time.

Homework Exercises

Once the class has read the story, they are now prepared to do the written homework exercises — exercises 2 through 5. They do them at home and return to class, and we discuss their answers. Since there is no single right answer to any question, I call on students to read their answers to the class. For variety they can read their answers to other students in groups of two, three or four. The important thing is that they understand the question and are able to give reasonable responses.

In exercise 4 of each chapter, students are to rewrite the story from a different point of view. For example, they must use the *we* form as if they were characters in the story telling it from their own point of view. Make sure to tell students to rewrite the story from the pictures not from the written story. In the early parts of the year, I have them look at the pictures and write out the story from a different point of view as I tell them the changes that need to be made.

The Class Invention

As in level one, we also have a day when the class invents a new story. I ask questions and, as the students say their answers, I write the story on the overhead. The second story in *Look, I Can Talk More!* deals with a girl who has social problems because she doesn't bathe. The class invention would deal with some of the same ideas. For example, you could make up a story about a boy who never showers after PE class. Ask the class why he doesn't have any friends. Encourage them to come up with outrageous ideas that will be part of the story. As I write the story on the overhead, each student takes notes.

This is a time to just let things flow and have fun. The students love making up wild things for the story. They compete with one another to see who can come up with the weirdest idea. The competition is what makes this work and makes it fun. You can guide the answers of the class. You can practice grammar or vocabulary. For example, ask all of your questions in the past tense or practice some of the difficult words from the chapter by including them in some of the questions. Maybe you want to practice the word *tip*. Ask them if Eva María receives a lot of tips at her job at Denny's or how much she gets from a family who spends $30 on a meal.

Once you have finished the story, have two or three students retell it from memory. For variety, I have all the students talk for 15 seconds and tell any part of the story. I also have the class chorally read the story in Spanish or have individuals translate the whole story to the class. Finally, the class takes a quiz on the story. Each student is allowed to use his/her notes during the quiz.

Other Class Activities

In exercise 8 in the *Look, I Can Talk More!* chapters, there are two sets of four blank boxes each. Tell the class stories that they draw in the boxes. Afterwards they retell the stories to each other and the class.

In every chapter in the book two more versions of the main story are presented (called Versions A and B), each consisting of six cartoon drawings each. If a transparency is available, project the drawings on the screen.[3] Otherwise, put up a poster that has them drawn on it, or have the students look at the pictures in the book. The first thing we do with one of these versions is have a class discussion about it in which we construct a story. The story always differs in its details with different groups. I ask the students about the people in the story. I get them to assign names to the people and places wherever possible. Finally, I have them act out the story with a student as the narrator.

At the end of each chapter, students make up their own stories from the pictures supplied in the first and last of six frames. They draw in the four middle frames. Later they come to class and choose actors to act out their versions of the story as they tell them. This is very inter-esting, since each person starts with the same beginning and ending. It is fun to see the wide variety of stories you get. I also have them write out their new stories. Then they go through the same procedures again with another set of six frames.

Chapter Test

The chapter tests in the second year are just like the first-year ones. They are unannounced vocabulary tests. This allows us to find out what students really know (long-term memory) instead of what they studied the night before the test (short-term memory). Students read target-language words and write the English equivalents. Vocabulary lists and tests for *Look, I Can Talk More!* are available separately.[2]

Although there is no future tense in the text, students receive an introduction to it late in the second year, and some even start using it in their writing.

As students do the numerous activities in each chapter, they encoun-ter and produce the same material in a great variety of ways. By the time they have finished the chapter, they have such a thorough grasp of the vocabulary and structures in it that they can generally produce them and manipulate them with considerable fluency.

Notes

1. Overhead transparencies for all the main stories, all Versions A and B, and all the strip stories in *Look, I Can Talk More!* are available in one packet from Blaine Ray Workshops. See Appendix B for address, etc.

2. Vocabulary lists and tests for Spanish and French are available both on CD and on paper from Blaine Ray Workshops (see Appendix B).

Chapter 7

The Third and Fourth Years

Since our students experience so much success in the first and second years, we continue to have relatively high sign-ups for the third and fourth years. We follow generally the same schedule in the third year as in the second. We teach a mini-story for two days and then do a reading for the following two days. We use books called ¡Mírame, puedo hablar muchísimo! (Neilson and Ray, 2005a); Look, I'm Really Talking!: French (Neilson and Ray, 2005b); Look, I'm Still Talking!: German (Ray and Neilson, 1994c); and Look, I'm Still Talking!: English (Ray and Neilson, 1994b).

Third-Year Storytelling

Vocabulary acquisition in the third year follows the same steps as in the first two years. Continue on with the basic steps of TPR Storytelling®, which are listed and described early in Chapter 3, by teaching and practicing it in context through personalized questions and answers, and personalized mini-stories. Even at the advanced level of the third year, almost all class time is spent on acquisition activities and not learning activities (see Krashen and Terrell, 1983). Through storytelling students also acquire most of the tenses of the target language. It is during the third year, however, that for the first time we briefly explain to students some advanced grammatical concepts and more emphasis is given to accuracy. (See Chapter 12.) Our grammar explanations deal with grammatical features which have already been acquired. Even if we are dealing with advanced concepts like the subjunctive, we teach them in a story first before giving explanations.

For each chapter we teach several mini-stories from *¡Mírame, puedo hablar muchísimo!* or *Look, I'm Really Talking!: French*. Since the students have learned the present and past tenses, they are now ready to start working on more advanced structures. As with stories at lower levels, our work on each story in a third-year class focuses on structure, a major key to the development of fluency. While doing so, we continue to make sure class stays interesting.

It is assumed that the students have already heard the future and the conditional many times in previous stories. They have likely heard the subjunctive since you have used the subjunctive previously whenever there was a need. Below is an example of how to deal with one slightly advanced structure.

Vocabulary and guide words (for both vocabulary and tense):

He needed to wear a costume.

He probably shouldn't go in.

You start your lesson plan with a problem. The problem for this story is found in the *Teacher's Guide for **¡Mírame, puedo hablar muchísimo!*** (Ray, 2005: 1).

Problem: A boy needed to wear a different costume to a costume party.

Below is the first paragraph of your skeleton story. In third year your skeleton stories are much more involved. They have lots of details. Your students still need to hear and understand lots of repetitions, but at this level more of them come in discussions about details. You first read the entire story to see the story line. Your goal is to teach the skeleton story to your class, but as always you will want the class to be able to suggest changes in the details of the story.

The paragraph below contains lots of interesting details. It suggests that your student would go to a store and buy a polar bear costume be-

112

cause it would not be common. It also suggests the boy lived in Puerto Rico. There is good information even in the first paragraph for your story. And there is so much more information that can be added. We don't know anything about Pepito. We don't know anything about where he lives in Puerto Rico or why he needs a costume. We don't know the time or the date of the party. All of these details can be established by you and the class and this is just the first paragraph.

Plan your story by writing down interesting facts for this story and identifying variables. List alternative variables and then brainstorm additional information that you will add to your story. If you want, you can even add a parallel character. As you go through the planning of the entire story, you will have many details and variables. You will also plan alternative variables just in case members of your class don't come up with any good suggestions when you have them guess.

When you teach the story, do it the same way you did it in lower levels. Have a student actor or actress come up to the front of the class. Ask the story. Add details. Let the story develop as you try to practice the basics of communication with your third-year class every day of class. Enjoy the new details as the story unfolds with the suggestions of your class members. The story continues until there is a resolution of the problem.

> There was a guy named Pepito. Pepito wanted to go out with his girlfriend. He invited her to a costume party. Pepito needed to wear a costume. He thought a lot about the costume details. He thought he should probably wear a polar bear costume. Since he lived in Puerto Rico, he thought a polar bear costume would probably be uncommon. That's why he went to the costume store and bought a polar bear costume. Then he returned home.
>
> Neilson and Ray, 2005a: 2 (translation)

You might also teach what we call passive mini-stories. These passive mini-stories are about students, but they use the new vocabulary. For example, if you were practicing the words for buying a costume, you could tell your students a passive mini-story. It might go like this:

Gringa [a student in the class] is very poor. She will want to buy a costume for Halloween, but she hasn't saved any money. It is only three days before Halloween, so she starts to save. In three days, she will have saved 13,433 dollars. She goes to Walmart and buys a good Halloween costume.

Passive mini-stories are quick little stories about your students that provide practice of the new words that will be used in the mini-story.

Circling in Advanced Classes

In advanced classes we circle only new structures and complex ones that our students are not processing quickly. We also ask questions about these structures that elicit creative responses. And we provide most of the repetitions by adding details and using the targeted structures as we ask about them and discuss them.

If you were practicing the phrase *she gave it to them*, you would "circle" that phrase. For example:

Class, did you give it to them? Did she give it to me? Did you give it to yourself? What did she give to them? Who gave it to them?

You would also ask questions that require creative responses. Using the same question as above you might ask, "Class, why did she give it to them?" If you ask for a creative response, you need to have a possible answer ready just in case the class doesn't come up with something interesting. For instance, you might say, "Class, it is obvious. She gave it to them because she doesn't like small dogs. She likes big dogs."

If the class is more advanced, your circling would involve the subjunctive (in Spanish, at least). For example:

¿Ella quiere que él la acompañe? (Does she want him to go with her?) ¿Ella quiere que él acompañe a su abuela? (Does she want him to go with her grandma?) ¿Ella quiere que él lo acompañe? (Does she want him to go with him?) ¿Quién quiere que él la acompañe? (Who wants him to go with her?) ¿Por qué quiere ella que él la acompañe? (Why does she want him to go with her?)

Read and Discuss the Extended Reading

There are four steps to the reading and discussion of an extended reading.

1. Translate the reading by paragraph. Do a choral translation in which you read a line and the entire class translates the line, or just call on a faster student and have him/her translate the paragraph. Be sure to have your students write in the definitions of words they don't know.

2. Ask the facts of the paragraph.

3. Create additional facts as you ask the class.

4. Create a parallel story based on the extended reading.

[In "Extended Readings" on pp. 76-77, we recommend a fifth step.]

Below is an example of the first paragraph of an extended reading for *¡Mírame, puedo hablar muchísimo!*

There was a girl named Pilar. Nobody liked Pilar because she always carried fish in her pants pockets. That's why she always smelled like fish. She wanted to spend time with some friends, but she didn't have any friends. She called her mom, whose house was near the ocean, and asked her for advice. Her mom told her that she needed more fish, and she was going to send her more fish from the sea.

In level three and four classes there are always more vertical-type questions (see "Vertical versus Horizontal Questions" at the end of Chapter 3). When you look at the above paragraph there are a lot of things that we don't know. We use our class time to establish these additional details.

Here are some examples:

We don't know much about Pilar:

Why does she have fish? She visited Australia when she was five years old and saw some fish.

Does she like fish? She liked most of them. But she really likes angel fish.

What kind of fish does she have in her pockets? She has an angel fish.

Where do the fish come from? It came from Playa del Carmen, Mexico.

How did the fish get to Pilar's house? It went on an airplane with a passenger named Dirk.

Does the fish have a name? Yes, the fish is named Bufford.

Another thread:

Does Pilar have any friends? She used to have three friends.

What happened to them? They liked fish, so they moved to the central coast of California. They wanted to live by a lot of fish.

Why didn't Pilar move? She wanted to, but she had a cat in New Mexico that needed her.

Does Pilar have any friends now? No, because she smells like fish and none of the kids she knows like fish.

Another thread could be about Pilar's mom:

Where does Pilar's mom live? Alaska.

Why does she live in Alaska? She likes fish.

What kind of fish? She likes salmon.

Does she have any salmon? She has a lot of salmon.

How many? 35.

Why does she have so many salmon? She wants to be in the Guinness Book of World Records for having the most salmon in a house.

You could also develop a parallel story about a boy in class:

Does Pilar have any friends? No.

Does Steve (a student) have any friends? Yes, Steve has 26 friends.

Why does Steve have so many friends? He is very popular.

Why is he popular? He doesn't have any fish in his pockets.

Why doesn't he have any fish? He just has money. He has a lot of money.

How much money does he have? Today he only has 14,000 thousand dollars, but most days he has a lot more.

How much money does he usually have? He usually has 43,000 dollars.

Why does he have so little today? He took all of his friends to Outback and they all ate salmon.

You are always trying to make the discussion of the stories interesting. When you can't think of any more details to add, just go on to the next paragraph and start over.

Weekly Schedule

Do an oral story on Monday and Tuesday and a written story on Wednesday and Thursday. On Friday do a timed writing and discuss a novel.

As in all storytelling, these activities can always be substituted for with other interesting comprehensible input. My students loved weekly class discussions about controversial topics. We discussed the news of the day. We discussed what was going on in the world and local news. It was always interesting. My job was to continue to ask questions about the topic.

Teach the Main Story

After you have taught the mini-stories, the students will be very well prepared for the main story from their book. Follow the steps of having students act out the story as you tell it and then having them retell it using the pictures on the screen[1] or a poster or the chalkboard or, if none of these is available, looking at the illustrations in their books. Make sure both you and they use the new vocabulary and the forms of the future tense. The first story in *¡Mírame, puedo hablar muchísimo!* and *Look, I'm Really Talking ! : French* uses a lot of future, since it was written expressly to provide practice with the future. Help your students learn the future verb forms through the story. Pick out some key guide words from the story and put them on the board. Have them retell the story using these guide words. It is the guide words that will help them develop the grammatical correctness necessary to speak the language with a high level of correctness.

Read the Main Story

Read the main story in class. Since you have taught the words in the story through the mini-stories and personalized questions and answers, personalized mini-stories and novel commands, the students should have an easy time reading the story. You can have the students translate the story to the class or have them read a paragraph and answer questions about the paragraph. You can also have them read a paragraph and ask you questions about it.

Do your discussion of the written story the same way you have done the other readings. Translate by paragraph. Ask the facts. Add other facts to the story. Create a parallel story. Make the discussion as interesting as possible. Look for threads of vertical-type questions to enhance interest of the class discussion (see "Vertical versus Horizontal Questions" at the end of Chapter 3). Continue the discussion as long as it holds your students' interest.

Chapter Test

The third-year tests are just the same as the ones used in the first two years. The first 80 questions are matching vocabulary (target language/first language). A story follows that is similar to the main story that the class has been working on. They read the story and do fill-in and true/false exercises about it. Vocabulary lists and tests for *¡Mírame, puedo hablar muchísimo!*; *Look, I'm Really Talking ! : French*; and *Look, I'm Still Talking ! : German* can be obtained separately, as can vocabulary lists for *Look, I'm Still Talking ! : English* (Ray and Neilson, 1994).[2]

Reading

Reading is an especially important activity in the third and fourth years. It is the designated activity for Wednesdays, Thursdays and Fridays in the improved five-day lesson plan (Chapter 11). See also Chapter 10, "Reading."

Essays and Class Discussions

Besides discussing the lives of your students, in the third and fourth years, discuss the topics of the 200-word class essays which are assigned every two weeks to be turned in on Friday. When students write an essay, they report that it is much easier to write about a topic after we have discussed it. Discuss world events, controversial issues and local happenings. Read the newspaper and look for things to discuss. Advice columns offer good discussion ideas. Here are some class discussion and essay topics:

1. Should students be allowed to wear whatever clothes they want to school?
2. Should school uniforms be required?
3. Should the drinking age be lowered?
4. Should all young people be obligated to serve the country in the military?
5. What can society do to diminish drunk driving?
6. Should the school year be lengthened?
7. Should you buy a car or go to college?
8. What are the advantages of a college education?
9. Should the government prohibit abortion?
10. Should the government censor movies?

11. Should mothers work outside the home?

12. Is rock music or hip hop a negative influence on our society?

13. Do clothes affect a person's behavior?

14. What is an ideal husband or wife?

15. Why is it important to have a sense of humor?

16. Why is it important to know another language?

17. Why do we explore space?

18. Should welfare be abolished?

19. What can we do to help the homeless?

20. Are parents too strict?

21. Should gambling be legal?

22. Should drugs be legal?

23. Is it important to be popular? Why?

24. How important is money?

25. Do you learn more in an easy class or a hard class?

26. Describe your life 20 years from now.

27. How would you change your parents?

28. Describe the ideal family.

29. Describe the ideal school.

30. Is it better to have a big family or a small one?

31. Is the United States obsessed with sports? Why?

32. What are the most interesting aspects of our school?

A good source for a variety of topics to discuss is *Conversation Inspirations: Over Two Thousand Conversation Topics* by Nancy Ellen Zelman (1996). Another is *Talk Your Head Off (...Write, Too!)* by Brana Rish West (1997).

When you have an essay due at the end of the week, discuss the topic on Wednesday in your class discussion (part of the five-day lesson plan). If the class is writing about how the future will be different, ask them questions that go along with the topic. Here are some sample questions about the following topic:

The Next Several Decades

1. What changes will there be?

2. What will life be like in 20 years?

3. How will technology change?

4. What about TVs, telephones, computers, household appliances?

5. What will cars be like?

6. What will society be like?

7. Will there be more or less crime? Why?

8. What will happen to your family?

9. What will happen to this high school?

10. How much will things cost? (e.g., a movie, gas, a hamburger)

11. How will travel change?

When students write the 200 words, I give them one half point per word. That means they get 100 points just for writing the 200 words (100 points maximum). Then I read the essays and give each student a correctness grade. I grade like this:

> 100 is for essays with few errors (less than ten).
>
> 80-95 is for essays that have the basics generally correct but they have a lot of errors. (The basics for Spanish, for example, are verb correctness and noun/adjective agreement.)
>
> 70 or 75 is for essays with constant basic errors.

As the year progresses, students are more willing to talk about their experiences and share their ideas. Building trust with students is crucial. You play the role of a moderator. Keep asking questions that will make your students think. Make them defend their positions. Whatever they say, make them support their ideas with evidence. This will help them develop critical thinking skills. Yes, they can think in their new language. If they say that parents are too strict, first ask why. Whenever you can't think of something to get them to talk, go to something more specific. For example, when the class is talking about strict parents, tell them you want to go to a party and you won't be home until two in the morning. What should the parents do? Should the kid be allowed to go? What factors are involved in a curfew? Have students take both sides. Have them be the parents and the kid. Have them discuss the party and what will go on at the party. Always continue to have each side support what it says with something more than feelings.

As students get more advanced, they can assume the role of moderator and the teacher can be a student. I personally love to sit in the class as a student. As a teacher, I always have to take the middle positions and ask questions to keep things going. When I am a student, I can finally express my opinions and say what I think. They are very different roles. It is much more interesting to discuss things than to do just about anything else related to the language.

Fran Peterson, a Spanish teacher in Bakersfield, divides her class into small groups for class discussions. She gives them a topic, and each group has to produce something. For example, one group will have to list ten reasons for going or not going to college in order of importance. Every member of the group must agree with the order of importance. If they don't, they keep discussing it until they agree or until they run out of time. After the group has agreed on a list, they may join up with another group. The two groups may compare their lists. They may then come up with a new combined list, again in order of importance.

Another way of framing a discussion is to have students use numbers to quantify things. For example, have them quantify their parents. A "ten" is the strictest possible and a "one" is the least strict. Where do their parents fall on this scale? A good person is a "ten" and a bad person is a "one." What does a person who is a "ten" do? What does a person who is a "one" do? You can elicit a lot of conversation by using numbers in this way.

In the fourth year it is expected that students will do more than just carry on a discussion. We expect them to speak correctly. This is a time when you can make a note of errors and tell the students the errors they make. These students are very advanced and should be speaking with few errors. So your corrections will be limited. Whereas in the first three years you make very few corrections because they seldom have a positive effect, at this level students are far more likely to make good use of them and apply them in their speech and writing.

The Fourth Year

In the fourth year we continue to use the five-day lesson plan (in Chapter 11). And more work is done on grammar and grammatical correctness. We "circle" the advanced structures, as above on pp. 112-113. The questions are repetitive so that those advanced structures sound right. As in earlier years, the correctness work is done primarily through retelling mini-stories in different tenses and from the points of view of various characters in the mini-stories and to specified characters in them and outside of them. This is the main role of storytelling at this level. See Chapter 12 for a discussion and many details about correcting grammatical features. In addition, we use essays (see above) and reading (see Chapter 10) to perfect advanced grammar. We don't use a textbook in the fourth year, but the students read a lot more than before.

Mark Webster, who teaches at Spring Lake High School in Michigan, says, "I teach my AP classes and level 4 classes the same way I taught a regular level 2 course, with TPRS™. I can just go a little faster when my low kids aren't so low. Just keep teaching to the eyes and to barometer kids (I still like this term). I treat my upper levels just like I treat my lowers."

Notes

1. Overhead transparencies for *¡Mírame, puedo hablar muchísimo!*; *Look, I'm Really Talking ! : French*; *Look, I'm Still Talking ! : German* and *Look, I'm Still Talking ! : English* are available from Blaine Ray Workshops. See Appendix B for address, etc.

2. Vocabulary lists and tests are available both on CD and on paper from Blaine Ray Workshops (see Appendix B)

Chapter 8

TPRS Teaching Skills

This chapter is an adaptation of a syllabus which was used at the fourth annual National TPRS™ Conference in Las Vegas, Nevada, in July, 2004. The syllabus was titled "New TPRS Skills and Techniques for Coaching Workshops" and was edited by Karen Rowan. Numerous TPRS teaching skills and techniques are described and exemplified below. Teachers who practice these techniques and thereby develop their TPRS teaching skills have reported ever greater success in their classes. Workshops at the annual summer National TPRS Conferences and at various locations throughout the year feature coaching on these techniques and skills. French examples were provided by Monique Gregory, German ones by Julie Baird.

CHAPTER CONTENTS   Page

Essential Skill: Repetitions   128

   1. Skill to practice: Circling (circle of questions — the main
      TPRS questioning technique)   128
   2. Skill to practice: Never making two statements in a row   135
   3. Skill to practice: Parking (versus moving quickly through
      the story)   135

CHAPTER CONTENTS Page

Essential Skill: Comprehensibility 136

1. Skill to Practice: Teaching to the barometer student 136
2. Skill to Practice: Teaching to the eyes 136
3. Skill to Practice: The pause 137
4. Skill to Practice: Responding to silence 137
5. Skill to Practice: Staying "in bounds" but keeping the
   story interesting 138
6. Skill to Practice: Translating reading 139

Essential Skill: Personalization 139

1. Skill to Practice: Getting details of your students' lives
   and using the details in mini-stories 139
2. Skill to Practice: Asking PQA details while reading 140
   Technique a: Passive mini-stories 140
   Technique b: Personalized questions and answers
   (PQA) 141
   Technique c: Culture 141
   Technique d: Teaching a life lesson based on what was
   taught in the book 141
   Technique e: Fact-checking 141

**Essential Skill: Keep Student Interest Through
   Believability** 142

1. Skill to Practice: Dramatizing 142
   Technique a: Coaching melodramatic acting 142
   Technique b: Overreacting 142
2. Skill to Practice: Exaggerating 142
   Technique: Everything is the opposite of the expected. 143
3. Skill to Practice: Specificity or vertical questioning 144
   Technique: The ladder of specificity or vertical
   questioning 144
4. Skill to Practice: Verifying the detail 145
   Doing One of Three Things: 145
   a. You listen to their responses and choose one. 145

CHAPTER CONTENTS   Page

  b. You say "no" to all of their responses and tell them   145
    the fact.

  c. You say "yes" to one of the responses and modify it.   145

  Technique: Almost technique   146

5. Skill to Practice: Student responses   147

  Technique a: Positive and negative L2 Responses   147

  Technique b: "How does s/he react?"   148

  Technique c: Everything is possible in German class.   148

  Technique d: Designating one responder   148

6. Skill to Practice: Keeping control of the story   148

  Technique a: "It's my story!" and "That's another story"   149

  Technique b: Never asking why   149

  Technique c: A brief explanation   149

  Technique d: Combining details   149

7. Skill to Practice: "TPRS Positive" at all times   150

  Technique a: Dealing with negative comments about   150
    students

  Technique b: Students are famous. Celebrities idolize   150
    them.

  Technique c: Exaggerated comparisons   150

  Technique d: Dealing with negative comments about the   151
    class

Essential Skills: Pop-up Grammar as Meaning   152

Skill to Practice: Pop-ups: Focusing on the meaning of   152
    grammatical features

  Technique 1: Pop-ups through stories   152

  Technique 2: Pop-ups through dialogue   155

  Technique 3: Pop-ups through PQA (personalized   155
    questions and answers)

  Technique 4: Pop-ups through reading (most effective)   156

ESSENTIAL SKILL:
REPETITIONS

1. Skill to practice: Circling (Circle of Questions — the main TPRS questioning technique)

In order to maximize acquisition of grammatical features and vocabulary by your students, it is essential to provide them with lots and lots of comprehensible input of every grammatical feature and of each item of vocabulary. Not only must you give them a lot of comprehensible input, but you must provide it in interesting ways so that they will stay engaged. The most effective and efficient way that we have found to do this is to provide "repetitions" of the grammatical feature and the vocabulary items through questioning techniques that focus on meaning. To do this, it is essential to make a single statement as part of a story and then to ask several questions about that statement before making the next statement that moves the story along. This means that you must stop the action of the story again and again as you are presenting it for the first time. Whenever you add a new detail, you go back and ask various questions about that detail and all previously presented details. "Scaffolding" is what we call this gradual process of adding a detail at a time and then asking numerous questions about all details presented up to and including the latest one.

PURPOSE: To provide enough "repetitions" of the new vocabulary and structures so that all your students will acquire (or internalize) them. In other words, you want them to learn this material thoroughly, to establish it in their long-term memory.

Every sentence has at least three parts:

A boy / wants to have / a bike.

Each part of the sentence should be "circled" separately. The new structure phrase in this sentence is *wants to have*. The "circle," an innovation of Susan Gross's, consists of:

1. a statement
2. a yes/no question about the statement — with a *yes* answer

3. an either/or question about it

4. a second yes/no question about the statement — this one with a *no* answer

5. (to begin to complete the circle) a repetition of the first yes/no question about the statement — with a *yes* answer

6. (and to close the circle) a repetition of the original statement

1. The first "circle" in this example deals with the third part of the sentence, *bike*:

Statement:	A boy wants to have a **bike**.	Ohhh.
Positive:	Does a boy want to have a bike?	Yes.
Either/or:	Does a boy want to have a bike a cat?	Bike.
Negative:	Does a boy want to have a cat?	No.
Positive:	Does a boy want to have a bike?	Yes.
Re-state:	Yes, the boy wants to have a bike.	

2. "Circle" part 1 of the sentence, *boy*, with no new information. This time, since the original statement has not changed, you start with the first yes/no question:

Positive:	Does a **boy** want to have a bike?	Yes.
Either/or:	Does a boy or a girl want to have a bike?	Boy.
Negative:	Does a girl want to have a bike?	No.
Positive:	Does a boy want to have a bike?	Yes.
Re-state:	Yes, a boy wants to have a bike.	

3. "Circle" the second part of the sentence, *wants to have*. Again, the statement has not changed, so you start with the first yes/no question:

Positive:	Does a boy **want to have** a bike?	Yes.
Either/or:	Does a boy want to have a bike or eat a bike?	(He wants to) have a bike.
Negative:	Does a boy want to eat a bike?	No.
Positive:	Does a boy want to have a bike?	Yes.
Re-state:	Yes, the boy wants to have a bike.	

4. Ask *wh-* question words to which the students already know the answer:

Who wants to have a bike?	A boy.
What does the boy want to have?	Bike.

3-FOR-1 (optional addition to the negative portion of the above circles):

This need not be done with every circle, but it helps to get three reps for the price of one:

Negative:	Does a boy want to have a cat? No, the boy doesn't want to have a cat. He wants to have a bike.	No.
Negative:	Does a girl want to have a bike? No, a girl doesn't want to have a bike. A boy wants to have a bike.	No.

Negative:	Does a boy want to eat a bike?	No.
	No, the boy doesn't want eat a bike.	
	The boy wants to have a bike.	

Advantages to giving a negative response with a 3-for-1:

1. It teaches how to do negation (very important in French, German, English and many other languages).
2. It gives you three reps for the price of one question.

Combine techniques:

Positive:	Does a boy want to have a bike? Yes.	Yes.
Either/or:	Does a boy want to have a bike or eat a bike? He wants to have a bike.	He wants to have a bike.
Negative:	Does a boy want to eat a bike? No. No, he doesn't want to eat a bike. He wants to have a bike.	No.
Positive:	Does a boy want to have a bike? Yes.	Yes.
Re-state:	Yes, the boy wants to have a bike.	

Fish for a detail with question words:

What color is the bike? Green.

Add details to the original sentence and recycle:

| Statement: | The boy wants to have a green bike. | |
| Positive: | Does a boy want to have a green bike? | Yes. |

Either/or:	Does the boy want to have a green bike or a blue bike?	Green.
Negative:	Does the boy want to have a blue bike? No, the boy doesn't want to have a blue bike. He wants to have a green bike.	No.
Positive:	Does the boy want to have a green bike?	Yes.

Then you "circle" again to add a detailed description of the bike, e.g., green with pink stripes, etc.

Fish for a detail with question words:

Who? What? Where? When? How much? How many?

Class, where does the boy who wants to have a bike live?	New Jersey.

Recycle:

Statement:	The boy who wants to have a bike lives in New Jersey.	
Positive:	Who lives in New Jersey?	The boy.
Either/or:	Does the boy who wants to have a bike live in New Jersey or Alaska?	New Jersey.
Negative:	Does the boy live in Alaska? No.	No.
Positive:	Does the boy live in New Jersey? Yes.	Yes.
Re-state:	Yes, the boy who wants to have a bike lives in New Jersey.	

Question word:

What kind of bike is it?	Someone says Schwinn and someone else says Harley.
Yes, it is a SchwinnHarley.	

"Circle" it:

Statement:	The boy wants to have a SchwinnHarley bike.	
Positive:	Does the boy want to have a SchwinnHarley bike?	Yes.
Either/or:	Does the boy want to have a SchwinnHarley bike or a tricycle?	A SchwinnHarley bike.
Negative:	Does the boy want to have a tricycle? No, he doesn't want to have a tricycle. He wants to have a SchwinnHarley bike.	No.
Positive:	Does the boy want to have a SchwinnHarley bike?	Yes.

Add a detail:

Does the boy who wants to have a SchwinnHarley bike like elephants?

Another option is to occasional pause for students to fill in the blank at the end of a statement:

The boy wants to have a _____.

Note: Notice the number of times a form of the phrase *want(s) to have* was used in the section above.

Practice the flow back and forth:

> yes/no
>
> what?
>
> either/or
>
> who?
>
> yes/no
>
> what?
>
> either/or
>
> where?
>
> fill-in-the-blank
>
> (and if language ability permits) why?

Two examples of fluidity in questioning:

> Does Susie want to kiss a big blue elephant? (Wait for response. Either agree with the students or say no.) Susie wants to kiss a big blue baby. Who wants to kiss a big blue baby? Does Susie want to kiss a big blue baby or a big blue elephant? What does Susie want to kiss? Does Susie want to kiss a big elephant?

> Does Roberto need money to buy a book? (Wait for response. Agree or disagree.) No! Roberto needs money to buy ice cream. Why does Roberto need money? Who needs to buy ice cream? Does he need to buy ice cream or a book? What does Roberto need to buy? How much money does he need to buy the ice cream? (Wait for class response. $15.) Almost! He needs $17. (Class: Ohhh!) Does Roberto need $15 or $17? Who needs $17? What does Roberto need? Why does he need $17? Does Roberto want to buy ice cream? What kind of ice cream? Does he like ice cream? Who likes ice cream?

134

To successfully practice the flow, you must teach to the eyes (see below) and watch for zero responses (see below). *How* and *why* questions should be delayed until students have the language ability to answer them. These questions require a creative answer. So we must be careful when we ask these types of questions. If you do ask a question that they don't have the skills to answer, answer it for them. For example, say, "Class, it is obvious. The boy has a bike because he lives in Alaska. All boys in Alaska have bikes."

2. Skill to practice: Never making two statements in a row

Practice making one statement (followed by "ohh!" in response by the class) and then following up immediately with questions about the statement. Have someone signal you if you make two statements in a row. When you make a statement, immediately follow it with a question.

"Ask the story" instead of telling the story!

3. Skill to practice: Parking (versus moving quickly through the story)

DIRECTIONS: Parking is staying in one place and getting reps. When you feel the urge to move forward in the story to the next plot development in the story, force yourself to stay longer. Milk the one location, one detail, or one sentence by asking questions with every possible question word to take full advantage of that one point in time in the story. The entire example up to this point has been an example of parking and it still needs more reps before the teacher would move on to the next point in the story.

PURPOSE: To keep on repeating the new vocabulary until all students have internalized it.

ESSENTIAL SKILL:
COMPREHENSIBILITY

1. Skill to practice: Teaching to the barometer student

DIRECTIONS: Check for comprehension with a barometer student on every word. Don't move on to new words until the barometer student comprehends completely. Make sure everything goes through the barometer student.

Coach the barometer student to tell you every single word s/he doesn't understand by using a signal (e.g., crossed fingers, time-out sign, punching fist into palm). Remember that students will still often not use the signal and you must constantly check for comprehension anyway. Tell the barometer student that her/his purpose is to slow you down. If s/he doesn't slow you down, s/he is helping you, her/himself and the class to fail. You may want to work with more than one barometer student at a time.

PURPOSE: To get the teacher to slow down to ensure total comprehension for every student. Comprehensible input is made comprehensible by pacing the class at the barometer student's pace. Never pace the class by teaching to the top of the class.

GO SLOW!

2. Skill to practice: Teaching to the eyes

DIRECTIONS: Practice teaching to the eyes of your students. To contrast whether or not you are actually effectively teaching to the eyes, practice looking above the eyes of the students. Teach to the tops of their heads or the back of the room. Look directly at one student and pretend that you are talking to that one student. Then talk directly to another student in another part of the room. Then look at the entire class. By looking into the eyes of individual students you will be able to assess their level of comprehension. In addition, your intonation will sound conversational and, hence, more interesting.

136

GO SLOW!

3. Skill to practice: The pause

DIRECTIONS: Say a question word. Point to it on the board. Pause. Point to each word and pause. Use a laser pointer.

PURPOSE: This is a crucial skill that is worth practicing often. It is an essential part of TPRS because it makes input more comprehensible. It gives students time to comprehend the question. Remember you only do this with slow processors. When your students are fast processors, you don't have to slow down. One reason that you do this is to give students enough practice so that you can go fast and they can understand faster.

SLOW!

4. Skill to practice: Responding to silence

DIRECTIONS: When you ask a question and get silence, you have to determine why.

A. Your first thought is: Did the students not understand?
    For example: The boy has to play.
                   Silence.

Go to the barometer student and assess through translation. Establish meaning. Did the student understand *the boy.... has to.... play*? If the student didn't know *has to*, point to it and its translation on the board. In case they're not already there, write them so that students who need to can check the meaning whenever they need to. Then practice *has to* with the class with a repetitive circle of questions.

B. Your second thought is: Was I (the teacher) speaking too fast? Very often students need time to mentally process what they hear in their new language.

C. Your third thought is: Could the students not think of an answer?

137

For example: How many pigs are there in Toadville?
                 Zero response.

In such cases you then give choices. Are there 41 pigs in Toadville or just two pigs in Toadville?

D. Your fourth thought is: Do the students not have the language to answer?

For example: How much is eight times ten minus 24?

The students don't have the language to answer the question, so they won't answer even if they understand the question. Don't ask questions of this sort, but if you do, just answer the question for them (56) or give them an either/or choice (Is it 56 or just 2.04?).

SLOW DOWN!

No matter how slowly you are going, if one person doesn't understand, it's too fast.

5. Skill to practice: Staying "in bounds" but keeping the story interesting

The "boundaries" are the locations, the language that the slowest processing student has already mastered, the guide phrases or words of the day, and completely comprehensible cognates.

DIRECTIONS: You have the ability to use any word you want. Just translate it and practice it. Whenever you introduce a new word, you will want to practice it unless it is a low frequency word. Of course, you don't want to introduce too many new words in one class session.

You are always looking for the balance between repetitions and interest. If students need more repetitions, then you spend more time going back in the story and asking previously established details. You also add a parallel character to get ever more reps.

If students are processing slowly (translating), you circle.

If your students are processing fast and producing with ease, then you work on adding details to the story and practicing more advanced structures.

PURPOSE: To keep it 100% comprehensible while always focusing on practicing the basics of communication.

6. Skill to practice: Translating reading

In TPRS foreign language classes above fourth grade (ages 9-10), reading includes translation into the students' first language.

DIRECTIONS: Do one of the following:

1. Have a student translate the entire reading to the class. Ask for volunteers and choose the fastest students to translate.

2. Have several students each translate a small part.

3. Read a phrase in the target language and have the class chorally translate the phrase. Continue doing this phrase by phrase through the entire reading.

We suggest that you not have students read in small groups. Translate as a class and then get to the discussion as quickly as possible. The discussion is what will cement the language in their minds. (See "Personalization" below.)

PURPOSE: To provide to all students, even the superstars, ample exposure (lots of repetitions) to more advanced structures through fully comprehended input. This will allow all students — some sooner, some later — to acquire more advanced structures.

ESSENTIAL SKILL: PERSONALIZATION

1. Skill to practice: Getting details of your students' lives and using the details in mini-stories

Examples: Gringa lifts weights at 5 a.m. every day.
Pato Loco plays basketball on the school team.
Marie gives piano lessons.

2. Skill to practice: Asking PQA details while reading

Ask personalized questions while reading mini-stories, extended readings and readers. While discussing the readings, personalize them by comparing students to the characters. Have students take on an utterly unbelievable role by asking unbelievable questions. With each question, practice acting as though the answers are completely believable..

For example:

Norma, do you have an elephant? Wow! That's great! (Act like she really does.)	Yes.
Do you talk with your elephant the way Paco does?	Yes.
In what language do you talk to your elephant, English or Elephant?	Elephant.
Do you dance with your elephant?	No, I don't!
No, Norma. That's not true. You *do* dance with your elephant.	Oh, yes.
Yes, Norma. But only on Thursdays.	Right.

Practice the technique of translating and discussing the reading. Discussing the reading means personalizing it. In the extended readings, most of the extended reading time will be spent discussing the students and their lives. This is crucial in order to keep the class interesting.

DISCUSSION TECHNIQUES:

Translate a paragraph at a time (for example, in *Pobre Ana, Pauvre Anne, Poor Ana, Bednaya Anya* or *Arme Anna*) and then move into a technique:

Technique a: Passive mini-stories (mini-stories which are for listening only, with no actors). Example:

Sonia la Bonita quiere ir a México igual que Ana porque quiere estudiar español en México por 29 años y 26 minutos. ¿Verdad, Sonia la Bonita?

(Sonia the Pretty wants to go to Mexico the same as Ana because she wants to study Spanish in Mexico for 29 years and 26 minutes. Right, Sonia?)

Technique b: Personalized questions and answers (PQA)

Guapo, ¿te gustaría ducharte con agua fría o agua caliente?

(Guapo (Handsome), would you like to shower in cold water or warm water?)

Technique c: Culture

En México hay un tanque de agua arriba de la casa. El sol calienta el agua durante el día y la familia tiene agua caliente.

(In Mexico there is a tank with warm water above the house. The sun warms the water during the day and the family has warm water.)

Technique d: Teaching a life lesson based on what was taught in the book

Poverty in Latin America. We tell our own personal experiences in foreign countries. Families that make $50 a month but wanted to save up their money to have us over for dinner. Places without running water. Bathing in the river. Going to the bathroom in the woods. Compare your stories to Ana's life and what she is complaining about.

Technique e: Fact-checking

Questions about the facts of what the class has read. Example: "What was the name of the boy?"

Discussions need to be fluid, not set in stone.

ESSENTIAL SKILL:
KEEP STUDENT INTEREST THROUGH BELIEVABILITY

1. Skill to practice: Dramatizing

Technique a: Coaching melodramatic acting

> Be sure students dramatize what they can in a melodramatic way. Students act out whatever can be acted out. Coach overacting. Coach perfect timing. (The boy gave the girl a cat. Stop and make sure this happens before going on with the story.) You are the director of a melodramatic improv play. Whisper outlandish directions to the actors so that they surprise the rest of the class. Take advantage of your hams and class clowns.

Technique b: Overreacting

> Act like things are real through facial expressions. Practice putting your hands on your head or opening your mouth in surprise.

> You: Class, what color is the cat?

> Class: Pink.

> You: Class, is that right? Is the cat really pink? Wow! Incredible! (or in Spanish) ¡Fantástico! ¡Increíble! or (in German) Toll! Unglaublich! or (in French) Formidable! Incroyable! Fantastique!)

> The weirder a student's response is, the more enthusiastic your response will be.

2. Skill to practice: Exaggerating

How much does a hotel room cost? How much does a book cost? How many minutes does it take to go to the moon? How long does it take to drive a car from San Diego to New York? How long does it take to run from Chicago to Miami?

Technique: Everything is the opposite of the expected.

Examples of how you can take the expected and make it unexpected:

A boy has a car. (He has a big cockroach in his car.)

A girl reads a book. (She reads books about how important it is to look at cats.)

The teacher likes to watch TV. (The teacher watches TV in the park with her dog.)

Take the opposing view. If you ask, "Does the girl want a big elephant?" and everyone says yes, say no. Then give a reason why: "No, the girl doesn't like big elephants because they don't fit in her car."

You:	Does the boy play a lot of football?
Class:	Yes.
You:	No. He doesn't play much football because he needs to sing to his elephant after school.
Class:	Ohhhhhhhh!
You:	Does the girl go to New York?
Class:	Yes.
You:	No, she goes to New Jersey. There is a small cat in New Jersey she wants to visit.
You:	Does the girl buy a house?
Class:	Yes.
You:	No, she doesn't buy a house. She buys a hotel. She likes hotels. She buys the Hilton Hotel in Bucksnort, Tennessee.
Class:	Ohhhhh!

3. Skill to practice: Specificity or vertical questioning

"Vertical" questions are ones that lead to other questions (see "Vertical versus Horizontal Questions" in Chapter 3).

Technique: The ladder of specificity or vertical questioning:

universe

world

thing

living thing

plant

flower

rose

blue rose

blue rose in front of a house

blue rose in front of the house at 314 Maple Street in San Antonio

then an event with this rose that makes it more specific

Example 1:

There is a boy.

Is it a human boy or an animal boy?

Is there an old boy or a young boy?

Is he a blonde boy or a brunette boy?

What is the boy's name?

Where is Jake from?

Is Jake from the U.S.A. or Mexico?

Where in Mexico?

Is he from the state of Chihuahua or the Yucatan Peninsula?

Where in the state of Chihuahua is the boy from?

Is he from the city of Chihuahua?

Where in the city of Chihuahua?

Example 2:

"The girl wants a gorilla."

She wants a gorilla from what country?

What city?

Where in the city?

The northern part or southern part?

From a zoo or from a restaurant?

What restaurant?

Where in the restaurant?

A male or female gorilla?

Big or small?

What color is the gorilla?

How many teeth does she want the gorilla to have?

How old?

What does she want the gorilla's name to be?

There are two 8-month-old, small, pink female gorillas named Frank with no teeth in the men's restroom in a restaurant called Delicioso in northern downtown Oaxaca, Mexico. Which one?

4. Skill to practice: Verifying the detail

When you ask a question students don't know the answer to, they guess. When they guess, you have to do one of three things:

    a.   You listen to their responses and choose one.

    b.   You say "no" to all of their responses and tell them the fact.

    c.   You say "yes" to one of the responses and modify it.

For example:

    1.   Class, how many ducks does John have?

        Students guess 5, 13 million, 2, 67 and 158.

        You can choose one of the guesses. If you do, you must say, "Yes, John has 67 ducks." Now you have established a fact of the story.

2. You can also say:

   "No, John has 15,280 ducks." (The class responds by saying, "Ohhhh!") Often when you say "no," you give an explanation. You might say he needs all of the ducks or he lives in Alaska, where there are a lot of ducks. An explanation lets the students see why their answer wasn't chosen. It also adds more interest to the story, especially if the explanation is an unexpected one.

3. You can also modify their guess:

   You say, "Almost, John has 5.6 ducks." (Class responds with "Ohhhh!")

Usually, when you modify the answer, you also give a reason: "There are .6 ducks because one duck lost one of his legs. It was a big leg."

We call this the "almost" technique.

Technique: Almost technique

Spanish: casi

French: presque

German: fast

You:	How old is the elephant?
Class:	Ten.
You:	Almost. He is 10.2 years old.
You:	How many miles did she walk?
Class:	One thousand.
You:	Almost. One thousand and 1.4 miles.
You:	How long did he wait?
Class:	Four minutes.
You:	Almost. 4.23 minutes!

Practice writing out the numerals as you say numbers. When there are 3.2 people, add a brief explanation of how that is possible. For example, explain that the .2 person is just two eyes.

5. Skill to practice: Student responses

Technique a: Positive and negative L2 responses

Post in your classroom in your target language:

English positive: Great! Super! Terrific! Fantastic! Wow! Interesting! Beautiful! What a beautiful girl! What a handsome guy! Of course! What a coincidence! Obviously! Oh, yes!

English negative: Too bad! Horrible! Yuck! Oh no!

Spanish positive: ¡Fantástico! ¡Chévere! ¡Estupendo! ¡Fabuloso! ¡Qué bueno! ¡Qué interesante! ¡Qué linda! ¡Qué guapo! ¡Por supuesto! ¡Qué casualidad! ¡Es obvio! ¡Síííííííííííííííííííí! ¡Me gusta (mucho)! ¡Increíble!

Spanish negative: ¡Qué malo! ¡Horrible! ¡Qué asco! ¡Qué feo! ¡Oh no, oh no! ¡Qué horror! ¡Qué barbaridad! ¡Qué lástima! ¡Qué pena! ¡Qué triste! ¡No lo creo!

French positive: Formidable ! O là là ! Mais oui ! Chouette ! Génial ! Super ! Hyper super ! C'est dingue ! Bien sûr ! Impec ! (short for *impeccable*) Quelle joie ! J'hallucine ! C'est l'hallu !

French negative: Quelle horreur ! Quel malheur ! C'est terrible ! C'est épouvantable ! Le pauvre ! Quelle cata ! (short for *catastrophe*) Misère ! C'est moche ! Ça craint !

German positive: Fantastisch! Sehr gut! Sehr interessant! Wie schön! Toll! Prima!

German negative: Schade. Schrecklich! Igitt! Ach nein!

Focus on making students respond to everything. Mini-stories are believable and "home run" stories when students react to every twist and turn that is added to the story by the teacher or the students. Take the attitude that everything you say is interesting and insist on a reaction after every statement. Students will be eating out of your hand. You can do this by just following the procedures explained in "TPRS Procedures" in Chapter 2.

Technique b: "How does s/he react?"

Spanish: ¿Cómo reacciona?

French: Comment il/elle réagit?

German: Wie reagiert er/sie?

Using this question makes a story appear real. For example, "How does the boy react when the girl cries?" Use "How does s/he react?" at any point in the story and use it often. Make the actor respond appropriately. Use it often to add interest and reality.

Technique c: Everything is possible in German class.

All in the target language:

You say: The plane flies from Denver to Las Vegas and crashes into the Atlantic Ocean.

Class: No! It's not possible.

You say: Yes. (Look serious and intent.) Everything is possible in German class. (Say it like you're really trying to convince them.)

Technique d: Designating one responder

Assign someone to say "¡Fantástico!" or "¡Maravilloso!" or "¡Qué bueno!" (Great!) (in French: "Fantastique !" or "Génial !" or "Chouette !" or "Super !") (in German: "Fantastisch!" or "Toll!" or "Prima!") or "¿De veras?" (Really?) (in French: "Vraiment ?) (in German: "Wirklich?") or "No me digas" (You don't say!) (in French: "C'est pas vrai !"). Von Ray assigns someone to do this. When he points to her/him with two fingers, s/he says it.

6. Skill to practice: Keeping control of the story

Students have to know it is always your story. It has to be your story so that you can keep it "in bounds." Students are not allowed to add to the story. They are only allowed to respond to your questions. When they try to add something on their own, these techniques help you keep control of the story.

Technique a: "It's my story!" and "That's another story"

Practice keeping control of the story by saying, "It is my story" or "That's another story," whenever their answers might take you "out of bounds." "It's my story!" tells the students they are trying to take the story somewhere you don't want it to go. "That's another story" says that they have a good answer, but it doesn't fit in this story.

Technique b: Never asking why

Remind students of the rule that they never ask why about your story. If a student does ask why, remind her/him that in this class you never ask why; you just say, "Yes, that's right." Then repeat the same statement or question again and have the student respond with "Yes, that's right."

Technique c: A brief explanation

Class, he didn't fly directly from Denver to Las Vegas. He flew all the way around the world the other way. The brief explanations can include adding any new little detail. Tell them he flew from Denver to Las Vegas, but first he flew to Salt Lake City because he wanted to talk to a duck in Salt Lake City. He likes to talk Duck with this duck in Salt Lake City.

This is a powerful technique, to be used often in your stories.

Technique d: Combining details

You:	What is the boy's name?
A student:	Bob.
Another student:	Eddie.
You:	Yes, his name is Bob Eddie.

7. Skill to practice: "TPRS Positive" at all times

Technique a: Dealing with negative comments about students

Do not let any student speak unkindly about a classmate ever, for any reason. When you hear such a comment, jump on it immediately and act like it was a misunderstanding. Make it believable. Our students are the smartest, bravest, handsomest, strongest, cleverest people in the world. Anyone who doesn't remember that clearly needs only to be reminded. If you hear a negative statement by a student about another member of the class, stop and clarify to the student in an exaggeratedly positive way that he has misunderstood. "Maybe you were thinking of Marie from math class. In this class, this Marie is far smarter."

A brief explanation:

"Marie won the Nobel Prize and the award for the highest IQ in the world. There are a lot of people named Marie, but none of the others are as smart as Einstein."

If the student continues to assert that Einstein is smarter than Marie, stop what you are doing and go whisper in the student's ear something like, "I will not let you ever say anything negative about a student in this class." Then go back to the front of the class and repeat the same situation. Make sure the negative student responds saying in the target language, "Yes, that's right. Marie is more intelligent than Einstein."

Technique b: Students are famous. Celebrities idolize them.

Students run into famous people on the street (but no idolatry of the celebrities is allowed). The famous person says incredulously, "The famous Marie from French class?!" (Coach as a choral response.)

Technique c: Exaggerated comparisons

Teacher: Who is smarter? Pamela Anderson or Marie from French class?

Technique d: Dealing with negative comments about the class

If you hear a negative comment by any student, take care of it right away. "Do we have to do another story?" "Can we play a game today?" "Do we have to do this?" "Can we do something fun today?"

Practice the following responses and use them for every negative response at any time in any class at any level.

Whenever you hear a negative comment about how you are conducting the class, you can say: "There are a lot of things I can do. All of my choices are worse for you. You can test me on that or just believe me."

"It really hurts my feelings when you say that. I feel like I don't want to teach. I don't want to hear that. Whether you want to do a story or not, don't tell me that. When you come into class, I want you to say [in the target language], 'Yeah! I like Spanish class.' " Have the student go outside and come in again and say that s/he likes Spanish class.

Model exactly what you want students to say or do. Then have them practice doing it. If several say, "Oh no! Do we have to?" tell them you don't like it when they say that. Say, "It is hard for me to teach this class. I don't want you to say that. We are all going to try that again and you are going to say, '¡Qué bueno!' " [French: "Super !" German: 'Prima!'] Then repeat the exact same situation and have them say what you just told them to say.

It is of prime importance that you listen for any negativity and take care of it *every single time*. There can be no exceptions.

It is MOST IMPORTANT that YOU are supportive, encouraging, loving, kind, the biggest fan, enthusiastic and focused on the success of each of your students.

ESSENTIAL SKILLS:
POP-UP GRAMMAR AS MEANING

Skill to practice: Pop-ups: Focusing on the meaning of grammatical features

At the beginning of Chapter 12 there is an explanation of why we use pop-up grammar.

Technique 1: Pop-ups through stories (1-5 seconds per pop-up)

In Spanish we suggest starting with the following:

A. Contrast the *e* in *come* and the *n* in *comen* (third-person singular vs. third-person plural):

"Class, what does the *n* do? What does just *come* mean without the *n*?"

This is a matter of getting students to understand and focus on the difference between *come* and *comen*. This is a major task. It won't just happen without focusing on it. You have to make it happen with your students. There are many opportunities to do this in the stories and in the readings. Focus on these verb endings and make sure *your students are focusing on them.* Don't be concerned with how long this process takes. It might take several weeks or months for your lower kids to really acquire this grammatical feature, but it is worth the effort and persistence.

B. Object pronouns. *Le* is the best one to start with.

Le dice or le dijo:

"Class, *dijo* means 'he or she said' and *le* means 'to him or her.' So you are saying, 'to him or her, she or he said.' "

Then, in a story or reading, you do your pop-ups. Use them at every opportunity. When you see *le,* you do a pop-up:

"El gato va hacia el chico y le dice [Class, what does the *le* mean?]: —Necesito un gato bueno."

Practice using the one-sentence pop-up and then going right back to the story.

In German we suggest starting with the following:

A. Contrast the *t* in *kommt* and the *en* in *kommen* (third-person singular vs. third-person plural) [See Spanish item A just a-bove.]

B. Verb in the second position with inverted word order.
"Am Abend geht der Junge nach Hause. Class, what sounds better, 'Am Abend der Junge geht nach Hause' or 'Am Abend geht der Junge nach Hause'? The second one is correct. The first one has English word order and doesn't sound right to German ears. Remember that the verb is always in second position in German sentences. If the subject isn't first, where is it? It follows the verb. Am Abend geht der Junge nach Hause."

C. Verb at the end of a dependent clause.
"Karl wirft die Katze auf den Boden, weil er ein böser Junge ist. Class, where's the verb after *weil*? It's at the end of the sentence, because *weil* is a verb kicker. It kicks the verb to the end of that sentence."

In French we suggest starting with the following:

A. Contrast the affirmative and negative. Ask students what does *il n'aime pas* means. Write it on the board so students can focus on the position of the negative. Then ask students how would they say *he likes*. Write *il aime* on the board for contrast. Do the same with verbs starting with a consonant. Explain the difference (use of *ne* instead of *n'*) only when students ask. There are many opportunities to do pop-ups on this while circling.

B. Contrast the *e* in *il/elle aime* with the *nt* in *ils/elles aiment* (third-person singular vs. third-person plural). Write them on the board so students can see the difference. Point out that the pronunciation is the same. Point out the plural forms of the pronouns.

"Class, what does the *nt* do? What does just *il/elle aime* mean without the *nt*?"

This is a matter of getting students to understand and focus on the difference between *aime* and *aiment*. This is a major task. It won't just happen without focusing on it. You have to make it happen with your students. There are many opportunities to do this in the stories and in the readings. Focus on these verb endings and make sure your students are focusing on them. Don't be concerned with how long this process takes. It might take several weeks or months for your lower kids to really acquire this grammatical feature, but it is worth the effort and persistence.

C.   Object pronouns. *Lui* is the best one to start with.

    Il/elle lui dit or lui a dit:

"Class, *il/elle a dit* means 'he or she said' and *lui* means 'to him or her.' So you are saying, 'he or she to him or her said.' "

Then you do your pop-ups. Use them at every opportunity. When you see *lui*, you do a pop-up:

    "Le chat va chez le garçon et lui dit [Class, what does the *lui* mean?]: — J'ai besoin d'un gros chat."

Practice using the one-sentence pop-up and then going right back to the story.

D.   As the final *-s* of the plural often is not pronounced in the French language, it is only through pop-ups and by writing the words on the board that we can help our students focus on the correct spelling. When you use a plural form, ask students what will be the ending of the word.

E.   Ask students why there is an *e* at the end of *une fille spéciale*.

F.   Have students focus also on the placement of the adjective after the noun in, for example, *des garçons intelligents*.

Technique 2: Pop-ups through dialogue

Practice getting other forms of the verbs internalized.

Get students to know the first- and second-person verb forms through dialogue and personal questions. An example of dialogue:

Class, the boy goes to the girl and says, "I want to dance."

The girl says, "Do you have an elephant?"

The boy says, "No."

The girl says, "I want to dance with an elephant."

In this dialogue, as in many, the speakers use first- and second-person verb forms. Use dialogue often in your stories. (This is not dialogue of the kind used in most language textbooks, dialogue which students memorize and practice saying word for word. Rather, it is dialogue as it is typically encountered in short stories and novels. In TPRS students don't memorize dialogues. They just listen and understand — comprehensible input.)

Technique 3: Pop-ups through PQA (personalized questions and answers)

You: Carmen, ¿quieres comer conmigo?
         (Do you want to eat with me?)

Carmen: Sí, quieres. (Yes, you want to.)

You now go to a pop-up:

You: You said, "You want to." If you are talking about yourself you say, "I want to."

You have said your pop-up in English. So now you go right back to the Spanish:

You: ¿Quieres comer conmigo?
                  (Do you want to eat with me?)

Carmen now answers: Sí, quiero. (Yes, I want to.)

The above two techniques enable your students to use verb forms in context correctly.

Technique 4: Pop-ups through reading (most effective)

Le hablaron a Carmen.

Sample pop-ups: What does the *aron* do in *hablaron*? What does the *le* do? Is there a redundancy in that sentence? What is the redundancy?

Los chicos fueron a la casa de los gatos azules porque los querían ver.

Sample pop-ups: What does the *r* do in *ver*? What does the *ían* do? What is the third *los*? What does the third *los* refer to? Did the boys want to see the house or the cats? Why? What does *fueron* mean? Do you notice that in Spanish we say "cats blue" instead of "blue cats"? Why do we say *azules* instead of *azul*?

When the students read, these pop-ups occur frequently. You might use them as often as every 20 seconds as a student translates to the class.

Chapter 9

How to Maintain High Interest and an Optimal Pace

In order to maximize the chances of success for every student, you must keep the class constantly both interesting and comprehensible for everyone at the same time that you keep the pace reasonable. Interest is the most important key of all. Not only is it important for the obvious reason that students will pay attention if an activity is interesting, but also, according to Krashen:

> A very interesting hypothesis is that we acquire best only when the pressure is completely off, when anxiety is zero, when the acquirer's focus is entirely on communication; in short, when the interchange or input is so interesting that the acquirer 'forgets' that it is in a second language. ... second language acquisition occurs when comprehensible input is delivered in a low-anxiety situation, when real messages of real interest are transmitted and understood. (1983: 298)

Interest

Students will want to listen to your class because you are making it interesting. Interest is a crucial factor in creating a classroom environment that students want to come to. If you did nothing but have them stand up and sit down, your students would do anything just to get out of your class and sign up for anything else.

The challenge from a teacher's perspective is to make a generally boring task — learning vocabulary — an interesting one. A few years ago, I had my students learn vocabulary through hand actions alone. Each word was taught through an action. I said, "meta," (goal) and the students lifted both hands in the air giving the signal a football referee uses for a field goal. I spent a great deal of class time just going over the actions. I found that students generally learned the words because I made them learn them. I continued to check for comprehension with the slower students until I was confident that the majority of the students knew the majority of the words. This technique worked well except for one problem: it was generally boring for the students. Now most of the class is reserved for fun activities like mini-stories, acting out mini-stories and personalized Q and A. Students do actions sometimes, but now I make sure my students don't just do actions endlessly. I always focus on the students and questions about them.

Maintaining Student Interest

There are many techniques we use to maintain student interest.

1. We do this mainly by asking questions. When we teach a mini-story, we are giving information about the story and asking questions. We vary the type of question constantly. We try to never ask two questions in a row that have the same type of answer. For example, if we have asked two questions where the answer is "yes," we would then ask an either/or question or a question where the answer is "no." Most teaching is done to the entire class. Likewise, most of the questioning is done to the entire class.

   By asking questions, you are actually checking the class to see if they understand. You can tell by their responses whether they understand or not. Whenever you hear a "zero response" (no one answers), you know the students didn't understand. You then must back up and make what you just said comprehensible. Even if you get a "weak response" from the class, you need to back up. Review or recycle parts of the mini-story again by asking the same questions again that you asked before. You can always go back at any point during the mini-story and recycle questions. Students won't feel this is boring because it will quickly help them to understand. You know they need more repetition when they give you a weak or zero response. Student responses hook students into learning the new language. During the mini-stories, students are responding hundreds of times a day. This is very engaging. Compare this to other classes where students sit mindlessly taking notes. In TPRS™ classes they compete one with another to see who can shout out the most interesting, funniest, coolest or cutest response to the questions from the teacher. *Questions that elicit this type of answer are particularly interest-provoking.*

2. We also maintain interest by humor. The BEP (bizarre, exaggerated and personalized) in our stories maintain high interest in our classes. Von Ray said, "We create interest with comprehensibility. We enhance interest with humor."

3. Another way we maintain interest is by having students involved in the teaching. Student actors are highly interesting. Seeing their facial expressions and having them scream and act sad or happy are delightful ways to keep student interest high.

4. A story line creates interest. When you have a problem or a plot, there is a natural interest to see what will happen.

5. Giving animals names adds interest. TPRS teachers need stuffed animals for their stories. I remember Frank the fish who appeared in so many of my mini-stories. Once he was vacationing at Machu Picchu. Another time he swam in front of a girl who was scuba diving in Maui. Frank the fish even sang in the opera in Florence, Italy. Von Ray had a bottle named Chuck who didn't move. He was a goalie. The kids played soccer against Chuck and built up their confidence

because they always scored a goal against the bottle Chuck. In a story at the end of the year, Chuck moved, much to the delight of the class.

6. The enthusiasm and excitement of the teacher maintain interest. If the teacher acts bored, the students will know the class is boring. If the teacher puts enthusiasm into her or his voice, facial expressions and gestures, students will feel the joy of the teacher. They will be much more interested in the class.

7. Personalization adds interest. It is funny when celebrities know our students on a first name basis. It is interesting when our student refuses a date with Britney Spears or Miss America. Our students are always smarter and more interesting than the celebrities.

Adding any personal information at all increases student interest. Talking about singers they like, movies they see or even friends and family adds interest. Going to a restaurant is general. Going to the Burger King on at 3700 White Lane is very specific and more interesting.

Comprehensibility

The second key is comprehensibility. If students understand what is going on in class, they will listen. It is only when they don't understand that they will turn off your class (i.e., not listen to what is going on).

Teachers often underestimate the importance of making the class comprehensible. If the class is not comprehensible, students won't listen. I have often heard teachers say, "They will get it." Of course they will get it if the class is comprehensible. How will they get it if the teacher doesn't make it comprehensible? The number one goal of any foreign language class must be to make the lesson 100% comprehensible. Stephen Krashen remarked on what a difference it made to him to comprehend everything as a student in a TPRS Mandarin class in the summer of 2007 (see his letter at the end of Appendix F).

I asked a girl once when she did not listen in class. I expected her to say that she didn't listen sometimes when I had them do too many actions. Much to my surprise she told me she didn't listen when she didn't understand. It takes more than just staying in the target language. Teachers must make the class interesting and comprehensible. While they may be able to keep the interest of the best students, it is extremely difficult, if not impossible, to hold the attention of students who just don't understand class.

The key element of TPRS is the questioning technique. Von Ray taught for a year using TPRS without understanding the questioning technique. He reported his slower students understood about 60% of class. After a summer of workshops, Von went back and did the questioning properly. The same lower-level kids now reported understanding over 98% of the class. Students need the repetitions provided by the questioning. Teaching a second or foreign language through TPR Storytelling® keeps students listening because it is comprehensible and it is fun and interesting.

How to Make Mini-stories Fun

How do you make mini-stories fun?

Take normal situations and exaggerate them. Turn small amounts of money into large amounts of money. Compare your students to movie stars. For example, today I told the class that Julie Uhl charges 20 dollars for a kiss. I told them that Beyoncé only charges a dollar. I said that the reason Julie (whose Spanish nickname is Sonrisa, meaning smile) charges 20 dollars is that she is 20 times prettier than Beyoncé. There is interest because:

1. There is exaggeration. The idea of paying for kisses is a funny exaggeration.

2. I talk about students in the class. It is so much more interesting to talk about actual students in exaggerated situations than some unknown characters out of a book in normal, everyday situations.

3. Usually there is an element of surprise. Keep the students guessing what will happen next.

If Class is Boring

What if you feel your class is boring?

Of course, a boring TPR Storytelling class may be very exciting compared to doing grammar exercises or other book exercises. Nonetheless, you want to keep it interesting. Give it your best energy at all times. Your students are worth it. You will feel better and so will they. Enthusiasm is contagious. They can't help but feel your enthusiasm. Keep reminding yourself that you are teaching somebody's son or daughter and they expect your best effort.

I remember having a class that I didn't feel was enjoying my teaching. I remember consciously thinking that I must force myself to be excited and to act excited even if I didn't *feel* excited inside. Over time it worked. Those students became more enthusiastic about the class. By the end of the year, that was my favorite class. I feel that, if I hadn't forced myself to be enthusiastic, it could have turned out to be a disaster.

Not every class is going to work out perfectly. Sometimes there are students that just don't want to be there. Nevertheless, if you give it your highest level of enthusiasm possible, they will give you their best effort and all will be rewarded.

Make the Students the Center of Your Class

Make your class interesting by talking about the students. You can be sure they are listening if you are talking about them. When you tell mini-stories, often make them center around the lives of your students. They will pay attention better and they will remember what you have taught better. We don't always make the stories bizarre. We often use things right out of our students' lives. The person in the story goes to a local park, goes to a rock concert of a group the students love, or goes to a nearby store that everyone knows. Bring in events from their lives.

Have mini-stories contain important school events or national events. Talk about food the kids eat. This is all part of "personalization."

Teaching for Mastery

I learned in college that learning is a relatively permanent change of behavior. That means if it isn't long-term, it isn't learning. We must teach to achieve long-term memory.

Mastery teaching is teaching a curriculum that is narrow and deep instead of a curriculum that is a mile long and an inch deep. Mastery teaching is practicing so the students master the material in class.

Some people claim that to function adequately in a language we need 1,800 words. Others suggest that only 300 to 600 words may be needed for fluency in a second language. The key here is to work on structure and not worry about vocabulary.

There are 1,300 to 2,000 words listed in most level one textbooks. An updated edition of one text now has over 2,500 words in the back. Textbooks are adding words when they should be taking them away. The implication is that you must teach all that vocabulary in one year. In addition, you would teach all the grammar. Students would also do the workbook exercises. Add in the reading and listening programs. It is easy to see how overwhelming a textbook program is and why few students continue on to upper levels.

Unannounced Tests

Since we are teaching for mastery, we need to have ways to see if our students are learning on a long-term basis. One way is to assess with unannounced tests.

It is hard for some teachers to understand that high student learning results from good teaching, not from good testing. A pig doesn't grow faster by weighing it more carefully or more often. It grows faster and better because it is fed well repeatedly. Whether we test or not, if we are teaching well, our students are gaining proficiency in the target language.

The whole reason for testing is different from the traditional model. In the traditional model students study for tests and, if they do well on them, they have supposedly learned the material (though they may have only managed to get it into short-term memory by studying just before the test). So the test is a motivator to get students to study and to attempt to learn. Students, parents and administrators expect tests and generally think they are necessary. Testing gives them the impression that students are learning.

In TPRS the function of the test is entirely different. We are not interested in what students have learned for short-term memory. We want to find out what the students have actually learned for long-term memory and what they haven't. This way we find out what material we need to deal with further.

We give unannounced vocabulary tests. These tests are not the only means of determining what we need to do more work on. We are continually assessing as we teach — checking barometer students' learning of grammatical and vocabulary items and noticing students' responses to our questioning. We also listen to students when they speak, and we read stories that they write and their timed writings. In the timed writings we can see what grammatical structures they have actually acquired, since they don't have time to think about rules.

We test by giving students vocabulary in the target language and having them translate those words to English. Some people wonder why we don't have them write the words in the target language. The main reason is that experience has shown that understanding of target language vocabulary correlates closely with acquisition of the language. So this is what we assess. And this tells us a large part of what we have not managed to teach well, so that we can do some more work on it and help the students to get it into their long-term memory.

Another reason we don't ask them to write the words in the target language is that we don't spend class time teaching spelling for mastery. Spelling is important, but teaching spelling for mastery would require a great deal of class time. I feel that is a poor use of class time compared to giving students more comprehensible input so that they will acquire more of the target language.

Pacing

One of the most important facets of the art of teaching with this method is pacing. It will take some experience to know how fast to teach the words. *Proper pacing can be achieved by making sure the class is comprehensible*. If all students are understanding everything, then you can be sure your pacing is fine. If students are only understanding 60%, your pacing is too fast. That might mean you just aren't asking enough questions using the new words.

The key is to be focused on making the class comprehensible while maintaining interest. To enhance interest, all you need to do is add more details. To make sure that material is more repetitive and therefore more comprehensible, be careful not to add too many details.

Chapter 10

Reading

We didn't used to emphasize first-year reading. That has changed. We have discovered that students can read quite early if they are given material at their level that is interesting to them. And we have come to realize that they learn faster and better when they do read more, at the same time that they are doing the many other things we do in TPRS™. Of course, reading has long been used as a means of learning languages, but not until recently in combination with TPRS techniques. The combination makes for a powerful learning package. So, we have been emphasizing reading more and more. We were slow in coming to realize the usefulness of reading partly because of a lack of interesting material at very low levels. To deal with this problem, we've been creating and publishing our own.

If students are going to be prepared for college Spanish, they must read outside of class. If you want to prepare your students for advanced college classes (3rd year), they must be able to read at a literature level. Only your best students will be able to do this, and you will want to give them that opportunity.

We have our students read stories, which we call "extended readings," and brief, easy novels. We have published *Mini-stories and Extended Readings for **Look, I Can Talk!*** (Ray, 2002a) (for first-year Spanish, French, German and English; at the end of this chapter there is a sample story from this book); *Mini-stories and Extended Readings for **Look, I Can Talk More!*** (for second-year Spanish (Ray et al., 2003), French (2004), German (2004) and English (2005)); and *Mini-stories and Extended Readings for **Look, I'm Really Talking!*** (for third-year Spanish (Ray and Neilson, 2005), French (2005) and English (2006)). Also noteworthy is TPRS teacher Gerhard Maroscher's *Short Stories: German 2.1 Reader* (2007) (for second year). The target words and phrases in it closely mirror those of *Look, I Can Talk More!* (Ray et al., 1997)

The following first-year novels, dealing with teenagers and topics of interest to them, are available (in order of difficulty, starting with the easiest):

Spanish:

Pobre Ana (Ray, 1999)

Patricia va a California (Ray, 2001b)

Casi se muere (Turner and Ray, 1998)

El viaje de su vida (Turner and Ray, 2000a)

Pobre Ana bailó tango (Verano, Moscoso and Ray, 2007)

French:

Pauvre Anne (Ray, 2000)

Fama va en Californie (Ray, 2002b)

Presque mort (Turner and Ray, 2002c)

Le Voyage de sa vie (Turner and Ray, 2001b)

German:

Arme Anna (Ray, 2001a)

Petra reist nach Kalifornien (Ray, 2003b)

Fast stirbt er (Turner and Ray, 2003b)

English:

Poor Ana (Ray, 2007)

Patricia Goes to California (Ray, 2007)

Russian:

Bednaya Anya (Ray, 2007)

Knowing When to Start

In order for students to be able to read at all, they must know 75% of the vocabulary. For them to read on their own, they must know 90% of the vocabulary. Simply do a word count of any section of the book. Have all your students count the number of words they don't know out of 100. Then they write that number down for you. You check the numbers and make sure your students can read before having them read in class or at home. We have found that students are ready to begin reading the easiest novels after a week or two of class.

Translating Out Loud

If some students in a class know at least 75% of the vocabulary in a book but less than 90% of it, we translate the book out loud in class. We avoid having students read the target language out loud. The reasons are:

1. We don't know if they really understand or if they just read the sounds of the words.

2. Mispronunciation of unknown words provides incorrect input and causes confusion.

3. We find that students learn repeated words when we translate that they don't learn when the words are read in the target language.

Better students are chosen to translate a page or two out loud to the class. All others read along while hearing the translation. It is impressive to witness students reading (translating) target language books as fast as they can read out loud in their first language. Another option for translating is for the teacher to read a sentence and the class to translate chorally.

After each paragraph is translated, it is discussed in class in the target language. Details of the plot as well as the culture are discussed. The discussion is meant to create interest in the plot by the students.

The Class Discussion

This has become a major emphasis of TPRS. In TPRS we focus on fluency structures and vocabulary (usually in phrases) that are needed to talk. These are very limited in scope, perhaps only several hundred words. We call this "small circle" vocabulary or "fluency" vocabulary.

In reading, though, students are exposed to literally thousands of words they may never use in speech. We call these words "big circle" words or "reading circle" words. When we translate, we just tell them the meaning of the big circle words instead of using valuable class time to learn words they won't need in speaking.

During reading, we spend a great deal of time focusing on small circle vocabulary. We do this by having a class discussion about what we are reading. The material we are reading gives us something to talk about. When we discuss the reading, we use small circle vocabulary.

First, the class discusses details of the reading. After a student has translated a paragraph, you ask questions in the target language about what s/he just translated. For example:

"What is the name of the boy? Where does he live? How many elephants does he have? Does he need a gorilla or another elephant? Who needs another elephant?"

Also personalize the questions:

"Do you need an elephant?"

If no one in the class responds affirmatively, ask one student if s/he needs an elephant. If s/he says no, tell the student that s/he does need an elephant. This leads into a discussion about the elephant the student needs. For example:

"Correct, class, John needs an elephant. Does John need an elephant? What kind of elephant does he need? No, class, he needs a mini-plastic elephant. Does he need one today or next month?"

Continue to get more information about your student and the elephant he needs. When you can't think of anything more to ask about this student and his elephant, just go on to the next paragraph and have a student translate it. After the second paragraph has been translated, go back and discuss it, just as you did the first paragraph.

Continue on with your discussion as long as it maintains the students' interest. All reading — the stories, the extended readings and the novels — are discussed in this manner.

Summary of Procedures for Reading

Below are the procedures we have found to be most effective for teaching reading. Step 3 of TPRS consists of these procedures.

- Give students a printed story.

- One person at a time **translates** aloud a paragraph the story while the rest follow along. Or the class translates each sentence orally after you read it in the target language.

- Make sure that all students understand everything as you go along and that they write the translations for any words they don't know above or beside those words. We have them write in the definitions in case they forget the meanings of the new words and to ensure comprehension.

- Use translation to explain grammar so that grammar is tied to meaning, not to grammar rules. (Use pop-ups; see Chapter 12.)

Paragraph by paragraph, discuss the reading in the target language:

- Relate the situation, characters and plot to students' lives.

- Ask if they have ever been in such a situation.

- Capitalize on the cultural information in the story.

- Use the story to teach life lessons.

- Give a short quiz on the reading.

- Students act out a scene if you're reading a novel.

- Discuss character development, choices and values.

[See also "Extended Readings" on pp. 76-77.]

Repeat these procedures for as many readings as you have. Treat extended readings and novels in this manner. The chart on the next-to-last page of this book shows all three steps of TPR Storytelling.

Making It Enjoyable

To make sure the students actually do the readings, students might be asked to write a small summary of the plot or take a short quiz. When they read independently, we always ask them to write summaries and/or take quizzes.

The main goal is to make reading in the target language enjoyable. We want our students to love reading. Therefore we are careful to avoid worksheets and other reading-related activities that kids hate. We want to make it fun to read. We don't want reading to be connected with lots of busywork.

I have heard that 70 percent or more of a literate person's vocabulary in his/her native language comes through reading. In the third and fourth years, most of the vocabulary is acquired through reading. Students need to read a great deal in order to continue to acquire lots of vocabulary. If your students can read more, they will acquire more vocabulary, their aural and reading comprehension will improve, and their accuracy in writing and speaking will too.

Second-Year Reading

For second-year North American high school students, we have a published a few brief novels. So far the following are available (in order of difficulty, beginning with the easiest):

Spanish:

Mi propio auto (Turner and Ray, 2003c)

¿Dónde está Eduardo? (Turner and Ray, 2002a)

El viaje perdido (Turner and Ray, 2001a)

¡Viva el toro! (Turner and Ray, 2000b)

French:

Ma voiture, à moi (Turner and Ray, 2004)

Où est passé Martin ? (Turner and Ray, 2005)

Le Voyage perdu (Turner and Ray, 2002b)

Vive le taureau ! (Turner and Ray, 2002d)

German:

Die Reise seines Lebens (Turner and Ray, 2003a)

Mein eigenes Auto (Turner and Ray, 2004b)

Langenscheidt has published numerous German "easy readers" that are usable in the second year. Some that have been used successfully are *Ein Mann zu viel* (Felix and Theo, 1991b), *Elvis in Köln* (Felix and Theo, 1999), *Oktoberfest* (Felix and Theo, 2002) and *Oh, Maria* (Felix and Theo, 1991c).

Many intermediate readers are available for this level.[1] They put the high-frequency structures and words (see "High-Frequency Words and Grammatical Features" in Chapter 2) in context, and they show the students how good their knowledge of vocabulary is. Another TPRS teacher visited my class once and was amazed at how much my Spanish II students knew. They needed almost no help to read the novel they were reading. Reading these novels has all the other positive effects that reading has for students at higher levels.

Third and Fourth Years

For students to enjoy what they read, the material must be interesting to them. To bridge the gap from intermediate foreign language learners to advanced learners, we have the students read the Spanish versions of American juvenile novels that many students have previously read in English. We have found some books at third- and fourth-grade reading levels that are more than suitable for third- and fourth-year TPR Storytelling students. Scholastic publishes very inexpensive books in Spanish such as *Class Clown* (Hurwitz, 1987 (*El payaso de la clase*, 1994)) and *Class President* (Hurwitz, 1990 (*El presidente de la clase*, 1993)). These two we have used for third year, as well as some of the books in the Goosebumps series such as *Monster Blood* (Stine, 1992 (*Sangre de monstruo*, 1995)). For fourth year we have had our students read *Ghost in the House* (Wright, 1991 (*Un fantasma en la casa*, 1993)), *Somewhere in the Darkness* (Myers, 1993 (*Un lugar en las sombras*, 1994)), *The Cricket in Times Square* (Selden, 1960 (*Un grillo en Times Square,* 1992)), *Dominic* (Steig, 1984 (*Dominico*, 1994)), *The Cat Ate My Gymsuit* (Danziger, 1975) and *Tuck Everlasting* (Babbitt, 1985) (*Tuck para siempre*, 1993)).

Thus far, we have published one book that is suitable for third and fourth year students. By Ecuadorian author Verónica Moscoso, it is available in Spanish, French and English versions:

> Los ojos de Carmen (2005)
>
> Les Yeux de Carmen (2006)
>
> The Eyes of Carmen (2007)

For juvenile books in French, one source is Scholastic Books of Canada (see Appendix B).

Langenscheidt also publishes several German "easy readers" usable at these levels, for example, for third year, *Das Gold der alten Dame* (Felix and Theo, 1991a) and *Einer singt falsch* (Felix and Theo, 1998), and for fourth year, *Bitterschokolade* (Pressler, 1986), *Die Ilse ist weg* (Nöstlinger, 1993), and *Yildiz heißt Stern* (Heyne, 1994 and 1996).

Some of the juvenile novels on the market are assigned a reading grade level by the publisher. The following is a rough guide to which reading grades are suitable for each year of foreign language:

2nd year	=	2nd and 3rd grade
3rd year	=	3rd and 4th grade
4th year	=	5th and 6th grade

All the above books are relatively easy to read and are of high interest to the students. Juvenile novels fill the gap between their present level and authentic literature. Generally, novels are more interesting to students than other reading materials, because there is a continuing story. The class can discuss the novel and write about it. They see how the characters of the novel evolve. In a novel certain words are often repeated.

In the third year and fourth year, the students read eight pages on Tuesday and then eight more on Friday in class. At home they read eight more pages after each of the class readings for a total of about 32 pages a week. Students can read novels of 100 to 150 pages in about a month. At 32 pages a week, they can read eight or nine books a year. Based on 20,000 words a novel, that is over 150,000 words.

After they read, we discuss the reading and have a quiz, which reduces their storytelling time a little. This is the only homework they have besides their biweekly essays.

Benefits of Reading

The benefits of doing a lot of reading are many. In addition to vocabulary acquisition, students pick up structure and morphology (endings), idioms and such problematic matters as the uses of *por* and *para* in Spanish; or of which verbs are followed by *à*, which by *de* and which by no preposition in French; or the various circumstances tenses are used in English, German, French and Spanish. Some such things they will have some familiarity with from the storytelling part of the class, others not. When they have done sufficient reading, many such things pop up correctly in their speech and writing. So there is gradual general improvement in correctness of both speech and writing. Their reading comprehension improves dramatically even in the course of reading a single novel. The breadth of material they comprehend aurally expands gradually but, in the long run, massively.

Some Tips

It is important that students understand the story line so that they will be interested in the book. We always focus on the content of what they are reading, and we don't worry about vocabulary as long as they get the gist and follow the story. Sometimes I also have them summarize each page that they have read on their own in the target language. And sometimes, instead of the quiz, they have a list of questions to answer at home.

Students usually have a difficult time reading the first two or three chapters of a novel, so we start out by having them translate those chapters for a few consecutive days out loud in class (taking a little time from the regular storytelling part of the class period). After that, students do their in-class reading silently.

Research and Experience

Research[2] and our experience show that students acquire vocabulary most efficiently by reading material that is both interesting to them and is at a level that is somewhat beyond their own, i.e., a level that includes some, but not too many, words that they are unfamiliar with. Only after experimenting with various approaches to reading, have we found that it is most efficient, effective and satisfying to use juvenile novels. In the third and fourth years we have them read a lot. In third year they read sixteen 250-word pages a week, for a total of five 100-page novels or about 125,000 words in the year. If the fourth-year students read ten 250-word pages a day five days a week, they can read eight 150-page novels in the year. This adds up to around 300,000 words. This approach is similar to that of Fluency First, which appears to be an unusually successful English as a Second Language program used at City College of the City University of New York (formerly known as CCNY).[3]

Krashen and Terrell (1983: 138-139) and experience indicate that vocabulary is acquired more rapidly if readers look up very few of the words they don't understand. We have found it practical to tell students to use the rule of thumb that, if they encounter the same new word three times or more without understanding it, then they can look it up. Otherwise, they shouldn't bother. I believe this is the only time students should use a dictionary. In TPR Storytelling we create *dictionaries in their heads* so that, like native speakers, they don't have to look up words and they can produce them in speech and writing when they want them.

176

Sample First-Year Extended Reading Story

There is a baby. His name is Harold. Harold is a baby that lives in Nome, Alaska. There are a lot of babies in Nome. The babies play a lot. They eat a lot. They yell a lot and cry a lot.

Harold lives in an elegant house. The house is big. It is one of the biggest houses in Nome. Harold likes the house because there are a lot of things in the house. Harold has 25 plastic elephants. He has 8 metal tigers. Harold likes the metal tigers. He also likes the plastic elephants.

Harold has a mother. The mother is a very good mother. The mother's name in Candice. Candice works a lot in the house. Candice likes being a mother. She likes working at home. She likes cleaning the baby when the baby is dirty.

Today Harold is very clean. Harold isn't dirty. Harold is in the kitchen. There are plates, forks, knives and a table in the kitchen. There is also a refrigerator and a stove in the kitchen. There is a microwave oven also.

Harold is hungry. Harold wants to eat. He goes to the refrigerator and looks for food. He opens the refrigerator. In the refrigerator there are many things. There are 22 liters of ice cream. There are 27 liters of chocolate milk. Harold is happy because there is a lot of food in the kitchen.

On the table there is more food. There are 33 bananas. There are 8 oranges and 7 pears. It is a lot of fruit for a baby. Harold wants to eat a lot but he can't eat 33 bananas and 22 liters of ice cream.

Harold takes out 2 liters of ice cream and 3 liters of milk. He takes out a bowl. He puts all of the ice cream in a bowl. He pours all the milk on top of the ice cream. It is a big bowl. He takes a banana. There is a plastic knife on the table. Harold takes the banana and cuts it in 13 pieces. He puts the pieces on top of the ice cream and the milk. He is happy because he has a lot of food in the bowl.

There is a problem. Harold doesn't have a spoon. He needs a spoon. He looks all around the kitchen but doesn't find a spoon. He needs to eat the ice cream with a plastic knife.

Harold starts to eat. He eats and eats with the plastic knife. When he eats, he has pieces of banana everywhere because he eats with a plastic knife. There is also milk and ice cream everywhere. It is a big problem.

Harold has on pants and a shirt. Now the pants and the shirt are dirty.

A lot of people think the mom is visiting a lion in Africa. This is not true. She is in the bathroom. There is no problem because the mom is a good mom. She listens to Harold when he is eating.

She goes to the kitchen and sees Harold. She looks at the kitchen. There is food everywhere. The mom is not happy but it isn't a big problem. Candice cleans the baby and cleans the kitchen. Now the baby is a clean baby. Also the kitchen is a clean kitchen. Both of them are happy because everything is clean.

from *Extended Readings for **Look, I Can Talk!*** (Ray, 2002)

Notes

1. For example, Kanter (1994). Very good second-year students can handle Hurwitz (1987, 1990, 1993 and 1994).

2. See Krashen (1989) and Krashen and Terrell (1983: 132-133).

3. See MacGowan-Gilhooly (1993a, 1993b: 3 and 1995).

Chapter 11

Improved Five-Day Lesson Plan

We have found the following plan to be far more effective and efficient than the plan we used earlier. It is a much better use of class time.

Monday and Tuesday

Mini-story (Step 2)

Wednesday and Thursday

Reading (step 3: translate the extended reading and discuss it)

Friday

Timed freewriting and reading (step 3: read/translate a novel like *Pobre Ana*, *Pauvre Anne*, *Arme Anna*, *Poor Ana* or *Bednaya Anya* and discuss it)

We suggest this five-day lesson plan as the ideal. One goal of a teacher is to be TPRS™ pure. In reality, no one is. Making a story last two hours requires a teacher to add lots of details to keep the story interesting. Beginning teachers aren't able to do that. It is a skill that develops over years. If you can only do 20 or 30 minutes of a story, you are doing well. The goal is to increase the time you're doing stories. As you get better, class discussions will be a regular part of what you do. Class discussions are a wonderful use of class time. They are engaging and are in the target language.

Freewriting

Every Friday the students do a "freewrite"[1] or "speedwrite." Fluent writers of the language are able to write 100 words in five minutes. Even many second-semester first-year students are able to write 100 words in five minutes. When students enter class they start writing and are given five to ten minutes to complete the assignment. At the end of the time they count their words. Their goal is to continue to write without stopping. They don't edit or correct during this time. They just keep writing. Students often are given a topic to write about. First- or second-year students write about:

1. their family
2. school
3. their favorite class
4. their least favorite class
5. an ideal weekend
6. their room
7. their car
8. their cat

Having them do timed writings without editing is an excellent way to assess fluency. When students have to write a certain number of words in a given time, it is easy to evaluate their abilities. And you can see how they are developing in both fluency and accuracy throughout the year. This is really a very good assessment tool. The accuracy of their acquired language can be appraised quite well, since they don't have time to think about rules. (It is best to consider writing conventions such as spelling, accent marks and other punctuation as a separate skill when you are evaluating accuracy through freewriting.)

Make sure you check students' freewrites, because they are the best way to find out what elements of the language you need to do more work on, which of course means that you need to (1) provide more repetitions through questioning and/or (2) do more "pop-up" grammar.

To third- and fourth-year students you can assign a topic based on the essay. For example, have them write about what travel will be like in 20 years. They too are usually given five minutes to write 100 words. They score a point for each word they write. You generally don't correct these. Record them, giving them a grade based on how many words they write.

Instead of assigning an essay topic, sometimes give them guide words to use in their five-minute writings. For example, write down five irregular verbs in the same tense and tell them they can write about anything they want but they have to use those words in their writing.

For more about freewrites and other timed writings, see "Timed Writings" in Chapter 5, "Storytelling in the First Year."

Note

1. Freewriting is a technique used in Fluency First (see "Research and Experience" in Chapter 10, "Reading"). See also MacGowan-Gilhooly (1993a: 4, 1993b and 25-26 and 1995: 13-15) and Rorschach (1991) in MacGowan-Gilhooly (1993b: 10).

Chapter 12

Teaching Grammar as Meaning

Pop-up Grammar as Meaning

Our current approach to grammar is far more effective than teaching grammar rules, and the results show it gets the job done far better than most, if not all, other approaches. The main features of it are:

1. providing numerous repetitions of grammatical features

2. making sure that grammatical features are fully compre-hended by means of what we call "pop-up grammar" or "pop-ups" and one-to-five-second grammar explanations

Pop-up grammar is an especially effective way of emphasizing the meaning of a grammatical feature in its actual context. Every gramma-tical element and every grammatical structure mean something. As we are dealing with a story or a reading, we focus on one or more gram-matical elements. We deal with grammar in this way because (1) it makes the grammatical features comprehensible and (2) it thereby leads to real acquisition of them.

We do not deal with grammar in any of the traditional ways, be-cause we believe they do not lead to real acquisition. These approaches to grammar are mostly what Krashen calls learning. While they often help learners to understand grammatical elements, they are not an effec-tive means of acquiring the elements. In other words, they aren't an efficient way to achieve correct speaking and writing. More talented students may acquire grammatical features whether they learn about them or not. They acquire them more quickly and with greater accuracy when pop-up meaning is used. We used to think that less talented students were not able to become accurate speakers of their new language. But we have discovered that, with the help of pop-up meaning, they actually do. It just takes them more time.

In practice, each pop-up is a quick question (or two) about a particular grammatical feature that appears in the context of a story or reading. The teacher interrupts the story briefly to ask the question and get an answer from the class. Then the story proceeds or the student(s) continue to translate the reading. Although a pop-up usually consists of a quick question and its answer, occasionally the teacher must give a short explanation or translation of the grammatical element being focused on. Examples of pop-ups are on pp. 150-154 in Chapter 8.

It is, of course, wise to focus on a limited number of grammatical features at a time.

Grammar Goals

There seems to be general agreement among language teachers that, sooner or later, language learners or acquirers should be able to produce grammatically correct language. Not all agree about when in the course of learning or acquiring the target language grammatical accuracy should be attained. Most language texts and most language classes spend a considerable amount of time at all stages on grammar explanations and grammatical accuracy exercises. Most assessment of language students, at all stages, gives considerable weight to grammatical accuracy.

I recently spoke to a girl who had lived in Sweden. She said, "I really didn't care how well I spoke Swedish because they understood me just fine." Many of our students are taking the class for credit and don't care at all about learning the language for fluency. But if the class is engaging, speaking another language will become attractive to most students. Speaking with complete accuracy is another thing. Even many motivated language learners have the attitude of the girl who lived in Sweden — errors are okay if people understand. It appears the passion for accuracy in students' speech is a teacher thing. Many teachers are passionate about accuracy in language and feel their students should share the same passion. But there is probably nothing we can do to make students be passionate about language accuracy. When I was in high school, I wasn't passionate about music. I was a sports person. As a senior, I took a semester of choir. I don't think there is anything that teacher could have done that would have made me want to sing in an opera.

What is a realistic goal we can have for our students?

I believe we can teach our students to talk with confidence . Because they are learners, their speech will unavoidably contain some errors. That being the case, we spend our class time doing productive and enjoyable activities like storytelling while continually encouraging correctness in ways that are meaningful to the learners.

Acquisition and Learning

At the same time, among language teachers there is much interest in and acceptance of the ideas of Stephen Krashen regarding learning and acquisition. Most teachers know that acquiring a language is what we call "picking it up." In specific reference to grammar, language acquisition is "an unconscious process of constructing grammar rules," sometimes referred to as "creative construction" (Terrell, 1982: 269). In Krashen's view, it is an unconscious effort. It happens when students are focused on the message and not on the form of the message, i.e., on the idea being expressed and not on whether it is expressed with correct grammar. Acquisition happens gradually, not all at once. It is evident that it has happened when an acquirer can regularly produce correctly in appropriate circumstances a form, structure or vocabulary item without having to consider whether it obeys a rule and without struggling to get it right. It just *sounds right* to the acquirer (see Burling, 1982) and s/he utters it with little or no effort. Another description of sounding right is that the acquirer has a *feeling of correctness.*

Learning for Krashen is the traditional process of studying grammar rules, verb conjugations and other word forms — what has commonly been associated with learning a language in school. It is "a conscious attempt to internalize grammar rules" (Terrell, 1982). Learning activities are ones in which the student is focusing on the form of the language. Any activity that focuses on how the message is given rather than the message itself is a learning activity. Anytime a student is producing the language while focusing on correctness, s/he is engaged in a learning activity. S/he is monitoring her/his speech while attempting to apply a rule already learned.

The Study of Grammar

What is accomplished by doing learning activities, by studying grammar? What teachers and students have traditionally thought is that studying grammar rules builds accuracy in speech. It seems so obvious, and yet it turns out there is little evidence to support this idea. The evidence indicates only slight transfer of knowledge of grammar rules into grammatical accuracy in speech (Krashen, 1992, 1994; Spada, 1986, 1987).

Grammatical accuracy in speech is a primary goal of grammar study, yet grammar study does little to accomplish this goal. Krashen hypothesizes that only three things are accomplished by studying grammar:

1. Understanding the grammar system of a language. (This is essentially an intellectual pursuit that a small percentage of students find interesting or worthwhile. It may have some practical application. If so, it is not the bringing about of correct speech production in any measure.)

2. Preparation for a test on grammar rules which a teacher or educational body thinks are worth knowing. (Usually most grammar rules learned for this purpose are soon forgotten.)

3. Allowing learners to use what Krashen (1994: 45-46) describes as a language monitor which they can use to make sure they are adhering to grammar rules as they speak. In

186

order to monitor and edit speech, three conditions must be met. The speaker must:

    a. know the grammar rule

    b. be focused on the rule

    c. have enough time to edit using the rule

It is obvious that meeting all three of these conditions does not happen for each word in our speech. It does happen occasionally, but only occasionally. There is rarely enough time. Even when there is, the first two conditions seldom occur. Many teachers and some students probably feel they are teaching and learning grammar not only in order for the students to build accuracy in speech (which barely happens at all) but also for students to be able to monitor their own speech. It is highly unlikely the rules learned will help much in monitoring speech unless the student has already acquired a lot of language. In such a case there can be some minor editing of speech. Even then, the editing may occur because the items in question sound right due to acquisition rather than because the appropriate learned rules are consciously applied.

Let's look at an example of the difficulty involved in applying grammar rules while speaking. To correctly say the Spanish equivalent of a seemingly simple sentence like *Our parents wanted us to be here*, a speaker would have to know a great amount of information and would have to make several lightning-fast decisions while saying the sentence (*Nuestros padres querían que estuviéramos aquí.*):

1. The vocabulary is the most important item. If the student doesn't know the words, s/he has no hope of being able to express this idea at all. S/he must know the vocabulary well enough to produce it almost instantly.

2. The student must know that *padres* means parents even though *padre* means father.

3. The student must know that adjectives must agree in gender and number with the noun they modify.

4. S/he must know the gender of *padres*.

5. S/he must know the correct past tense to use in this situation.

6. S/he must know the third-person plural form of this past tense for the verb *querer*.

7. S/he must know that *querer* followed by a change of subject requires the use of *que*.

8. S/he must know that *querer* followed by a change of subject requires the use of the subjunctive after *que*.

9. S/he must know that *querer* in the past requires that the verb following *que* be in the past subjunctive.

10. S/he must know that the verb *estar*, not *ser*, is required when speaking of the location of people or things.

11. S/he must know the first-person plural past subjunctive form of the irregular verb *estar*.

If we assume a computer-brained superstar student knows all the words, all the rules and all the forms, we see that this still is not enough. The student must also be focused on the need to apply all of these rules. And s/he must be able to apply the rules quickly enough so the person listening will remain patient enough to still listen. While this may seem like an extreme example, the concept is valid. To speak correctly, the person would have to edit every sentence s/he utters. S/he would need to edit and correct every word s/he utters. It is obvious that even for the most intelligent of the intelligent this whole process is virtually impossible. It is obvious how much more trouble an average student would have pulling this off after learning all of the above.

Only Comprehensible Input?

There is general agreement that production of grammatically accurate speech is one of the primary goals of language study. And yet, if Krashen is right about how grammatically correct speech is achieved, in most language classes and texts there is a great deal of time spent on activities which do not lead to it.

So, if learning grammar rules doesn't lead to grammatically accurate speech, what does? Krashen (1994) presents convincing evidence that comprehensible input is what leads to the great majority of acquisition of language. He also believes that nearly all language is acquired rather than learned. What we need to do then, above all, is to provide a great quantity of comprehensible input in a variety of ways.

If we were to take this idea to its logical extreme, all we would do in language classes would be to provide comprehensible input. The Natural Approach purports to do something close to this, although in practice most practitioners seem to include many learning activities. The "narrative approach" proposed by McQuillan and Tse (1998; see "What's New in This Edition and in TPRS (Preface to the Second Edition)" at the beginning of this book) would come much closer if implemented fully. The "listening approach" of Brown and Palmer (1988) does in fact go all the way, providing only comprehensible input.

We agree with Krashen that input must be emphasized. If we could give our students 6,000 words (100 words a minute) of comprehensible input in every class throughout the school year, then we could give our students a million words a year of comprehensible input.

On the other hand, if we put our students in groups doing output activities, the students would:

1. speak slowly

2. use very simple words and structures

3. use language that has already been acquired and, as a result, would be getting virtually no new input during that time

Looking at the numbers, it can easily been seen what is most efficient in learning a foreign language — comprehensible input.

To get our students to hear and understand a million words, we could simply teach them a few phrases and use those phrases over and over. Too boring. So we must have a specific plan that will frequently provide students with *new* interesting comprehensible input. Krashen warns that providing too much new input could result in *less comprehensible* input due to new-input overload and a probability of considerable boring content.

In TPRS we include speaking activities, although the great majority of them are not learning activities, since students and teachers focus on the content and not on the correctness of the language. Usually they are, in some measure, acquisition activities, since they generally entail listening as well as speaking. However, this is not the main purpose of them. The main purpose of them is neither learning nor acquisition, but the building of confidence in speaking. Speaking helps to make a student feel like a real speaker of her/his new language, as Krashen has pointed out. Practice in speaking over time seems to also decrease the speaker's anxiety or, as Krashen puts it, it "lowers the affective filter." Confidence is a significant ingredient in fluency (although, oddly enough, there is no experimental evidence that fluency per se results from speaking). The speaking activities we use contribute to the development of fluency by gradually both (1) improving confidence and (2) increasing speed of delivery of utterances at least to a point where it is close to normal.

Some activities are neither acquisition nor learning activities. Speaking is not always a learning activity. Sometimes it is just expression, communicating, output. It is also performance of the speaker's competence, as linguist Noam Chomsky (1965) famously put it. It is an indication of the level of competence of a student in the language, allowing assessment of what features of the language a student has acquired — a valuable assessment tool.

Targeted Vocabulary Words and Grammar

Many targeted vocabulary words in TPRS are actually phrases. Many of these phrases contain significant grammatical features such as the word order of a noun-adjective combination or of an object pronoun-verb combination or (in English) a two-word preposition or (in German or English) a separable verb. Students are required to use these as they retell mini-stories. This is an important and effective technique for the accurate acquisition of grammatical features.

190

Explained Grammar

After the classical TPR phase, starting with the first storytelling chapter, we briefly explain new grammatical features that appear in them. These explanations are usually extremely brief — one second or so. In the third and fourth years we explain to students some advanced grammatical concepts such as certain uses of the subjunctive. Certain elements of grammar are acquired later than others. Traditionally curriculum makers (textbook writers and most teachers) and test makers such as those of the Educational Testing Service have wanted specific elements to be learned and/or acquired by a certain point. Textbooks and teachers have dealt with grammatical features in a more or less traditional order, an order that is not the same (at least for any commonly taught language) as the natural order of acquisition of features that Krashen and we agree occurs.[1]

Developing Ease of Expression

In timed writings, or "freewrites," and in class discussions, students are given the opportunity to express themselves and develop ease of expression. We have class discussions every Wednesday, Thursday and Friday. We do freewrites every Friday. During this part of class we get our students into higher levels of production both in speaking and writing.

A Radically Practical Approach to Grammar

This approach to dealing with grammar is a radical departure from the usual. In most language teaching, grammar is taught explicitly from the beginning or almost the beginning. In the typical current-day non-TPRS classroom where non-TPRS textbooks are used, point after grammatical point is studied and drilled without regard to students' ability to produce correct real speech or writing involving these grammatical points. Students study (or at least are exposed to) one or more points, are tested on them and then move on to one or more other grammatical points, whether they have demonstrated any degree of mastery of them in real communication or not. Our view is that these practices actually slow down and detract from the overall process of the acquisition of a language.

Some teachers might not want to teach without explicit grammar instruction because students make errors early. But, the fact is that students make early errors under any system. It is just that with our approach they are actually talking much earlier (as opposed to parroting and doing grammar exercises), so they are bound to make more errors. If the teacher understands what students will be able to do at level four, s/he will be much more tolerant of early errors. It is much easier for students to handle explained grammar once they have acquired most of the more basic grammatical features of a language — a powerful reason to delay the explicit teaching of grammar.

Emphasizing rules early forces students to slow down their speech and edit it more, meaning that they may always be editing when they speak. A byproduct of learning is hesitancy, which is the opposite of fluency. The earlier the learning, the more the hesitancy. And the more grammar points students are taught in, say, a month, the more hesitancy there is, because they monitor their speech much more. Ignoring rules for the first many months allows fluency to develop. When students have acquired a considerable amount of language and are rather fluent, learning can begin to be useful. They can then use rules to edit or monitor fluent speech. However, in my experience, it generally takes a lot more input than we have time for in a school setting for even the best students to be able to edit their speech without undue hesitancy.

Students want to be able to communicate in the language, but if a year passes and they see they can't, many drop out. Among those who stick with it for a second year, if they can't speak to any degree by the end of that year, many more give up. So, what is achieved by spending time on grammar early? One major result is to discourage large numbers of students from "learning" a language. Certainly this is not the intention of anyone who believes students should learn grammar from the beginning. Certainly it is not the intention of anyone who writes textbooks or who makes up exams to measure competency at various levels. Nonetheless, it is a significant result.

Another effect of putting off learning grammar is that the longer you do so, the better your students will learn it. For one thing, the language they have acquired will make it easier for them to understand the grammar, since they can actually "see" it in their own speech. For another, no matter what you emphasize, some of the lower students will have disappeared, so you will be working on grammar with a more select group of students, many of whom will be good learners.

The Importance of Having Students Use Vocabulary Words and Phrases

It is imperative that you display new vocabulary words and phrases when you teach mini-stories, especially as students get more advanced. Students tend to go back to level one speech if they aren't required to use the words that are in front of them as they retell a mini-story. When they are required to use them, students use the advanced verb conjugations instead of talking around them. The same is true of other grammatical features that appear in targeted vocabulary items. Using the words and phrases in context helps students get a feeling for using them correctly. Later they start showing up in their spontaneous speech.

Note

1. There is much evidence that there is a natural order of acquisition of grammatical features by second language learners of all languages (see Krashen, 1977, and Krashen and Terrell, 1983: 28-30). The order is not absolute. Rather, it functions by groups of features that are acquired more or less at the same time. Once one group has been acquired, another group follows it. Of course, it is still dependent on comprehensible input, since obviously if a learner is never exposed to a particular feature, there would be no way for her/him to acquire it.

Chapter 13

Student Rapport

Perhaps the most important part of teaching is getting along with the students. Most teachers know that one key to the job is getting the students on their side and getting them to learn by making the activities fun. That, unfortunately, is more easily said than done.

Get to Know Your Students

Whatever method you choose, somehow you must get information about your students' lives. You will put this information to good use in class. You talk to the class about individual students. It doesn't matter how you get the information, only that you know it and use it at appropriate times during the class. Everyone has things they are interested in. One day a student came into my class at noon and spent a lot of time telling me about her coin collection. She had traveled to many places and had collected coins from various countries. With pride she told me about some of her prized coins. This same girl had organized a talent show for a small town in Pakistan the year before she moved to the United States. She felt great pride in her efforts. With this information I was ready to talk about her in class. No student has ever come up to me and asked me not to talk about him/her in front of the class. They are proud and happy when I showcase their accomplishments in front of the class.

If you teach high school, read the sports sections of your local paper for information about your students. Let the class know that Amanda Bernal won all three of her matches in tennis last night and that Kevin Lyon caught a touchdown pass plus three other passes. Let them know if a student makes all-league or not. I promise you they will want to understand your class if you are talking about them.

Extra Credit

When my students take their first test of the year, I tell them that they can always have two points extra credit by writing about themselves. I let them write to me in English or Spanish. I spend a lot of time answering those comments. I always try to build up their confidence in themselves. I remember the information they share with me and, if appropriate, I brag about them to the class.

When students are negative about what I do, I ask them not to say negative things in class. If they say class is boring, I tell them not to say that. If they don't want to do what I have planned, I tell them to not tell me about it.

Amy Knupp

One year I had a girl who was negative every day she walked into class. Amy let me know my class was her most boring class of the day. She told me that it was even more boring than biology (the ultimate insult). After listening to her for many months, about March I told Amy that I had a goal for her. I didn't want any more negative words the rest of the year. I offered her something (I can't remember what) in return if she would keep her part of the bargain. She did and I felt when she left my class she was much more positive. She came back the next summer and had signed up for Spanish 3. She told me she had been in Colombia for the summer and had been able to speak and understand a lot of Spanish. I said, "That is great. You will be excited about learning Spanish this year."

She replied, "I will not."

Amy came into my class two years later to tell me about a summer Spanish program she had been to where she pledged to speak only Spanish for five weeks. She wanted me to tell other students about it. I felt great pride in her progress.

Sometimes entire classes would make negative remarks. When I heard that, I would do my best to stop it. Many times when I handed out books (*Look, I Can Really Talk!* (Ray and Neilson, 1994a)) in my third-year class, the students would breathe a collective negative sigh that said, "Oh no! Do we have to?"

Sammi Plottner

That was when I would tell them the Sammi Plottner story. Sammi was kinder to me than any student I have ever had. One time she came back from lunch and brought me a muffin. She gave me candy bars (I really didn't need them) and other gifts. Sammi was just a kind person. At the end of the year, students give teachers scholarship recommendation forms. Sammi gave me hers. I couldn't help but write things that let the reader know that there was something special about this girl. Though there were many deserving students in the school, Sammi was the one kid who was most deserving. Awards night came and went. I was not able to attend but asked someone about it. His comment was "It was the Sammi Plottner show." I then tell my classes that I know they don't like everything we do, but even if they don't like it, they need to act like they do. Now when I hand out books, the entire class yells, "Yippee! I like these books." We all know it is a joke, but it is a positive one. I feel good and they do too.

One day I was talking to a student from another high school. I asked him who his favorite teacher was. He said that it was his Spanish teacher. I asked him why. He responded, "Because she talks to me." What a simple recipe for success with your students. Talk to them.

Shake Their Hands at the Door

When your students enter the room, shake their hands. Go up to one and ask about his family or his day. Ask about what he did last night or about sports. Ask if he has a girlfriend or if he gets along with his mom. Find out if his parents are divorced. If so, does he live with his mom or dad? These are simple questions, yet they show that you care. When students leave the room, stand at the door and give them a warm, two-handed handshake. Compliment them on their nice clothes. Tell them you are glad they are in your class. Above all, smile.

When I first started teaching, I taught at a small high school in Northern Idaho. I walked down the hall and not one student said hi to me. It was like ice. I went to another high school and things were better but still pretty much the same. I just didn't know how to get along well with the students. I finally read *How to Win Friends and Influence People* (Carnegie, 1981).

That book had a great impact on my life. I started practicing the ideas Dale Carnegie taught. Those ideas worked like magic. Students responded to my warmth. After teaching for fifteen years, I was finally voted "Teacher of the Month." Many teachers received that award year after year, but for me, I felt it came because I had finally learned how to put my students first.

I love getting to know my students. I want to let them know I care.

Chapter 14

Adapting a Textbook for TPRS

Those of us who encourage teachers to use TPR Storytelling® are frequently asked, "How can I use this method with the textbook my school makes me use?" We asked Karen Rowan and Susan Gross for their opinions. (See Appendix A, "TPR Storytelling Presenters.") The majority of this thoroughly revised chapter was written by Rowan.

The Real Issue for Textbook-Using Teachers

Susan Gross taught French at Cheyenne Mountain Junior High School in Colorado Springs and is a TPRS™ workshop presenter. Gross says, "The real issue for most teachers is not vocabulary, but grammar. They think they have to do the grammar in their adopted textbook. Even though the book's grammar lessons very likely do not follow the *natural order of acquisition* (see note 1 at the end of Chapter 12), they feel that the grammar sequence is sacred because it is 'in the book.' Once they understand how to teach grammar through stories, they are likely to be much less apprehensive about it."

Essentially, what she is saying is that, if you use TPRS to teach stories which contain many examples of the grammatical features you want to be acquired (and the features are simple enough so that they don't come before their place in the natural order of acquisition), your students will acquire them better than they will if you explain the grammar to them and have them do learning exercises. You simply include the grammatical features that you want students to acquire in the stories that they work on. You keep on including them in more and more stories until they seem very natural to your students. After this goes on for a while, these features start to appear in their speech as they are expressing themselves in their own words. This is when you know that they have been acquired.

An important technique that we use to make sure that students start to use grammatical features, and new vocabulary too, is listing the target structures on the overhead or chalkboard. Some grammatical features need explanation, so we quickly explain them when we list the words for them. We start doing this soon after storytelling begins. We do not drill them or have students do worksheets or exercises in a textbook — learning activities that do not bring the results we're looking for.

Gross goes on to say, "Nevertheless, these teachers want and need a grammar syllabus. (See "The Grammar Covered in Three Years in the Look, I Can Talk! Series" in Appendix E.) No matter what Krashen says, grammar is where the rubber meets the road for the vast majority of textbook-bound teachers." (See all of Chapter 12.)

As we say in Chapter 12, TPR Storytelling methodology is a radical departure from the usual grammar-centered curriculum. (If you have not yet read Chapter 12, "Teaching Grammar as Meaning," we urge you to read it now.) The fact is that your students are likely to learn their grammar just as well and probably better with TPRS than with any of the usual alternatives. Consider what Sue Steele wrote on August 26, 1998 (There is a letter written earlier by her in Appendix F.):

> With my students' skills in grammar getting worse and worse, I felt I had to find a way of teaching French that did not rely on my students to have had a good grammar background. TPRS does that for me. They listen first, then they speak, then we write, and then discuss the grammar. In fact, they ask the grammar questions. They are using direct and indirect objects by the 6th/7th week. They are using pronominal verbs at this same time. They ask questions, I explain. Then we go on. Their writing

skills at the end of one year are phenomenal. For their exam, they had to write a children's story of at least 200 words. I have kept them all. They are just so good. I have showed them to several people, and other French teachers have been in awe.

I have had to change my teaching in order for my students to be successful. I had been searching for the last 10 years or so. It had to be something that I felt that taught the grammar but would not be so painful for both my students and me. Something that would keep students involved in learning French without dropping out because they have felt so helpless since they did not understand the grammar. This method at least keeps the students involved in their learning. They are part of the learning experience since they get to write their own stories. They help me come up with signs. They love knowing that they are participating in their learning. I am no longer teaching to cover a language but to help my students learn a language. I no longer care if I have not covered what I should have covered by such and such a time. I care that my students can speak, write, read, and comprehend. They are not afraid of the language.

I am a grammarian. I am determined that my students know their grammar. This method is working for me and my students. It was hard for me to change. It was very frightening. The results have satisfied me. My standards are very high. I am known as a "hard teacher." I am still a drill sergeant in my classroom. A very happy drill sergeant!!!!!

Sue Steele

Brighton High School

Brighton, Michigan

While we believe that following a grammar-driven curriculum actually slows down and detracts from the overall process of the acquisition of a language, we offer some suggestions here for adapting a textbook.

Several Options

There are several options when adapting a textbook to teach through TPRS. We describe three below. All of them deal with both grammar and vocabulary. All of them presuppose that you have taught at least 50 to 150 words through classical TPR before you begin to work on storytelling. (See the beginning of Chapter 5, the third-to-last paragraph in this chapter and Appendices D and G.)

Notice that what we are recommending is that you adapt your textbook to work with TPRS, not the other way around. All of the options we describe can work. TPRS is a comprehensive method that leads to successful acquisition of the target language. Using it piecemeal will not bring this about.

Occasional use of TPRS will, on the other hand, at least give students more comprehensible input than they would have received otherwise. While it is true that this would help them to acquire *some* language, it is also true that frequent exposure to comprehensible input yields much, much more acquisition. If, at the same time, the teacher avoids making discrete grammar explanations that are not in context, students' fluency tends to develop without impairment.

Vocabulary lists in textbooks often exceed 100 words per chapter. Texts often have more than 15 chapters. This quantity of vocabulary approximates the active vocabulary that most adults have in their native languages. According to Jim Trelease (1982: 21), adults use an average of 1,800 different words in everyday speech. The most frequent vocabulary words are obviously the most needed words. They are the most frequent words because they are used every day by all speakers in all social environments. The same is true of all basic grammatical features. Focusing on these words and grammatical features by providing them via lots of comprehensible input is what our experience has shown leads to early fluency. Diluting the input by spending more time on less essential vocabulary and grammar doesn't just delay fluency; it doesn't lead to it at all. Teachers should liberally reduce vocabulary lists. Whether looking at the text chapter by chapter or looking at two to four chapters at a time or looking at the text as a whole, low-frequency vocabulary should be eliminated.

Don't forget that your textbook may cover some grammar points in an order which deviates from the natural order of acquisition. So you won't want to spend time on features which students can't acquire before they have acquired certain other ones (see note 1 at the end of Chapter 12).

Why Adapt a Textbook to TPRS?

According to Karen Rowan, who has adapted four textbooks in their entirety to date, you definitely should not do this. Rowan presents TPRS coaching workshops which include textbook adaptation instructions, and is the co-owner with Blaine Ray of Fluency Fast Language Classes, Inc. She is also the author of the Prentice Hall TPRS textbook adaptation ancillaries for *Paso a paso* (2000 and 2002) and *Realidades* (2004 and 2008) and the editor of the *International Journal of Foreign Language Teaching*. Unless there is absolutely no other viable option, do not adapt your textbook to TPRS, she says. It is time-consuming, difficult and takes a great deal of the pleasure out of both teaching and TPRS. The grammar syllabus of the textbook inhibits the natural order of acquisition. The only situation where it makes any sense to adapt a textbook and write your own stories is when use of a non-TPRS textbook is required and a good TPRS ancillary is not available.

Option 1: Use TPRS materials and use the textbook series as a supplement

There are three ways to do this:

A. Whenever possible, use TPRS materials that were already written such as the *Look, I Can Talk!* series (see "Ministories" in Chapter 5, "Storytelling in the First Year;" the beginning of Chapter 6, "The Second Year;" the beginning of Chapter 7, "The Third and Fourth Years;" and the list of available TPRS materials in Appendix K) and use the textbook as a supplement. Some of the most valuable elements of textbook series are the ancillaries, such as the videos and readers and resources for teaching art, history and culture.

You can use *Look, I Can Talk!* (in French, German, Spanish or English; Ray, 1990) and give assignments from the textbook as homework. Take the last five minutes of class to tell your students what they need to do in the book. Your students will understand the text exercises so much better because of the TPRS that you do in the classroom.

Rowan cautions that one important drawback to this method is that going over homework the day after it is assigned is time-consuming. Because this is not an input activity, time that could be spent on acquisition is spent on grammar explanations. We recommend you use as little time as possible doing this.

B. You can also follow the order of the chapters in *Look, I Can Talk!* and choose themes from your text that will meld easily with the content of *Look, I Can Talk!* With this option you are not adapting your text chapter by chapter but, rather, by theme, with the understanding that your class will not "cover" the entire book. Remember that you are not adapting TPRS to your textbook. You are adapting your text for TPRS.

C. Alternatively, use *Look, I Can Talk!* and then take the last two or three weeks of the semester and cover all the material in the textbook. Teach the class the grammar they will need to know and have them study any vocabulary you think is important.

Gross had good success with racing through the textbook at the end of the year. "The students thought it was a kick to do a chapter every two or three days. They were flabbergasted to discover that they had actually learned a whole book's worth of French without realizing it." Mary Holmes had good results doing this in 2001-2002. See her posting in Chapter 15. Rowan also taught her students to use verb charts and conjugate verbs vertically in preparation for other teachers' expectations.

It is important to let colleagues know that you are covering the text and that your students will be prepared for the next level. It is also important to have the support of a principal or someone above you. For more on this, see the answer to the question "What should I do if none of the other teachers in my department teach with this method?" on p. 239 in Chapter 16. It is also wise for teachers to keep a high profile with parents. Parents marvel at the rapidity with which their children are learning to speak a second language.

Option 2: Use TPRS textbook ancillaries

If you cannot use TPRS materials, explore the options available in textbook ancillaries. A few publishing companies have worked with TPRS teachers and authors to create valuable, legitimate and useful ancillaries. Even if the textbook you are using has only a small ancillary that doesn't provide enough stories so that you can adapt the text adequately to TPRS, peruse it anyway for any small gems it might contain, such as illustrations that could be used to inspire a good story. It is possible to use a TPRS supplement from a series other than the one from which you are teaching.

Using TPRS materials that are already written is less time-consuming and generally simpler. TPRS is a very low-maintenance methodology and can require very little planning and very little grading when teachers do not have to create their own materials from scratch.

Rowan provided the following guidelines to help in choosing and using TPRS supplementary books:

10 Things to Look for in a TPRS Textbook Ancillary

1. How many pages is the ancillary? A meaty supplement means more to work with. One that is only a few pages long probably indicates it's not as useful and was created as a sales gimmick, not a serious TPRS aid. Some ancillaries have short vocabulary lists, illustrations and stories that are about three sentences long. They provide insufficient support for the teacher who wants to teach primarily with

TPRS, but interesting resources for teachers who dabble in TPRS.

2. When was the ancillary written? TPRS has changed a lot over the years. Recent ancillaries are more likely to be consistent with current practices, which are more effective and efficient than earlier practices.

3. Who wrote the ancillary? Is it an experienced TPRS presenter/teacher who is on the MoreTPRS listserv or someone who works for the publishing company who is not a TPRS teacher? Is the name on the front of the book actually the author? Some companies have used the names of reputable TPRS teachers, but had the books mostly ghostwritten to get them out faster. Blaine Ray has written forewords to several textbook ancillaries. This should not be seen as an endorsement of the text but a confirmation that the publishing company gave credit where credit was due and speaks well of their integrity.

4. Is the vocabulary for each story presented as isolated vocabulary words like *letter* and *write* or as structural phrases like *writes a letter*?

5. Did the book use all of the vocabulary from the textbook — a smattering of vocabulary from the textbook or only the high-frequency words? Books with too little will be difficult to use. Books that teach all of the words are likely to be too bulky because they are using a lot of low-frequency vocabulary.

6. Is vocabulary recycled throughout the ancillary? Vocabulary that is presented only once and never recycled indicates that either the book uses low-frequency vocabulary that wouldn't naturally show up in later stories and/or that the grammatical scope and sequence is driving the stories, isolating discrete grammar items in their own chapters.

7. Is the ancillary following a grammatical scope and sequence? The more loosely-tied the stories are to a gram-

matical syllabus, the more natural-sounding the stories will be.

8. Look over all of the levels. If the level 2 and 3 books use simple structures and basic TPR, they probably weren't written by an experienced TPRS teacher and probably won't be very useful for TPRS. The procedures suggested for each level should not be exactly the same.

9. Are there reading materials provided in the form of mini-stories, extended readings or readers? (If not, supplement with the *Pobre Ana* series. Reading is an essential part of a strong TPRS program.)

10. Regardless of which ancillary you are perusing, none exists that provides an adequate introduction to TPRS. The introductions and directions are not intended to be a replacement for a workshop or for this book.

Option 3: Create your own materials

Using a textbook that has not been adapted is the highest maintenance way to use TPRS and it is not recommended unless it is unavoidable because planning time will be drastically increased. It is somewhat easier for the teacher who can think on her or his feet and create stories from personalized questions and then write them down later. Teachers who want to script their stories out ahead of time will increase their workload considerably. This is, however, an excellent way to train yourself and is used by many TPRS teachers in the beginning.

For those who really want to adapt their texts, here is the process that Rowan used to create the Prentice Hall textbook adaptations:

1. Paring Down the Vocabulary List

Mark Davies, author of *A Frequency Dictionary of Spanish* (2006: 2), says that most frequency dictionaries were created using written language as a guide. Thus, the word *poesía* becomes high-frequency in Spanish. Much of Davies' book is based on spoken language. The 100 to 200 highest-frequency words should be taught first in any language.

Virtually all structures — simple to advanced — can be taught using the most crucially necessary words.

a.   Some chapters can be eliminated almost in their entirety if the theme involves rarely used vocabulary. Car parts, camping terms and exotic fruits generally fall in the realm of the 5,000th to 10,000th most common words in any language. Eliminate them guilt-free and use the saved time to provide more comprehensible input on essential vocabulary.

b.   Each chapter's vocabulary list can be pared down considerably if it is cross-referenced with a frequency dictionary. Don't want to put in the effort? Determining low-frequency vocabulary is largely a function of common sense. If you've never heard it outside of a classroom in the last 20 years, it may be safe for your students to live into their mid-20s without it.

c.   Cognates should be recognizable without translation or a high number of repetitions. Teachers will be able to communicate in full sentences with a broad variety of vocabulary quickly by using cognates. Be mindful of false cognates. True cognates do not need to be presented in TPRS structures, and can even be presented in reading. A cognate should only be considered a usable cognate if it is comprehensible to the pacesetter (barometer) students. Otherwise, writing aurally unrecognizable words such as *hamburguesa* on the board generally converts the word to a usable cognate.

d.   Some words such as action verbs and classroom objects can be taught more quickly with classical TPR. Pare down your list with a little aerobic TPR at the beginning of a chapter, teaching three words at a time and gradually increasing the number. (See Appendix G for an explanation of how to use TPR.) A general rule of thumb is that a word can be taught through TPR if its meaning is transparent without translation. Still, write the words and definitions on the board to avoid possible confusion.

2. Creating Mini-stories

    a. Make a list of important language structures

       Select the highest-frequency vocabulary and the most important structures to teach in a mini-story. Examples of structures at different levels:

       Basic:

          wants to go

       Intermediate:

          would have to buy

          will be hungry

          she got along well with her

          he takes a shower (Spanish: él se ducha; Spanish structure in English: he showers himself)

       Advanced:

          X wanted her to go with him (Spanish: X quería que ella le acompañara; Spanish structure in English: X wanted that she go with him)

          it was important for her to leave (Spanish: era importante que ella saliera; Spanish structure in English: it was important that she leave)

          he gave it to her

          he did not give it to her; he threw it at her

          she did not accept it; she threw it at him

    b. Personalized questions and answers, using one structure

       Choose only one structure to use the vocabulary in context in personalized questions and answers (PQA). Use the target structure in each question and begin a conversation with the class. See the section on PQA in Chapter 5 for some ideas. The verb forms will change to the second-person familiar or formal and the first-person singular and may also include the first-person plural or the second-person plural. Begin with whatever seems to lend itself most easily to conversation. For example, don't ask, "What did you give to someone else?" — which is impersonal and uninteresting. Instead, you might say, "What did you give your best friend for her/his birthday?" or "What was the worst gift anybody ever gave you?" — which would lead to potentially interesting conversations.

Pursuing conversations through personalized questions and answers while using the target structures is the simplest way to teach vocabulary and structures. Students need a high number of repetitions of vocabulary in context in order to acquire it. Many times, interesting questions will inspire ideas for stories.

c. Creation of the mini-story

Two ways to create a story:

i. Let the personalized questions develop into a story that you create "on your feet." If the story isn't a home run, you will have still provided ample comprehensible input.

ii. Prepare a story in advance by scripting it. The simplest story structure is:

X has a problem. S/he wants / needs / lacks Y.

S/he goes to location 1 to look for Y. S/he doesn't find it.

S/he goes to location 2 to look for Y. S/he finds it. S/he is happy.

The story must (a) have a problem to be solved, (b) be compelling and (c) be personalized. It is helpful to use students in the class and/or celebrities as characters in the story. Exaggerated movements, motions and numbers add pizzazz. Each mini-story should have about three new structures. As a group, the mini-stories will include all of the new vocabulary words the students need to know for the chapter. These are the basics. For a much more thorough treatment of this question, see "Preparing a Mini-story" and "Creating a Story for Class" on pp. 32-34 in Chapter 3 and all of Chapter 4, "Developing a Mini-story Through Questioning."

3. Creating Extended Readings

Use already written extended readings whenever possible.

To write your own extended reading, use the list of vocabulary structures and write them at the top of a page. Then write the story as it happened in one of your classes. Use the names of your students. Use the same vocabulary words multiple times to get adequate repetitions of the structures. If the story was a home run in class, it should be a home run on paper. Consider changing some of the details for variety. If you absolutely can't come up with a compelling ending, leave it blank and write it together in class using the students' ideas

Final Essential Considerations

We *caution* you that if you spend time teaching grammatical features that are found in textbooks early but really are not acquired until much later, you will be wasting your time and your students'. Whether students have learned a rule or not, they will very probably not apply it when they express themselves in speech until they have acquired certain other grammatical features that precede it in the *natural order of acquisition* (note 1 at the end of Chapter 12). Remember that students *acquire* grammar mainly through comprehensible input, not through *learning* rules. And each student acquires grammatical accuracy at her/his own pace. Examples of grammar points that usually occur in first-year textbooks but which students do not acquire until much later are: the uses of *ser* and *estar* and the personal *a* (in Spanish), the uses of *the* and *a/an* (in English) and the partitive (in French). Stick with basics like verb-form correctness and noun/adjective agreement (in French and Spanish). These are features that are acquired fairly early.

Regardless of what text is being used or which option is chosen, at the very least some form of the first TPR list should be taught via classical TPR before storytelling begins. (See Appendix D, the beginning of Chapter 5 and Appendix G.) Once you have taught most of the words from the first list, you will be able to use these to create interesting, surprising, even captivating stories. For example, students generally need to know the words *give*, *say* and *throw* in early stories, even though they aren't introduced until the later chapters of most textbooks. (If you are using *Look, I Can Talk!*, this is even more important, as the preliminary list of words is used frequently from the very beginning).

There is perhaps no component of a TPRS curriculum that is more crucial and essential than a reading program. Regardless of what materials you are using to create stories, investing in readers or novels that are comprehensible is paramount. Since most textbook programs do not have readers like the *Pobre Ana* series by Blaine Ray, most of the teachers who come to textbook adaptation workshops or participate in discussions on TPRS textbook adaptation listservs use the Blaine Ray readers to supplement their programs. (See Chapter 10 on developing a reading program.) Rowan notes that she can tell the difference — from the speaking and writing of the students — between a TPRS program with a reading program and one without. Reading is even more essential when students are using adapted TPRS materials.

The most dangerous trap a teacher can fall into is to believe that s/he can continue teaching pretty much the same way s/he has been. The problem with this is that textbooks are grammar- and output-based. Generally, teachers who try to make TPR Storytelling fit the text — by using reading comprehension stories that are in the text as TPRS stories and/or by teaching grammar explicitly — are ultimately unsuccessful because they are trying to do the impossible — which can only lead to frustration. Those who adapt their text to work with TPR Storytelling generally succeed, and they and their students love the difference.

Chapter 15

The More TPRS List

In August, 1999, Michael Kundrat and Kristy Placido started a TPRS™ listserv. I believe this has done more to train teachers in TPRS than all the workshops we have presented. The list has turned into an invaluable resource for teachers around the world to learn TPRS. It allows them to get immediate answers to their questions. There are now about 5,000 members on the More list.

The More TPRS list can be joined by going to:

http://groups.yahoo.com/group/moretprs

All should be aware of the following guidelines:

1. Members of this list should be trained in TPRS (workshop, video or some other manner of training)

2. Members should be practicing TPRS teachers (although some of us are retired from teaching or are full-time presenters, methods instructors, etc.)

3. Members should be willing to learn from each other and promote a supportive, kind and helpful atmosphere that we have all grown to love about this list!

Below are some excerpts from the list.

From: "Carmen Andrews-Sanchez" <sancca@e...>
Date: Thu Sep 21, 2000 7:50 pm
Subject: Why I love TPRS!

Ok, I know that most of you don't need to hear this, but I just am bursting at the seams with my love for TPRS! This is long, so I won't be offended if you delete without reading! :)

Last night was our Open House. I have never had so much fun in 6 years of Open Houses. Anyway, I had planned to talk really specifically about the whys of TPRS, etc., and I just got so carried away I couldn't even finish in the 10 mins that I had with each class of parents. We always end up with students that come to open house, which I think is weird, but this year I just used them! I had a volunteer from each class come up and after I quickly introduced myself in Spanish, I told the MINI-STORY with the boy who's afraid of falling cats and had a student act it out. Meanwhile, the parents eyes were huge — having to listen to all of that Spanish. Anyway, I then told them that when I first began teaching how I had used TPR and had great success at using a lot of Spanish in my classes.

In about the 2nd semester, I hit the grammar in the book and had a hard time using as much Spanish. My students always learned a lot about the language, but they could never really use it, and I had been searching since to try and find the way to get my students to speak Spanish. I told the parents that I was embarrassed, that for 5 years I stood in front of parents at Open Houses and invariably a parent would ask, "Will my student be fluent in 4 years?" and I would have to say that "A few will be, but, unfortunately, most will not." I told them from the bottom of my heart that I think that this is WRONG! It is wrong for foreign language teachers to say that we can't teach students what our JOB is to teach them!

I said that I didn't mean this as a criticism of other teachers, as we have terrific teachers at our school. I told them that I went to a workshop this summer and found my answer how to get kids to speak Spanish — TPRS. I explained the steps to them. I told them about unannounced tests. I told them why I don't give much homework — basic-ally, that it doesn't do them much good anyway! Aside from the re-search (which is pretty strong), I know firsthand that most students copy their work from someone else or do their homework during the 5 mins. before class or are trying to cram it in between sports, families, etc. All of the parents were extremely supportive of the small amount of homework. I shared some of the other class activities that we did. I was funny — the parents smiled and laughed through the entire presen-tation — even the students who are usually bored to tears during Open House (making me always wonder again why they come!) were en-gaged in the presentation and nodding to their parents, etc. One parent in my 6th period class said, "When the bell rings, I'm having so much fun I want to stay and learn Spanish!" (just a funny note - this mom had orange hair in 2 big ponytails and reminded me totally of Cindy Lauper — her daughter is pretty much the exact opposite - pretty aver-age as far as clothes and things go! :)) When I was finished in each class, parents told me how much their children loved my class. One parent told me that there son (an average ability kid) comes home EVERY DAY and acts out that day's story and tells it to them in Span-ish, even though they don't understand a word of it. I did not have one negative comment from parents and very little skepticism. Funny, when I was the one that told Blaine when I registered for the confer-ence that I was skeptical because I still couldn't see how you could use TPRS with the upper levels...and, while I believed the basics of the methodology, I needed to see it to believe it! I walked out of Open House bursting at the seams with joy. I finally feel like I am a great teacher. Do I have a lot to learn? Sure I do. And so do my students! And I am excited and love teaching them every single day.

Are there days when they just aren't into it? Of course there are...but, there are many more where I see their eyes looking at me with interest and I am so proud of them when they can retell the story. Today I was bouncing off the walls with joy — when after putting "mientras" [while] in 3 stories and pretty much every kid left it out when they retold — today, in EVERY class a kid said while he was in Spain, he bought a lottery ticket — and I had never put it in today's story! How awesome is that? They took 10-word vocabulary quizzes today and the class averages were 80%, 85%, 86%, and 91%!!!! How much do I love TPRS? More than I can even express in words (even though I have written many, many today!) Another (TPRS) teacher said to me that most of her kids' freewrites are pretty good, but some made absolutely no sense — and she wondered how I was 'grading' them and how my kids' freewrites were. I pulled a girl's paper who has had a lot of trouble so far this year — she really was missing a big chunk of what she should have known from Span. 1 — like today she asked me what day I was tutoring and — when I said "lunes, martes, miércoles y jueves" — she looked at me like I was from outer space. Anyway, I pulled her freewrite out thinking that it would be a good example of a student's freewrite that wasn't very good - her first freewrite had 29 words. Today's was over 100 words and really only had minor errors in it but was almost completely understandable!!!!! I know that I have a long ways to go, but I just get excited about getting better because my kids are so much better than when I was teaching with the textbook! I just feel like I have seen the light and my whole life as a teacher has taken on new meaning. This is really what it means to be a teacher, isn't it? I am so happy that I literally shed tears over this stuff. Thank you, Blaine!

Carmen :)

From: gringostar@aol.com (Jeff Brown of Long Beach)
Subject: Re: Student complaints/long

I am sorry to hear about your fifth year students complaining and such. I teach in a high risk school and sometimes believe that complaining from students is the norm and not the exception. One of the things I have been doing this year which works real well is, I have been letting the kids vote on what they want to do. Some days, I have two lessons for them, one for storytelling and one from the book. Then I let them vote, and almost always they vote for the stories as opposed to the book. Therefore, if we vote, they cannot complain. If they say, 'This story is boring,' then I say 'Well, you make up the story.' Or I say, 'I know. As soon as you hear my story, you can make your story and tell it to the class, and then we can vote on whether it is more boring than my story.'

Date: Thu, 7 Mar 2002 22:02:52 -0600
From: Dan Cox <dcox@po-1.w-marshall.k12.ia.us>
Subject: another comment on success

The timed write and success threads have popped up in recent posts and I wanted to comment. Writing is one area that my kids have really excelled at as a whole when it comes to quantity. At least 90% of my level one kids are writing 120 words in ten minutes and many write quite a bit more. I attribute a lot of the success to constant praise/rein-forcement and a student's inner desire to be the best. We celebrate when individual students achieve "personal bests", and there is a group of kids who compete hard each week to earn the distinction of being the top writer at their level.

In Spanish one I have two kids writing in the low 300s and a couple more on their heels. The same holds true in level two. The top kid has been writing from 350-380 words in ten minutes. Something I didn't think was possible finally happened today. He got knocked off by a fellow classmate that wrote 402! We were amazed and celebrated with her.

The success of the very top kids also has a way of raising the bar for the rest of the class. They want to do well even if they can't get to 300 or 200. I also give the incentive of one extra credit point for writing 100 words more than the required level (150 right now in level two) and two extra credit points for 200 words over that level.

So, even though my day ended on a bad note, it's nice to reflect back on the positives that happen each day.

Dan in Iowa

From Jalen Waltman

I just want to say that as horrible as the year began last year with my fellow Spanish teachers, it ended on a very vindicating note for me in May. Our principal decided, no doubt under pressure from someone, to give a test to one of my classes and one of the other Spanish I teacher's classes (who were taught grammar-style with the textbook.) The test given was a book test straight from Dime's testing materials, to which the principal added an essay question upon my request. Without going into all the details surrounding the test, here were the "official" results: Out of 60 questions, my class's average score was 27.64 correct; the book class's average was 28.25 correct. This was NOT INCLUDING the essay question, which he said he didn't know how to figure into the score. The essay was graded by one of my fellow Spanish teachers, one who had strong reservations about and objections to my use of TPRS. She made up a little scale of 0-4 with 0 being "no attempt" and 4 being "no problems with grammar, clear to native or non-native." On this scale, my class average on the essay was 2.32 and the book class was 1.22 (a score of 1 indicated "not enough info, mostly grammar errors" on her scale.) My class, incidentally, did a little better on every section of the book test EXCEPT for the fill-in-the-blank with the verb conjugation part, which they collectively bombed bad enough to allow her class to score just a fraction of a percentage point above mine. This is particularly miraculous, I think, considering 3 factors: 1) the principal (randomly) managed to choose my weakest, least mature class to take the test; 2) my students had never seen the textbook all year; and 3) this was my first year to teach with TPRS. His comment to our department at the end of the year meeting was, "both teaching methods have strengths and weaknesses, judging from this test. The strength with the book method is conjugating verbs, and the strength with TPRS is writing." HA! The irony in that statement astounds me.

Journal of a TPRS Teacher — Why I'll Never Go Back

By Jalen Waltman

This is the story of just one of my students from last year. There are several others just like it.

"Jeff" was the kind of student language teachers usually dread to see, the kind you only get in Spanish I because they never go on to Spanish II, the kind who are only there because there aren't enough electives to go around. He was a skater, a pot-smoker, anti-social, anti-authority. From the first day of school he gave me the kind of look that let me and the rest of the class know we'd better leave him alone in his tormented little world. He'd come to class in baggy pants hanging the customary 8 or 10 inches below his waist, skulk into his chair and put his head down. If he ever did look up, it was with a threatening scowl designed to keep everyone at a distance. I never bothered him much or tried to make him look up and participate, though I usually don't allow someone to have his or her head down. The class understood. Jeff was in a different category.

That was the routine for him for most of the fall semester. He skipped class every so often and was suspended once or twice, but when he was in class, he kept his head down. I left him alone and made up my mind not to hold it against him. Who knew what kind of home life he had, what difficulties he'd been through in his 15 years of life? No, I never felt angry at him for his behavior. I just kept teaching my class with the new method I'd learned that summer at a Blaine Ray/Susie Gross workshop in Edmond — TPRS.

When I began the school year last year with the decision to start using TPRS exclusively — no textbook — neither my students nor I fully knew what to expect. I fumbled with the method a great deal for the first several months, with more positive attitude than skill, and found to my delight that from day one I had my students in the proverbial "palm of my hand" even when I didn't know exactly what I was going to do next. The difference from textbook-and-grammar teaching was mind-boggling. There had never been so much laughter in my classroom, and I probably laughed more than anyone. Many times the lesson came to a complete halt while we all had a good laugh, sometimes with tears in our eyes. I saw students who NEVER would have enjoyed or been even remotely successful in my former classroom come alive, participate, and learn. The TPRS classroom had a niche for everyone — the brains, the meek, the bold, the happy, the troubled. As it turned out, there was even a niche for Jeff.

One day last November, I had told the class a story in Spanish about a girl who goes to the pet store and buys a cat who turns out to be a very, very bad cat. I scanned the class for a student I had never called on to retell the story back to me. My eyes landed on Jeff, and before thinking, I heard myself say, "Jeff! You've never told me a story. Yes, Jeff. I want YOU." Jeff didn't move for a couple of seconds, and then slowly raised his head, his scowl as dark and menacing as ever. The rest of the class caught its breath. Only their eyes moved from him to me. Their collective unspoken thought — which I read perfectly — was, Mrs. Waltman, what are you doing? Jeff sat silently glaring at me. Well, I thought, I had made my bed, and I was going to lie in it.

"Come on, Jeff, you can do it," I pressed. He finally spoke. "I wasn't listening to the story." "That's okay, I'll help you," I returned, smiling encouragingly. "The story starts out with `There is a girl.'" He studied me for a minute, probably considering whether to protest further or just put his head back down. I pushed again. "You know how to say it. Come on. 'There is a girl.'" At length, Jeff opened his lips and muttered, "¿Hay una muchacha?" The rest of the class stared at me wide-eyed, little amazed smiles forming on faces. They (and I) couldn't believe it. I never let my shock show. I pushed for more, acted like it was perfectly normal that Jeff had just uttered a complete, perfectly grammatical sentence in Spanish, after months of having his head on his desk in class. "She goes to the store," I prompted him. "¿Va a la tienda?" he replied. My heart raced. "She buys a cat." "Compra un gato." "She gives the man 10 dollars." "Le da dinero." Okay, that works, I thought. I gave him a few more sentences, and he quickly translated each one. When he'd gotten through about half of the story, he stopped abruptly. "Can somebody else tell the rest?" he growled and put his head back down on his desk. It was too late, though. I saw the little grin about to form on his lips just before his face disappeared onto his folded arms. Yes, it was too late. Now we knew — we all knew that he had been sitting there with his face on his desk, learning Spanish. The class and I exchanged a glance that said, "Wow!" and I called on someone else to finish the story.

Several weeks later, I made up a little vocabulary game which we played in teams ("countries"). Jeff was in Venezuela. When it was Jeff's turn, he found he almost always knew the answer. This delighted and surprised everyone, including Jeff. He began to let his enthusiasm show the second time we played the game. This anti-social, normally unfriendly guy would transform into a most serious game contender. He'd chide his fellow Venezuelans when they'd answer something wrong, usually with a "you suck!" which they found quite amusing. I'd gently ask him not to use "naughty words" in class, but with a smile on my face to let him know I wasn't mad at him. He eventually began to apologize to me whenever he'd slip and say an inappropriate word. When we began to get Jeff's participation in class, we got the "real" Jeff, language and all. But I didn't really mind so much, because it was so magical to see him find success in class, to actually crack a smile. One of the other Venezuelans, Laura, came up to me after class one day. "Isn't it incredible to see Jeff participate like that?" she asked me. "It's amazing," I agreed. You don't know how much! During the spring semester, Venezuela starting choosing Jeff to be the captain of any game activity since he usually knew the answer and was so much fun to watch participate.

I think the most miraculous moment of all was the day Venezuela, Peru, and Spain — the three "countries" in Jeff's class — had to compete in a dance contest. Venezuela's dance was the "merengue" which I quickly taught them just before they had to compete. Venezuela — including Jeff — hurriedly assembled their desks into a stage and asked if they could dance on top of them. I shouldn't have let them, but I did. They got up there — Jeff included — and danced the merengue with everything they had. They won the dance contest.

Jeff's test average for the year was 80. He made an 82.5 on the year's final exam. All of the credit for his success goes to TPRS and my bumbling use of it last year. It creates the kind of classroom learning experience and atmosphere where kids of all kinds can find success and feel positive about a foreign language. I can't tell you what kind of miracle it is to see that happen. You have to see it for yourself. And as for me, I'll never go back to anything else I've tried. I guess you could say I've "found my niche" too.

From: "Julie Baird" <baij@wawasee.k12.in.us>
Subject: Re: What is my problem?

Liz asks: How can I make my class more interesting?

Sometimes you have to fake the enthusiasm. If you are enthusiastic, your kids will catch the emotion and also become enthusiastic.

You have to pretend that each MINI-STORY you do is real and happening at the moment. Don't go through the motions. Enjoy the MINI-STORY with the kids. Laugh at the dorkiness of the story.

Use your voice to convey a lot of different emotions during the day: surprise, excitement, confusion, awe, etc.

You are an actor on a stage and you need to draw the kids into your own theater. You need to give them a wonderful performance so that they will want more.

Having said all that, there are times when we get a combination of kids that just don't respond. I have one such class this year. It is so discouraging because I know it is not me. I have a wonderful time with my other classes and this group of kids just refuse to enjoy the class. They rebel against learning and that is their decision. With this class I tried to go away from TPRS but my conscience wouldn't let me. I can still reach them with TPRS better than I can with books, worksheets and other learning tools. The class is not enthusiastic, but my job is not to entertain them or even make sure they like the class. With this class I still try to be the best actor I can be, but my goal for them is to learn German.

From Kristy Placido <placido@cablespeed.com>:

One more thing that I'm thinking about today...

You know how seasoned TPRS teachers are always talking about loving the kids and, if a student is difficult, it means that you need to show more love? Well, I have to admit that this whole concept has been the hardest for me to learn. Of course with some kids, the love comes easy. With others, it is hard! But the more I do this, the more I find that love and respect are really the key to this whole process. Nothing works well if it is done without love! I have been making a special effort lately to reach out to some of the kids that normally probably don't feel much love from school or their teachers. I'm finding that by being "more human and less teacher" the kids reach out to me too.

It is so easy to forget to give that extra smile or to ask about something that is going on in the kid's life. But the rewards for making those little efforts are so great. I talked to my students about my little dog getting hurt this week. Animals are such an easy way for people to connect! I've connected with so many kids this week just by talking to them about their pets and sharing with them about my dog. On Friday my class was trying to get me to stop the "lesson" by asking me questions about my dog. I told them we could talk if we did it in Spanish. It was really fun and it was nice to use our second language for meaningful talk at the 2nd year level! I'm so proud of those kids!

I hope I can continue to remember to take time for those little "connections" every day! If you are new to TPRS, please make sure you focus time on the kids' lives and experiences. Those are so much more important than anything else you can talk about. Even if you are bad at being bizarre and your stories are kind of boring, the kids will love you and love your class if you care about them and talk about their lives!

Have a great week everyone!

Kristy

Date: Thu, 08 Feb 2001 17:55:06 -0000
From: thompsonmb@islc.net (Michael Thompson)
Subject: 6 words a day on the block: week one

A couple weeks ago I asked how to accomplish 6 words a day on the block without trying to fit in two active mini-stories (difficult at best, and I'm realizing not a good idea--it's the old teach two lessons on the block mistake, pretending that you have two separate days when it's really one big lesson). I got excellent suggestions from Kirsten and Teri, and I've adapted their suggestions to my own style. For anyone else who is struggling with the block, give a format like this a try:

1) gesture the first three words, and "play around" with the words for 10-20 minutes, depending on student interest (and the length of your block). Playing around for me is a combination of PQA and one or more passive mini-stories which are sometimes spontaneously acted out (unplanned). Assess the words one final time, and then

2) follow procedure 1 to teach the second set of 3 words. Try to have a different emphasis during presentation; for example, I like to have little or no acting during the first set, and have acting during the second to keep their attention. The passive mini-story of course can be milked.

3) 5-day lesson plan activity for 10-15 minutes

4) return to the words, and finish the steps with a mini-story containing all 6 of the day's words.

I have been really seeing lately the POWER of great acting. If I can get those kids to really put on a show it makes the story just come to life. If the actor is dull, it can be the best mini-story I ever thought of and it will flop. So I have been working harder at coaching acting lately and I think it is paying off. I actually had a different actor re-act a story when one kid was acting in a really lame way. (Ok, before anyone says I'm mean, I GENTLY chided the bad actor and jokingly told him he needed to pep up if he ever wants an academy award. Trust me, the kid can take it!) The second kid (a girl who played the part of a boy) was enthusiastic to try to be extra dramatic the second time through. Today, another boy in the same class got up and did a fabulous acting job! It really carried the whole story! I am trying hard to make it a real honor to be an actor and the kids are responding!

From Blaine Ray <Blaineray@aol.com>:

What is your solution for págames [pay-me's] when the whole class isn't participating with gestures? Do you give the whole class a págame?

Kids not doing gestures kinda creeps up on you. One kid will stop doing them and then another. Pretty soon you have the whole class not doing them. You can't really give the whole class a págame.

What you can do is explain to the class that you found out you were doing this all wrong. Tell them you found out that it is crucial for learning that they do the gestures. Explain that from now on gestures aren't optional, they are required. Explain to them that they can have a day off anytime they want. (See the previous post about taking a day off.) By telling them they don't have to do the gestures but they do have to take a lower grade or make it up, shifts all the pressure off you and puts in on the kid. He has to decide whether to work or not. In that way you don't have to force them to do the gestures.

You do have to watch diligently and make sure they are ALL doing the gestures or taking the day off. After a while I ask each day, "¿Quién quiere el día libre?" [Who wants the day off?] If any one student is not doing gestures, I then say, "Págame."

Again, tell your students you were doing it wrong. Explain to them why and then follow through religiously. It will make a big difference.

Blaine

From Nikki McDonald:

At 05:44 PM 2/24/00 -0500, Kathleen?? wrote:

How many mini-story's do most people do each day? . . . It's these little stories that are making me crazy. I think it's especially tough because I teach first and second year, so they don't know that much. Any suggestions?

Try giving three words--any three--to someone else: a husband, a colleague, a child, a friend. They DON'T have to speak Spanish (or French or German). Ask this person to use these 3 words in a sentence or two. Ask them to do it again. And even ask for a third scenario if neither of the first two pans out. My husband is getting great at coming up with mini-stories that I can flesh out. Yes, it takes time to turn them into stories; but once I have an idea that grabs me, the story writes itself. This isn't the answer, but it may occasionally give you the jump-start you need.

Nikki

From Von Ray <chilenopo2000@yahoo.com>:

Hello fellow TPRSers! Although this is my first "official" year teaching TPRS, I've slowly been converted step by step throughout my lifetime. I know Blaine pretty well. After all, he is my dad. My dad taught me a great insight this past weekend. I was home watching a tape from a couple years ago when he taught in the classroom setting. The main thing that I noticed was that he totally cracked himself up throughout the entire mini-story even though the kids didn't laugh all that much. Of the four classes I have this year, 3 of them seem to think that I'm one of the funniest people on the planet while the last class wouldn't laugh if I went to them and tickled them. But after watching my dad's class, I decided to go all out and try to be as funny as possible with this particular class. The story was a complete home run. Once I committed to cracking myself up, they laughed a lot more. Even though they didn't laugh nearly as much as my other classes, the class was 10x more enjoyable for me. As I lay in bed Monday night thinking about the almost perfect mini-stories, I simply started laughing out loud at some of the humor from the day. Boy, are those days special! And at this point of the year, there can be no holding back when it comes to the humor.

From: Susan Gross

Ken,

It is kinda scary taking the first few steps, isn't it? Congratulations on giving it a try. Once you get going it does become more natural seeming, so hang in there!

My level 1s have been complaining that they "can't understand all the things" I'm saying. I have repeatedly told them not to try to understand it all. They still insist that if they can't understand it all, they can't understand anything.

Ooooops! They need to understand *everything* you say. If you allow yourself to talk "over their heads", they will become bored, have side conversations, complain, and rebel. This is a danger signal! The reason it is hard to do TPR Storytelling in level one is that they can't understand very much. That is why Blaine says that TPR Storytelling is lots easier to do in levels 3 and 4. Our goal is to provide 100% comprehensible language all period long. Be aware that even when you use only words they know, there will STILL be a significant portion of the class that does not understand what you are saying. If you use words they *don't* know, then *everyone* will feel lost at least some of the time! You don't want that.

From: \<mholmes@mcs.cnyric.org\>
Wednesday, May 22, 2002 7:22 AM

Hello,

I teach first year French and Spanish in upstate NY and I have to tell you a little about my year. I used TPR in September and October and TPRS for the rest of the year. NY state has a topic oriented curriculum, so I went thru each chapter in LICT and added extra vocabulary that was pertinent to the topic. I also went thru the books I am supposed to use, "Allez Viens" and "Paso a Paso", and incorporated vocab from the chapters into the LICT stories. My students will go next year to a VERY traditional setting, so for the last three weeks we have been marching through the books. All I did was: go over the vocabulary from the book, do the audio and video activities from the chapter, and then I gave the chapter test. We marched thru 10 chapters of Paso and 8 chapters of Allez Viens. (those are the chapters I am supposed to "cover" in a year) My results were spectacular. We didn't use the book until these last three weeks. Almost all of my students had a 90 or above average on the chapter tests. They were reassured because they could see how much they had learned. They are now familiar with the format they will be required to use next year so the high school teachers should be happy. Everyone is happy. This method really works by any standard, just trust yourself and your students.

Mary from Syracuse

From: "vpargolf" <vpargolf@yahoo.com>
Date: Mon, 05 May 2003 18:48:59 -0000
Subject: [moretprs] Nat'l. French Exam celebration

Well...using TPRS I had two eighth grade students score 76/80 and 72/80 to lead Colorado/Wyoming on the high school (level I) version of that exam. (4th and 8th scores in the nation).

After two years I am just now starting to "get" it. Relying on the book would not have produced these results. Thanks to my workshop leaders, Susan Gross, Von Ray, and Karen Rowan, and to the awesome posts of Blaine, Moco Loco, etc.

I see now how stories naturally emerge from PQA. This trust that a story will emerge, drawing from but not relying on my mini-story for the day, is new to me, and powerful. Now I can focus on the kids. Hey, it only took me 26 years!

It is not about results, but having fun. Yes, I can have fun in the classroom, and I can love what my kids say, just like a mother who loves what their babies say, to paraphrase something Susan told me recently.

Ben Slavic, Littleton, CO

In an email dated September 14, 2004, Mr. Slavic added:

My middle school 8th graders participated in the high school level I version of the National French Exam last March. Five of them scored, out of 70 poss. questions, 68,65,63,63, and 62. These were the top five scores in Colorado. The 68/70 was one of only 18 scores among 22,451 participants nationally. All five were nationally recognized as top ten scores. When asked, I attribute these results directly to TPRS.

Date: Sat, 2 Oct 2004 05:13:42 -0700 (PDT)
From: Blaine Ray <blaineraytprs@yahoo.com>
Subject: Visit to East High in Denver yesterday

I spent the day at East High yesterday teaching classes.

They have been a TPRS school now for several years. It is interesting to see how well they are doing. Their numbers show just how much TPRS has influenced their department. They have been doing TPRS for about 7 years now. New teachers commit to teaching this way.

I taught all levels of classes yesterday. It is interesting that I can't tell the level of class by teaching it. Bryce Hedstrom was there and tallied my questions. In a level four class I had 45 statements (often followed by correcto?)

There was a ratio of 5 questions to every statement.

I asked

51 si/no	30 who
7 fill in the blank	8 where
63 either or	28 why
12 what	3 mistakes of fact

There were only 7 barometer checks because the kid was good. There were 49 pop ups during the class.

Blaine

Date: Sat, 2 Oct 2004 05:34:15 -0700 (PDT)
From: Blaine Ray <blaineraytprs@yahoo.com>
Subject: A class with four levels in one -- Amazing new information

Last year at a workshop I suggested the ideal format for teaching language would be to have all classes mixed with all levels. I have always hoped someone would try the experiment and do it. Last spring Meredith went to her principal and got it approved. They are now into the 6th week of this class.

Yesterday I got to teach the class and talk to the kids. It was so interesting.

First of all, at the workshop Thursday I asked Meredith how the class was going and what she had learned so far. She said, "My fours have been the big winners so far. They have made the most improvement."

This statement was shocking to me. How could this be? I would predict the fours would make the least progress because you are teaching to the level one kids and going slow enough and being repetitive enough that even the level one kids can understand. So the idea that the fours would make the most progress in this class blew me away. We are so clueless as teachers about what it takes to learn to speak in class. This shows me that even advanced students need repetitions and focus on the basics of the language and that they will get the most gains from the basics instead of always pushing them beyond their level.

I taught the class yesterday. I talked to the students beforehand. I asked many of them why they took the class. Almost every one said he/she really wanted to learn Spanish. Some level 3 students thought they would learn it better in the experimental class. They also spoke very highly of the teacher.

Teaching the class was very interesting. I identified one level one student to be my barometer and moved him right in front of me. Bryce also tallied this class.

In this class, my ratio changed. Now I had 30 statements and a ratio of 3 to 1. Over half of my questions were yes/no or either/or. I believe this was because of my focus on the level one barometer student. I went to him many times during the class. He truly slowed me down and made my questions easier.

I couldn't feel who were the advanced students. At the end of the class I asked the level one students to raise their hands. I was very surprised. There was no indication to me that those particular students were level one students. (except for the barometer)

This class was truly amazing. I am so excited about it. I truly believe this will prove to be a great great success and a model for other schools. I would absolutely LOVE for my child to learn in this multi-level class. I am convinced we will get maximum gains here.

They tested these kids before the year began. They are going to test them again at the end and compare their gains to gains of their other TPRS students in the school. I think we are going to see some amazing numbers.

I talked to the class yesterday about how things will get better and they will learn more and more as the year progresses. It was so exciting to see. ....

We filmed this class and either one or two others. We are going to copy these classes onto DVD and sell them. I am hopeful we can sell them for 10 dollars for you that are interested. I will let you know when they are available.

Blaine

Date: Tue Jan 29, 2008 5:21 pm (PST)
From: Mark Webster <mwebster91@charter.net >
Subject: articulation with colleges

We have a TPRS program (7 teachers) and we use Blaine's program (LICT, More, LIST, and his novels, and Gale Mackey's Grammar CD) and Joe's program in the upper levels (Album, some of Joe's handouts, etc). We are a 820 student public school with 17% free lunch. 93%+ of our level 4 kids test into 201 or 202. 95% of our AP kids place into 202 or junior level (when permitted by the college/university). The program will continue to improve as we improve and refine.

We have analyzed course descriptions/grammar structures taught at each level at a number of local colleges and universities. It seems pretty much the same in the first two levels (100-200). I find it difficult to align curriculum in upper levels with 300 level courses in college because it's so varied and changes as professors move around. Some colleges are super grammar focused and do tons of fill-in activities and the kids hardly read anything (per former students). Other colleges are more acquisition based. Some of our kids are absolutely "over prepared" for some colleges. They place above the courses offered. At larger universities with larger L2 programs, the rest perform as well as or better than their peers — as TPRS educated students.

We've decided to just teach the best we can (using the TPRS system) and read as much as we can every week (levels 1-4/AP). We've added cultural tidbits along the way delivered via stories, out of class/summer reading, music, powerpoints, maps, etc.

Mark Webster
Spring Lake HS, MI

Chapter 16

Frequently Asked Questions about TPR Storytelling

Doesn't this method require a lot of energy?

In order for the students to get the input necessary to learn the language — at least in the beginning levels — the teacher must provide it.

At a recent workshop, Susan Gross, a SWCOLT (Southwest Conference on Language Teaching) foreign language teacher of the year, pointed out that the real problem with teacher energy is dealing with students that aren't learning. They are bored with the book and they don't want to be in your class. They show with their faces that they don't want to be there.

On the other hand, what a contrast to have students excited about coming to class and learning Spanish, French, German or English through stories!

All in all, it is worth the energy that you give. Student achievement is our number one concern. We feel very good about what they accomplish.

It can also be assumed there will be less paper work for the teacher. In this system there is not a lot of homework assigned. In addition, the students generally take fewer tests than in other classes. These two factors not only reduce the amount of time the teacher spends correcting papers but also allow more time on task for the students. Nancy Núñez, who teaches high school in Tatum, Texas, and is using TPR Storytelling, said, "I have a life now — I don't spend 90% of my time grading papers." Others have told me it was hard for them to get used to walking out of class when the bell rang since they had no papers to grade, but they finally did get used to it.

Of the thousands of teachers who use TPRS™, I don't remember one complaining about the energy involved.

How can I use this method with a text?

This is such an important question for many teachers that we added an entire chapter on it in the second edition. We have revised it for the fifth edition. Most of the content of the chapter was provided by Karen Rowan, who gives workshops on this topic. Please see Chapter 14, "Adapting a Textbook for TPRS."

What if my department mandates certain grammar structures?

There is a common assumption that just because certain grammar structures have been covered that the students have internalized them. I have found that not to be the case. Krashen has expressed the opinion in many workshops that language is nearly all acquired. He says there is no study that shows the gains from grammar-based teaching last longer than three months. This has certainly been my experience. The fact that a student can fill out a worksheet on the present tense does not necessarily mean that s/he knows the present tense in the sense that s/he can use it correctly in fluent speech. Any teacher can cover concepts. I have covered the past tense in an hour. With this method we don't attempt to cover anything. We teach the language for fluency. It takes some time to get that fluency.

If a test is given at the end of the term, you might try what one teacher did. Since it was a department test, she taught the information on the test through stories. The test was given annually and each year the school averaged 65 percent on the test. Her students took the test and averaged 85 percent. Make sure that your students are given the same test that others are given. Teach the material through storytelling and compare the results.

Some schools have tried TPR Storytelling® as a pilot program. Jo Hodgson, from Gilbert, Arizona, is a junior high teacher using TPRS. Her students were so advanced that, when they went to high school, they were moved ahead one year. The high school came to her and hired her to pilot a program for the high school the next year. Often just getting the administration to let you try it will produce such dramatic results that it will be there to stay.

How have students done on standardized tests?

We have found that classes that take national standardized tests consistently score better than the national average. Joe Neilson of Salpointe Catholic High School in Tucson had a class that took the National Spanish Exam after only six months. The class had no grammar instruction yet averaged 67 percent on a test where the national average was 41 percent. Other classes have taken the National Spanish Exam, and all have averaged higher than the national average. None of these classes had studied grammar.

At Stockdale High School in Bakersfield, California, where I used to teach, we had eight students pass the Spanish AP test after only two years. They were true beginners in Spanish when they came to Stockdale and they passed the test at the end of their sophomore year. We had over 60 students who started as true beginners pass the AP test in three years. They did so with very little homework and in four years or less. Stockdale is a public school with 1,900 students.

Donna Tatum and Jean Amick at Kentucky Country Day School in Louisville gave the national French exam. Their students placed 1, 2, 3, 4, 5, 6, 7, 9 and 10 in the state. They also had seven national placers on the same test out of 12,000 students who took the test.

Kirsten Calkins has had 38 special ed students pass the NY State tests. Not one special ed student from her school had ever passed the Spanish state test previously, yet not one of her special ed students has failed the test. She had a 100% passing rate among her second-year students on the third-year test. To our knowledge, this had never been done before.

Von Ray had one student score 54 out of 60 on the National Spanish exam. Several others scored 50 or higher out of 60.

Janette Holman had her fourth-year TPRS class take the AP test. Eight out of nine passed. The same year her non-TPRS fifth-year class took the test. Only three out of 12 of them passed.

Connie Vargas and Donna Lubick had a student who was great at learning languages. He had five years of traditional French, three years of TPRS Spanish (with Connie) and one year of TPRS German with Donna. At the end of the year he took three AP tests. He got a 4 in French, a 5 in Spanish and a 5 in German.

Ben Slavic had his middle school students take the high school national French exam. His top four middle school students beat all of the high school students in the state of Colorado. His top student placed third in the nation, getting 68 out of 70 on the test. One of his errors was due to an error on the test. He was the only one of 20,000 students who took the test that found the error. Neither did the seven native-speaking French teachers who had proofed the test.

The following year, the student took the AP test and got a 4.

Do you ever speak languages other than the target language? Why?

In classical TPR there is little need to use any translation. The meaning of all of the commands is usually apparent to all.

When you use words that when modeled may be interpreted in more than one way, e.g., *walk* and *go*, it is essential that you ask students to translate individual words to see if they know their meanings. You are constantly trying to find words they don't know. When you find a word or words that one student doesn't know, you make a note of it. You practice those words even more.

It works best to use translation to find out what words students don't know. Sometimes they know the action without knowing the meaning of the word.

If you are teaching an ESL class with students who speak many first languages, you can't use translation, at least not so much as in a class where all or nearly the students speak one language. Carol Gaab, who teaches ESL in the Phoenix area, suggests using illustrations, photos, props and scenarios in lieu of translation to help make sure vocabulary is understood clearly.

Some people criticize the use of translation in the class. They say that the target language must be spoken at all times in the classroom regardless of the cost. There are two times when the target language is not being acquired in the classroom. One time is when the teacher is speaking a language (e.g., English) other than the target language. The other time is when the teacher is speaking the target language but the students don't understand.

This is crucial for understanding this method. Students need to understand the target language. Anytime they don't understand, they will not listen. There must be high interest in the content of the class, but there also must be a language-rich environment that is understood by all. (See "Use of Translation" and other parts of Chapter 2.)

The main reason for using translation is to make sure that every student understands the vocabulary and the grammatical features. Another reason you do translations is to find out, in the fastest way possible, who knows what vocabulary. The language is really not acquired by doing the actions. We do the actions so that the vocabulary can be acquired. Then the stories, which are the true acquisition part of the class, will be understood. In other words, language must be acquired in context. There are two basic steps: (1) acquire the vocabulary and (2) acquire the language.

What are some tips to make this work?

First make sure that all students are always engaged. Have fun and just practice the language by focusing on the details of the story. Students aren't even aware of the language because there is so much emphasis on the details. Exaggerate common things in size, shape, cost and speed. Have fun. Lighten up and go with the flow. Let students speak out to the class in the target language. Get used to having a noisy class-room with a lot of spirit and a lot of learning.

When do I start teaching grammar?

You should delay most grammar! Joe Neilson calls this understanding the big picture. If you know where your students are going to end up, it is easy to allow them to be where they are. First-year students can gradually acquire only very basic aspects of grammar, beginning with third-person singular verb forms, followed by first-person singular ones. The more you emphasize correctness, the more hesitancy you will get.

Grammatical correctness can come from retelling stories from different perspectives. It is all right to start to work on correctness at any time as along as you do it through the stories. It is important to teach students how to speak correctly. We have found that correctness is most easily acquired through mini-stories.

You always say things grammatically correctly, so your students will get used to hearing them said correctly. Gradually they will begin to imitate you so that their speech will grow in correctness. If your students don't have a particular grammatical concept internalized by a certain time, just practice it some more through stories. They will get it with practice unless, of course, it is a structure that is too advanced — one that is beyond their level.

In *The Natural Approach* Krashen and Terrell (1983: 28-30) discuss the natural order of acquisition. Krashen hypothesizes that there is a predictable order in which grammatical components of the language are acquired. No amount of worksheets, games or practice exercises can change late-acquired items into early-acquired ones. Teachers expend a great deal of effort trying to force their students to learn grammatical concepts that are late-acquired.

We now start TPRS with the past tense. We have found that delaying the past tense results in the present tense becoming engrained to such an extent that it is difficult to get most students to start acquiring the past. The only way to overcome this is through editing, which is pretty much a short-term memory activity. Instead of letters the present becoming so engrained, we now teach both past and present at the same time, contrasting them in the spoken and written versions of stories and in discussions. (See "Creating a Story for Class" in Chapter 3 and "Teaching a Second-year Mini-story" in Chapter 6.)

Do I have to start at the beginning of the year?

No!!! Start tomorrow. Jump in and get wet. Use the precious time you have to teach your students in the best way you know how. Try it.

Many teachers have thrown away the books after a Saturday TPR Storytelling workshop and gone into the classroom Monday and changed the entire way they teach. They have reported back their enthusiasm. One teacher reported that she could hardly sleep because of her enthusiasm. She said she would wake up nights thinking of how she could apply these ideas.

Other teachers, after a year of applying this method, have reported having tremendous success. One man said he was going to give up teaching — until he found TPR Storytelling. Now he is excited about his job and loves the progress he sees in his students.

What should I do if my students haven't had any TPRS training?

If they are first-year high school students or weak second-year high school students, start with the first-year mini-stories and use *Look, I Can Talk!* (Ray, 1990; available in Spanish, French, German and English). If they are in kindergarten through third grade, use Carol Gaab's *¡Hola Niños!* (1999), *Salut les enfants!* (2000) or *Hi Kids!* (2002). If they are third- to sixth-graders, use Valeri Marsh and Christine Anderson's *¡Cuéntame!* (1995a) or *Raconte-moi!* (1995d). If they are seventh- or eighth-graders, use their *¡Cuéntame más!* (1995b), *Raconte-moi encore!* (1996b), *Tell Me More!* (1998) or *Tell Me More! Japanese Adaptation*, Chapter One (1999). Also for Japanese middle school students, you can use *Japanese in Action* (1998) by Laurie May and Kaoru Kimura. For seventh- or eighth-graders (or fifth-, sixth-, ninth- or tenth-graders) who are learning German, you can use Michael Miller's *Sabine und Michael*, Level 1 (1999) or Level 2 (2000). If they are good second-year high school students, start right in with *Look, I Can Talk*

More! (Ray et al., 1992; available in Spanish, French, German and English). Teach each story very well, and your students will feel very good about your program.

Please note: In addition to the materials mentioned here, there are many more TPRS materials available now with which you might start teaching. See "TPR Storytelling Materials and Other Helpful Resources for the TPRS Classroom" in Appendix K.

We have had students check into our program with no TPR and they do just fine. One student said to me, "I have learned more in a week and a half here than I learned in a year and a half at my other school."

Should I use this program with my present book?

I would suggest not combining the book and TPR Storytelling. There is not enough time for both. If you must teach the book, take the vocabulary and grammar from it and teach them through TPR Storytelling. You will have much more success. Joe Neilson reported that he tried using the book and supplementing it with stories. He said it was a big mistake and he would never try it again. He said he would teach material from the book through TPR Storytelling. See Chapter 14, "Adapting a Textbook for TPRS."

If you adapt the book, select the vocabulary carefully. Teach fluency vocabulary, the words students need to know so deeply that they can say them with little or no hesitation when they are expressing themselves. See "The Fluency Circle" in Chapter 2 and "The Class Discussion" in Chapter 10. Categorize the words in order of importance and make sure you use TPRS to teach only the very most important words. Ask yourself, "How common is this word? Can you be fluent in Spanish without this word?" If it is an essential word, teach it through TPRS. Other words are *passive vocabulary* words. They are acquired through listening and reading. Don't teach those words for fluency. Just see to it that students understand them, translating them when necessary. They will pick some of them up.

What should I do if none of the other teachers in my department teach with this method?

I say there is no excuse for teaching grammar rules to the detriment of your students just to please other teachers. If you had your own children in class, you would want them to truly learn to speak the language, not just learn about the language. Again, take the material and teach it well through TPR Storytelling. If any of your colleagues are open to this, show them the video *Introduction to TPR Storytelling* (Ray, 2007) and offer them written material. Often what happens where one teacher teaches from a grammar-oriented text and others use TPR Storytelling is that the students try to get out of the textbook class and into the TPRS class. A school district once called and asked me to do a workshop. They said so many students were dropping out of the grammar-oriented class that they wanted me to come back and train the other teachers in this method.

Make sure you have the support of your administrator. If s/he is lukewarm about the whole idea, try to get her/him to let you try this on a one-year trial basis. Have students from your class and the textbook class take a national standardized foreign language test at the end of the year. Let her/him decide which method is better by evaluating the results of standardized tests. Be sure to get this cleared before you start. Many teachers have had problems by not letting their administrators know about the experiment they were doing. Most administrators would agree to a pilot program in which you test *all* kids at the end. If the administrator won't let you compare your students to others, at least you can compare your students to the national average. This is very convincing.

Why do students like learning this way?

Success! Success! Success! Students feel good in class. They feel like they can learn the language. They feel good about themselves. I have found that students with very little or no language experience have a great deal of confidence in using the language. A few years ago I took my daughter to a workshop to demonstrate her language ability. It was in November, so she had had about two months of experience in the language. She told the group of foreign language teachers some of the stories she had learned in class. She told the stories using the names of my students in the stories. When she told the stories, I visualized the actual students in class acting out the story. (This method is so visual that I just automatically did this.)

Afterwards I asked the teachers to give her a topic to write on. She wrote a complete essay in five minutes. I read the essay to the teachers so that they could see her errors and how well she could write. Their comments showed how impressed they were with her. One teacher said, "I'm so glad you brought your daughter along to let us see the potential for our students." Later on that daughter took a trial AP test. She had one of the highest scores in the history of our school after just two years of Spanish.

Nothing motivates like success. Students sign up for the following year in high numbers because they feel good about what is going on in class.

Do you have to have a dynamic personality to teach this way?

Some might feel, after attending a workshop, that they have to be a Steve Martin type to make class fun. In reality, you just have to use the steps of TPR Storytelling. Students will learn by doing mini-stories. Some teachers have expressed fear about using this method because they felt they didn't have the right type of personality.

Much more important than personality is simply showing, in your own way, your interest in your students and what they do and say. See Chapter 5, "How to Maintain High Interest and an Optimal Pace." All of TPRS is success-oriented. If making your class dynamic is a real concern you have, we suggest you try TPRS and see how the results affect your classes. This book and the More TPRS List (see Chapter 15) are a couple of good sources of support for any kind of problems you might have in teaching with TPRS. Even if you're not fabulously dynamic, do you think there's a better approach that will help your students to become fluent speakers of the language you're teaching? If you get good results, you're doing a good job and you can be proud of what you're accomplishing. That's what counts, not dynamism.

Many have reported that they use props effectively to take the focus off of themselves and put it onto the props. This is a good idea anyway. Get as many props as possible, and your students will learn some words more easily, connecting the words directly to the props. The students will focus on them, and the class will be more alive, fun and interesting.

Do you practice pronunciation?

Pronunciation is a progressive thing. Students will improve as their exposure to the language increases. In TPRS they hear the same word so many times in so many contexts before the need to produce it that they nearly always are able to pronounce every word adequately if not very well. Hearing a word well and many times are the most important keys to good pronunciation. If you make sure both of these things happen, you rarely need to concern yourself with pronunciation. An early emphasis on pronunciation is usually counterproductive, because it makes students focus on how the sounds are made instead of focusing on producing meaningful language. Achieving good pronunciation is more difficult in some languages than others. Another factor is the first language of the learner. (Also see *Learning Another Language Through Actions* (Asher, 1996: pp. 3-38 to 3-41).)

When do the students see the words?

We have found no downside in letting students see the words as they learn them. The upside is comprehension. We always err on the side of comprehension.

When do you correct?

If what the student says can't be understood by a native speaker, we correct her/him. We start teaching verb correctness in the first year through mini-stories. We do this by retelling them in the first person. We correct to the students' level. When a student says, "I s/he goes," we correct, especially if the error was made by a good student. Generally speaking the better the student, the more we correct, because better students usually can make better use of corrections. There's no point in correcting a student who will not be helped by the correction.

We continually teach the basics of the language through stories. We use stories to teach verb correctness as well as noun/adjective agreement. If a student gets the verbs and agreement generally correct when s/he talks, s/he is an advanced student of the language.

What are some advanced techniques used in TPRS?

We are currently doing some advanced workshops — workshops for experienced TPRS teachers. Many teachers have been doing TPRS for years and are interested in expanding their repertoire of TPRS techniques. Some of the ideas that we deal with in these workshops are described below. Most of them are also described elsewhere in this book. Designating them as advanced is really a subjective choice. The main idea is that there are other good ways to accomplish our goals, carrying out the principles of TPRS. We think it is very important to use class time efficiently while sticking to these principles, so we emphasize the use of the techniques we have found to be most efficient.

1. Add subplots to your stories. You can always add another twist to the plot. The character can do something else or you can add another character in your story. These additions give you lots of opportunities for more repetitions of the words.

2. Recycle within the story. Whenever you feel like it, you can go back in the same story and recycle questions. You are free to go back to any point in the story and review that portion again. When you go back, you physically go back to the location in the classroom where that part of the story took place. If it took place in Celeryville, Texas, you go to the area of your classroom that represented Celeryville.

3. You have to be aware of good answers from your students and react with enthusiasm to the good responses. This is the key to high interest when the novelty of TPRS wears off. When you hear an interesting or funny response to your question, act excited or thrilled to have such a great re-

sponse. Say, "Wunderbar!" or "Super!" or "Formidable!" or "¡Fantástico!" Let the class know the response was superb, a home run.

4. Act like all the details of the story are real. Sell the idea that these things are all real to your students.

5. Find out about the lives of your students. Get details from their lives in the stories. Any detail about any student will add interest to your stories. Locations (e.g., where they go to movies), events (e.g., Jill won homecoming queen), songs (e.g., current number one song), sports (e.g., John plays basketball), pets (e.g., Susie's cat named Tweetie) or things (e.g., Jared's pet rock.) You can get this info before class, from student questionnaires or from PQA.

6. Relax and go with the flow. Teach students, not curriculum. You are not wasting time if you are in the target language and having fun. Some days you might not even get to the story. You might be so involved in PQA that you just enjoy the day. But you are still using the words and using the language. It is fun. Enjoy it.

7. Passive mini-stories. Passive mini-stories are "one-word stories" that generally aren't acted out, although they can be. They are little stories you tell about a student that just use one of the target vocabulary words you are teaching. They can be very short or longer. They can be repeated. They can be repeated with variations. They are not retold by students. They are only for listening, to provide more comprehensible input. Therefore we call them passive mini-stories. Here is an example for the target word *grab*:

   A boy grabs the book. The boy runs to the door. Monica cries.

8. Make factual mistakes as you retell as story (such as saying "banana" instead of "arm"). Students can shout out their corrections.

9. Let the students fill in a blank orally in every sentence as you retell a story; you say, for instance, "The monkey is sleeping in the _____ ," and pause for the students to shout out the missing word.

10. Be demanding. We want students to be accurate. We always correct to their ability. If the student knows something and says it wrong, we say, "Try that again." That just means he knows it but wasn't focusing on it. We want our students to speak very well. We need to have high expectations. We can't give them outs. Hold them responsible for every minute of class. Calling on students in a predictable order is teaching to a lower standard. We want each student to be held responsible for each minute of class. At the same time we want every student to know that we care that s/he succeeds.

What are some good homework activities?

Good homework activities are:

1. Retell the story to an adult and have the adult sign a paper that says the student told him/her the story.

2. Write out the story.

3. Draw out the story.

4. Write a new story.

5. Write a new ending to the story.

6. Read. Read. Read (something which is interesting to the students that is at or slightly above their language level).

7. Read the rest of the extended reading.

8. Read any novel on your own.

Chapter 17

Advantages of TPR Storytelling

There are numerous advantages to TPR Storytelling that are rarely found in other methods. The most important is that students can remember the grammatical features and the words. They get enough exposure to them through the stories and through TPR that they are able to remember them and speak the language. Another way to put this is that they actually acquire the grammar and the vocabulary. The stories are simple and it is actually difficult to forget them. If students can't remember what has been taught in a class, it doesn't matter what is taught.

TPR Storytelling develops fluency[1] with accuracy. Students acquire the language in a fun way that enables them to speak. In the process they develop an "ear" for what sounds right. As a result, they learn to speak the language so that it sounds right to them (see Burling (1982)). This process closely resembles that of first language acquisition. No other language-learning method seems to come so close.[2]

TPR Storytelling is fun. The stories generally are exaggerated and ridiculous. The humor makes students laugh and promotes better long-term memory and a positive attitude towards their new language.

TPR Storytelling is interesting. Since it is centered around the students' lives, it is more likely the students will be truly interested in the content.

Students in TPR Storytelling classes generally get better grades, according to many teachers who have taught this way after teaching with a more traditional approach. I have heard of many instances of students who got a D in a traditional class and then got an A in a TPR Storytelling class. It seems obvious that most students would be successful, since we spend the majority of the class time working on essential structures and vocabulary. If students are thoroughly familiar with basic vocabulary and structure, having experienced it numerous times in various ways as meaningful input, there are positive consequences. They are able to comprehend it in normal-speed speech. They are able to produce it when they need to in speech and writing. As they do this, they are developing fluency in both speech and writing. When students can both understand and produce meaningful spoken language, they know they are acquiring it. They feel successful and they are successful.

Karen Rowan, who teaches at Colorado Springs School in Colorado Springs, Colorado, says, "84% of my students received A's or B's on the first test. My dropout rate is 0. My attendance has improved. The kids like my class more. I have seen my students' writing and speaking improve at a rate I never thought possible."

In *TPR is More Than Commands* (1998: 84) Seely and Romijn say:

The results of using storytelling as a major strategy along with TPR are outstanding — perhaps unequaled. The results in regard to spoken production are especially noteworthy. Little if anything compares as an instructional strategy that

    a.   develops the ability to speak freely, that is fluency

    b.   encourages students to use their imaginations and creativity

    c.   thereby encourages them to take on a large part of the responsibility for learning

    d.   builds their confidence in speaking

TPR Storytelling can accomplish very important things that perhaps nothing else can. It is a systematic, entertaining, low-stress way of internalizing pieces of a "cognitive map" of grammatical structures, or of internalizing a "holistic pattern of how the language works," to use a couple of Asher's terms.

We keep attempting to improve TPR Storytelling, and we have made great strides. We are at a point where I think that we probably have all the major elements in place. I believe that future improvements are likely to be minor. Of course, I could be wrong.

We keep attempting to improve TPR Storytelling, and we keep finding ways to make it even better. We keep thinking that we are at a point where we probably have all the major elements in place and that future improvements are likely to be minor. I still believe this. Be that as it may, with creative ideas coming from so many teachers — as this edition goes to press in March, 2008, there are nearly 5,000 members of the TPRS listserv — we can expect that there will continue to be positive developments in the method.

Notes

1. Zev bar-Lev's method called SILL (Sheltered Initiation Language Learning), in my experience (Contee's), develops fluency and has a number of unique features. See bar-Lev (1993) and consult languagebazaar.com. It has been used mostly in colleges and adult schools. Maureen Breen's Funetics technique apparently also gets good results in fluency and accuracy. It has been used mainly in high school. See Breen and White (1996 and 1998). Elizabeth Kuizenga Romijn's Recurrent Action Grammar successfully develops both fluency and accuracy while using TPR repetitively in unique ways. See Romijn (2008). All of these approaches are fun, too.

2. One approach that might is described in Brown and Palmer is book *The Listening Approach* (1988).

Glossary

acquire, acquisition

This verb and this noun refer to the process of "picking up" elements of a language so that they remain in long-term memory and are easily understood when heard and are readily produced by a speaker when s/he needs to use them to express what s/he intends to. They are contrasted with *learn* and *learning*.

acquisition activity

This is any activity in which students focus on the message or meaning of language that is comprehensible to them. They do not focus on correctness in acquisition activities.

adaptation

This is the term that Asher uses to describe the phenomenon of students' no longer responding to commands with the interest and delight that they do early in classical TPR. The term comes from biology.

assess, assessment

Usually we use *assessment* as a synonym for *comprehension check*. It can also mean: test to find out what students have acquired and what they haven't.

barometer student

See *slow-processing student*.

BEP

Bizarre, exaggerated and personalized. We find that most personalized mini-stories are more effective if they have these three characteristics. Some teachers prefer the term *unexpected* instead of bizarre.

bezahl

German for *pay-me*. See that item.

big circle vocabulary, big circle words

See *reading circle*.

break down and **breaking point**

At times we try to test the limits of what a student or a class can accomplish. When we reach a point where they cannot do something adequately, we say that they *break down* and that we have found the *breaking point*. Then we retreat to just short of that point and attempt to prepare the student or class to be able to succeed at what they could not do when they broke down at the breaking point.

brief explanation

A quick explanation about a grammar point, made to ensure comprehension of the meaning of the point. See pop-up.

chain commands

Two or more commands given one after another before any physical response is made.

circle (verb)**, circling**

To use the technique of asking several questions about a statement and then completing the circle by repeating the original statement. See Chapter 4 and the beginning of Chapter 8 for examples and details.

class invention

A story invented by a whole class responding to questions put to them by the teacher.

classical TPR

The use of commands with real action responses. The actions are often full-body responses and sometimes are pantomimed. This is contrasted with *gestures* or *hand TPR*. In this book TPR, or Total Physical Response, is the same as classical TPR.

comprehensible input

Language in the target tongue which students hear or read that is understandable to them.

comprehension check

A quick assessment of whether one or more students comprehend certain material aurally.

easily-taught word

A word that can be taught for recognition with a single exposure to it.

extended reading

A story based on the target material in a story which has already been worked on with TPRS techniques. The purposes of it are to provide additional repetitions of the target material and to provide the other benefits of dealing with a reading with TPRS techniques. A sample is at the end of Chapter 10.

five-day lesson plan

The plan for doing specific activities each day of the week in 55-minute classes.

fluency

In this book the word *fluency* nearly always refers to the ability to express intelligibly in speech (without reading) what one wants or needs to without undue hesitancy or difficulty. The concept includes the ability to produce one sentence after another in "connected discourse." It does not refer to grammatical correctness or native-like pronunciation, nor does it refer to being able to understand the speech of a native speaker. Only occasionally does it refer to native or near-native ability to speak or write a language.

fluency circle, fluency vocabulary

The words, phrases and structures needed to talk, also called "fluency vocabulary," "small circle vocabulary" and "small circle words." There may be only several hundred that are indispensable. See also *reading circle*.

freewrite, freewriting

For a specified brief time, usually from five to ten minutes, students write on a topic given by the teacher or on a topic of each individual's choice. They do not revise or correct what they write. Also called "speedwrite" and "speedwriting." See "Timed Writings" in Chapter 5.

gesture

A TPRS gesture is a physical response to a command or vocabulary item usually with a hand signal which represents the concept which is being taught. For example, *run to the window* can be done by making a window with two fingers of one hand and having two fingers of the other hand "run" to it. Occasionally a gesture may be a facial expression instead of a hand signal, or the respondent may simply point to something or someone. The contrasting concept is *classical TPR.*

guide phrase, guide word

(1) A target grammatical element or phrase or a target vocabulary word or phrase, i.e., one that is being repeatedly used orally to provide sufficient comprehensible input of it so that it will be acquired by students. (2) A word or phrase which students are required to use in a story they are creating or in something they are writing. (3) A word or phrase listed with others, all of which may change in form when a mini-story or main story is retold from the perspective of one or more characters in the story and/or is retold in a different tense.

hand TPR

See *gesture* above.

high-frequency words, vocabulary, structures and **grammatical features**

Those most needed for a language learner to be able to express herself/himself. See *fluency circle.*

home run

An impressive success. In TPRS this term is often applied to a story that develops in such a way that the class responds with remarkable exuberance.

horizontal question

A question the answer to which does not lead to more questions about a specific topic. See also *vertical question* and "Vertical versus Horizontal Questions" at the end of Chapter 3.

in bounds

A teacher is in bounds when s/he makes sure that all students are able to understand everything that s/he is saying. See "*In Bounds* versus *Out of Bounds*" in Chapter 2.

internalize, internalization

These words refer to the process in which students become thoroughly familiar with vocabulary items (and other features of their new language) via aural comprehensible input. When a student has internalized an item, usually s/he is able to produce it in speech.

invention

See *class invention*.

learn, learning

We use these both in the ordinary, everyday way and, often, in the Krashenian sense of somehow getting to " '[know] the rules,' [have] a conscious knowledge about grammar." (Krashen and Terrell, 1983: 18).

learning activity

Learning activities are ones in which students are learning rules, they are making a conscious attempt to internalize them, or they are focusing on the form of the message rather than the message itself. Whenever a student is producing language while focusing on correctness, s/he is engaged in a learning activity.

low-frequency words, vocabulary, structures and **grammatical features**

Those least needed for a language learner to be able to express herself/himself. See *reading circle*.

milk (verb)

To get the most out of a situation or statement, especially by providing a large number of repetitions of a guide phrase through questions.

mini-situation

See *personalized mini-situation*.

mini-story

A short story used as a vehicle for acquiring vocabulary and structure through comprehensible aural input and for providing an efficient and interesting way to begin expressive use of new vocabulary, morphology and structure.

model (verb)

To perform an action (or make a gesture that represents an action or concept) in order to demonstrate the meaning of a word or phrase. The teacher models TPR words or phrases as s/he presents them for the first time and later only when necessary.

monitor (verb)

To check one's own speech to see whether it is grammatically correct.

novel command

A command which students have in general never heard before and which contains elements they are already quite familiar with or can easily comprehend (such as cognates). In TPR Storytelling we nearly always use this term for commands that in addition contain a specific new vocabulary item which we want students to acquire. Typically, many novel commands are given one after another to provide comprehensible input of one particular item in various contexts. Though they need not be, many are bizarre and entertaining.

out of bounds

A teacher is out of bounds when any student is not able to understand anything that s/he is saying in the target language. See "*In Bounds* versus *Out of Bounds*" in Chapter 2.

pacesetter

See slow-processing student.

págame

Spanish for *pay-me*. See that item.

park, parking

To stay or staying at each of the three locations of a mini-story long enough to ask enough questions so that students hear as many repetitions of the guide phrases of the mini-story as can be beneficial. Or, to keep on dealing with a particular detail or sentence long enough to provide the maximum benefit from it.

passive mini-story

A mini-story which is told for the purpose of providing comprehensible input of one or more vocabulary items in context. It is passive because usually it is not acted out. Often it is a very brief story that provides comprehensible input of a new phrase, word or grammatical feature that will be used in a mini-story. See number 7 on p. 243 in the answer to the question about advanced techniques.

pay-me

Blaine developed a way to keep students' speech in the target language. When they speak their native language without permission, the teacher says "Pay me" in the target language. The system is described at the beginning of Appendix I.

paye-moi

French for *pay-me*. See that item.

personalized questions and answers
(PQA or personalized Q and A)

A brief session in which the teacher asks the students questions about themselves and in which specific new target structures, other grammar features and/or vocabulary are used in most questions to provide comprehensible input in a real context. Questions may be directed to the whole class, for anyone to answer, or to specific individuals. The answers may be short or long.

perspective

Telling a story "from perspective" is telling it from the point of view of one or more of the characters in the story or telling it to one or more of the characters. It may also mean telling a story in a different tense from any point of view.

point of view (POV)

See *perspective*.

pop-up and pop-up grammar

Quick questions that the teacher puts to the class about grammatical features when they occur while dealing with a story or a reading. Also, very brief explanations of grammatical points. The purpose of them is to get students to focus on the actual meaning of a word instead of the general meaning of a word. For example, in Spanish (in a specific context) *quiere* means *she wants* and not just *want*.

PQA

See *personalized questions and answers*.

practice (noun, verb)

A special meaning in TPRS of *practice* is hearing, or to hear, targeted material as comprehensible input. Repetitions of the material are what provides the practice.

process, processing, processor

When a sentence is heard by a student, the student processes the various sounds and words in it in order to understand it. The student is the processor. Various factors influence the speed of processing, which is a significant factor in how fast the teacher orally delivers specific comprehensible input to students and in how many repetitions are needed to bring about normal speed in processing.

reading circle

The thousands of words that are in readings but are seldom or never used in everyday speech. Also called "big circle." See also *fluency circle*.

recycle, recycling

Asking questions which have been asked before for the purpose of providing more repetitions of structure and vocabulary.

relaxed write, relaxed writing

A writing assignment in class for a specified period of time — usually 10 or 12 minutes — in which students can ask questions about vocabulary or grammar and can look up whatever they want to. See "Timed Writings" in Chapter 5.

repetition

The special use of this word in TPRS refers to providing one of many oral/aural occurrences of a targeted vocabulary item or a grammatical feature in a meaningful context as comprehensible input.

response time

The time that it takes a student to respond physically to a command or another vocabulary item s/he is expected to respond to.

retell (noun)

A retelling of a story.

role reversal

The giving of commands by a student to the teacher.

script (verb)

To write down the questions before class that a teacher plans to ask while teaching a mini-story.

slow-processing student

One of a small group of students in a class whose aural comprehension the teacher checks at times to determine whether the teacher is speaking faster than students can process. These students play a vital role in helping the teacher slow down. Also called a "barometer (student)" or a "pacesetter." See also *process, processing, processor* and "Barometer Students" in Chapter 2.

small circle vocabulary, small circle words

See *fluency circle*.

speedwrite, speedwriting

See *freewrite, freewriting*.

target grammatical element, item, phrase, vocabulary, word

One that is repeatedly used orally for the purpose of providing sufficient comprehensible input of it for it to be acquired by students. Sometimes the terms *guide phrase* and *guide word* are the same thing.

timed writing

There are two types. See *freewrite, freewriting* and *relaxed write, relaxed writing*.

TPR, Total Physical Response (noun phrase)

Commands with full physical response to them. In this book we use this limited definition, though TPR elsewhere is sometimes a broader concept — movement along with related words. See "Novel Commands" in Appendix G; "Teaching the Words Through Gestures (Hand TPR)" in Appendix H; and Seely and Romijn (1998: 1). See also *classical TPR* and *gesture* above.

TPR (verb)

To teach (a word or phrase) with TPR. We say, for example, "TPR (the word) *kiss*" and "TPR it."

TPRS word, vocabulary, structure and grammatical feature

A target grammatical element or phrase or a target vocabulary word or phrase, i.e., one that is being repeatedly used orally to provide sufficient comprehensible input of it so that it will be acquired by students.

vertical question

A question the answer to which leads to more questions about a specific topic. See also *vertical question* and "Vertical versus Horizontal Questions" at the end of Chapter 3.

Appendix A

TPR Storytelling Presenters

All of the listed presenters do workshops on TPRS in general. Specialties are indicated with a •. Presenters who are listed without a • also may have some specialties.

Debra Allison
Foster City, CA
4dallison@gmail.com
tinyurl.com/SpanishTutor
Spanish
• mixed-level classes
• adult TPRS classes

Carmen Andrews-Sánchez
Silverado High School
Las Vegas, NV
carmen@inputmatters.com
chezsan@gmail.com
Spanish
• beginner and advanced
  workshops
• coaching
• upper levels, including AP

Scott Benedict
Silverado High School
Las Vegas, NV
702-577-1245
scott@teachforjune.com
teachforjune.com
Spanish, German
• grading

Barbara Cartford
3141 Dean Court, #602
Minneapolis, MN 55416
612-408-7342
barbaracartford@hotmail.com
Swedish, Spanish
• middle school, high school and
  adult learners
• workshops
• coaching

Laurie Clarcq
Marcus Whitman High School
Rushville NY 14544
1617 Route 245
Stanley, NY 14561
585-526-7047
Spanish
lclarcq@mwcsd.org

Dale Crum
Littleton, CO area
morningdog@aol.com
dcrum@jeffco.k12.co.us
• Classroom Management
• *Tools for Teaching* by Fred Jones

Leslie Davison
Dillon Valley Elementary
Breckenridge, CO
lesliedavison@hotmail.com
Spanish
• elementary
• dual language / dual immersion /
  bilingual
• adult students

Jason Fritze
Independent consultant
Laguna Beach, CA
(615) 945-8504
jasonfritze@mac.com
www.comprehensibleinput.com
Spanish, French
• comprehensible input
• reading strategies
• professional research
• second language methodology

Carol Gaab
TPRS Publishing, Inc.
P.O. Box 11624
Chandler, AZ 85248
800-877-4738
carol@tprstorytelling.com
Spanish, ESL
• elementary
• middle school

Diane Grieman
Blue Oak School
Napa, CA alegria_3@yahoo.com
Spanish, French
• circling
• personalization
• coaching
• coaching coaches

Susan Gross
Susan Gross Educational
  Workshops
Colorado Springs, CO
susie@susangrosstprs.com
www.susangrosstprs.com
French
• educational consulting
• reading
• effective grammar teaching
• classroom management

Piedad Gutiérrez
Hillside Elementary School
Montclair, New Jersey
pgutierrez@montclair.k12.nj.us
www.TPRSofNJ.com
Spanish
• TPRS basic and advanced skills
• culture and language together
• lesson planning and textbook
  adaptation
• podcast and handcrafted stories
• learning centers in language
  classrooms

Bryce Hedstrom
219 McLeod Ct.
Loveland, CO 80537
970-290-4228
Behedstrom@yahoo.com
Brycehedstrom.com
Spanish
• reading
• music

Mary Holmes
2561 St Ret 43
Aaverill Park, NY 12018
315-559-5348
French, Spanish
mgholmesbike@yahoo.com
• using storytelling in music and
  literature

Melinda Kawahara
Lindy Lizard English House
Kagoshima, Japan
mel40ryu40mi10sei6@polka.plala
 .or.jp
lindylizard.com
English, Japanese
• teaching young learners

Janice Holter Kittok
Educator in Service, LLC
Box 607
Delano, MN 55328
763-972-2791
jankittok@frontiernet.net
www.educatorinservice.com
Spanish, Swedish
• culture and storytelling
• content-based instruction
• K-12 curriculum development

Marjorie LaBella
Clinton Central School
Clinton, New York 13438
2labellas@frontiernet.net
315-831-5322
French

Lynnette Lang
Wheaton Academy
West Chicago, IL
44 w 972 Berner Rd
Hampshire, IL 60140
847-354-0155
French
• AP
• backwards lesson planning
• TPRS training

Gale Mackey
El Dorado Unified High School
 District
Placerville, CA
530-306-7565
cuentista@aol.com
Spanish
• music

Todd McKay
505 Crestwood Lane
Downingtown, PA 19335
610-873-7774
484-432-2558
thmckay1@aol.com
Spanish

Michael Miller
Sabine und Michael German
 TPRS materials
2418 Hagerman St.
Colorado Springs, CO 80904
719-635-0017
fax: 719-785-5755
michael@ sabineundmichael.com
www.sabineundmichael.com
German

Pablo Muirhead, Ph.D., and
 Jacqueline Muirhead
Milwaukee Area Technical
 College
Milwaukee, WI
3726 N. Morris Blvd.
Shorewood, WI 53211
muirheap@matc.edu
muirhepa@yahoo.com
414-297-6412 (work)
414-861-9990 (cell)
Spanish, German, Indonesian
• integrating culture
• critical world language pedagogy
• culturally-relevant pedagogy
• standards for foreign language
 learning

265

Joe Neilson
4147 East Whittier St.
Tucson, AZ 85711
(520) 327-5103
jrnombligo@aol.com
Spanish

Diana Noonan
World Languages Coordinator
Denver Public Schools
900 Grant St., Room 600
Denver, CO 80203
diana_noonan@dpsk12.org
diananoonan@gmail.com
720-423-3295
303-908-5407

Kristy Placido
Fowlerville High School
Fowlerville, MI
517-223-6095
placidok@gmail.com
placido@cablespeed.com
www.kristyplacido.com
Spanish

Blaine Ray
8411 Nairn Road
Eagle Mountain, UT 84005
toll free: 888-373-1920
fax: 888-RAY-TPRS
BlaineRay@aol.com
www.BlaineRayTPRS.com
Spanish

Von Ray
3809 St. Andrews Drive
Eagle Mountain, UT 84005
toll free: 888-373-1920
chilenopo2000@yahoo.com
Spanish

Deb Read
Oregon-Davis Jr. Sr. High
Hamlet, IN
hm: 574-936-6930
wk: 574-867-4561 ext. 323
www.readthewriter.com
deb@readthewriter.com
French, Spanish
• PowerPoint
• beginning learners
• TPRS basics
• TPR basics

Karen Rowan
Karen Rowan Workshops, Inc.
PO Box 165
Manitou Springs, CO 80829
719-389-0405
karen@tprstories.com
www.tprstories.com
Spanish
• adapting textbooks to TPRS
• coaching
• teaching Fluency Fast

Elizabeth Skelton
41888 Cottonwood Creek Road
Crawford, CO 81415
970-921-3867
ellbeth@bethskelton.com
German, Spanish
• ELL / ESL / EFL
• foreign languages
• TPRS in content courses
• reading

Ben Slavic
6451 W. Arbor Ave.
Littleton, CO 80123
303-995-0526
303-730-1789
benslavic@yahoo.com
www.benslavic.com
French

Maggie Smith
School for International Training
Brattleboro, VT
mffsmith@gmail.com
French

Donna Tatum-Johns
Kentucky Country Day School
Louisville, KY 40241
donna.tatum-johns@kcd.org
H (502) 426-7144
W (502) 814-4373
French
• reading
• coaching

Dr. Shelley Thomas
Middle Tennessee State University
Murfreesboro, TN
615-898-5757
shthomas@mtsu.edu
French, ESL
• brain-based learning

Pamela B. "Daisy" Tingen
Monroe Academy
Forsyth, GA
P.O. Box 408
Milner, GA 30257
770-358-4928
French
allwisemom@yahoo.com

Andy Trimiño
FL Consultant
Springdale, AR
atriminoster@gmail.com
Spanish, French
• TPRS stories — long or short?
• reading and writing
• story creation
• beginning TPRS teachers

Pat Verano
Argentina para vos
Medrano 179 (1722)
Merlo, Buenos Aires
Argentina
argentinaparavos.com.ar
Spanish, English, Mandarin
    Chinese, French, German
• acting out songs

Robin Young
World Languages Specialist
Mesa Public Schools
Mesa, AZ
480-472-0268 (wk)
reyoung@mpsaz.org (wk)
480-286-0426 (hm)
robsings@yahoo.com (hm)
French
• basic TPRS strategies
• enrichment activities
• effective assessments
• integrating non-fiction in reading
    and TPRS

Elaine Winer
Deerfield High School
Deerfield, Illinois
224-632-3184
ewiner @dist113.org
Spanish

Inga Zúñiga
Orange Avenue School
Cranford, NJ
zuniga@cranfordschools.org
Spanish
• coaching
• acquisition theory
• multilevel classes

267

Appendix B

Where To Find It

TPR STORYTELLING MATERIALS

The main source is:

Blaine Ray Workshops
8411 Nairn Road
Eagle Mountain, UT 84005
Local phone: (801) 789-7743
Tollfree Phone: (888) 373-1920
Tollfree fax: (888) RAY-TPRS
 (729-8777)
E-mail: BlaineRay@aol.com
www.BlainerayTPRS.com
www.BlainerayTPRS.com

Especially for elementary school and middle school TPRS™ materials:

TPRS Publishing, Inc.
P.O. Box 11624
Chandler, AZ 85248
(800) TPR IS FUN = 877-4738
Fax: (480) 963-3463
TPRISFUN@aol.com
www.tprstorytelling.com

See Appendix K for several other sources.

Command Performance
 Language Institute
28 Hopkins Court
Berkeley, CA 94706-2512
Tel: 510-524-1191
Fax: 510-527-9880
info@cpli.net
www.cpli.net

Many of the other Command Performance Language Institute distributors listed on the final page also carry selected titles. Just ask.

Sabine und Michael
Michael Miller
2418 Hagerman St.
Colorado Springs, CO 80904
(719) 635-0017
Fax: (501) 421-1495
michael@mail.sabineundmichael.
 com
www.sabineundmichael.com

Sky Oaks Productions
See the final page of this book.

A LIST SERVE

MoreTPRS List
http://groups.yahoo.com/
 group/moretprs

FLUENCY FAST LANGUAGE CLASSES

Karen Rowan
Fluency Fast
P.O. Box 165
Manitou Springs, CO 80829
866-WWW-FLUE(ncy)
 (866-999-3583)
719-633-6000
fax: 719-389-0406
www.FluencyFast.com

SELECTED PUBLISHERS

Academy of Reading Publications
products now available through:

Lindamood-Bell Learning
   Processes
416 Higuera Street
San Luis Obispo, CA 93401
(800) 233-1819
www.lindamoodbell.com

Kendall/Hunt Publishing Co.
P.O. Box 1840
Dubuque, IA 52002
(800) 228-0810
www.kendallhunt.com

Pro Lingua Associates
P.O. Box 1348
Brattleboro, VT 05301
(800) 366-4775
www.prolinguaassociates.com

Scholastic of Canada
(800) 268-3860
(905) 883-5300
www.scholastic.ca

TPR SPECIALISTS

James J. Asher
Sky Oaks Productions
Los Gatos, CA
See the final page of this book.

Melinda Forward
PO Box 1317
Sandia Park, NM 87047
toll free: (866) 750-1181
melindaforward@yahoo.com
www.melindaforward.net

Carol Gaab
Chandler, AZ
See Appendix A.

Todd McKay
Downingtown, PA
See Appendix A.

Elizabeth Kuizenga Romijn
Northern & Southern California
Command Performance Language
   Institute
Berkeley, CA
(510) 524-1191

269

Appendix C

Research on TPR Storytelling

In a note to graduate students who contact him, James Asher says:

What remains to be explored are the parameters of TPR Storytelling. We need carefully designed research studies to answer fundamental questions such as [numbers added]:

1. Is there a significant difference in performance between students who experience stories that are exaggerated, bizarre, and surprising compared with stories that are mundane?

2. Is there a significant difference in performance for stories that are goal-directed (e.g., How to give directions to a taxi driver, How to buy a ticket on the train, How to find your way to the hotel, restaurant, police station, etc.) compared with stories that are not goal-directed?

3. Is there a significant difference in storytelling performance between students in elementary, high school and college?

4. Is there a significant difference in performance between students who experience mini-stories compared with a standard length story?

5. How many stories are optimal before adaptation sets in? (Adaptation may be measured by student resistance as indicated by remarks such as, "Please, not another story," "Can't we do something else today?," etc.)

6. What is the optimal mix between classical TPR, storytelling and other linguistic tools such as grammar explanations, patterned drills, etc.?

7. How do storytelling students perform on standardized proficiency tests? Do they outperform students in traditional classes? If so, by how much?

8. What are the correlations between predictors such as academic aptitude, school grades, age, socio-economic status, etc., and the criteria of performance as a result of storytelling?

I can see scores of exciting research projects for a master's thesis or a doctoral dissertation focused on developing scientific answers to these important questions about TPR Storytelling.

Note: Performance can be measured in short-term retention, long-term retention, and attitude ratings by students. Performance can also be assessed by ratings of proficiency in speaking, reading, and writing by teachers who do not know what kind of training each student has experienced. This is called a "double-blind" study.

(personal communication, August 18, 1998)

Mark Webster, who teaches Spanish at Spring Lake High School in Spring Lake, Michigan, has written a Master's thesis (2003) in which he has assembled a significant body of information about TPRS™. In a small survey of some teachers whose high schools are using TPRS, he found evidence suggesting that (1) there is far less than average[1] attrition (drop-off in enrollment from one level to the next) in high schools which have programs using TPRS in all or most classes and (2) attrition has declined significantly in programs that have converted from textbook-based instruction to TPRS. His research also found unusual success on the Advanced Placement exam by students of TPRS teachers.

In regard to preparedness for college level courses, in the fall of 2002 two former students of his "were asked to write 150 words in 30 minutes for a sophomore level Spanish class at Hope College [in Holland, Michigan]. Both completed the task in five minutes...the professor approached [them] to see why they had finished so soon. He found both papers complete and with minimal errors after the summer vacation. Many of the other students required all of the time permitted." (p. 49) Webster concludes, "TPRS students are more than prepared for college. At campuses all over the country, professors are frustrated with the lack of communicative skills students have in their classes. ... TPRS students can communicate in the target language." (p. 50)

Notes

1. See Draper and Hicks (2002).

Appendix D

Vocabulary Lists:
TPR and Most Frequent Words

Classical TPR Phase

The following list is intended to help with the pre-storytelling phase for true beginners. We don't mean to suggest that it should be used in its entirety. How long this phase lasts is at the discretion of the teacher and can vary considerably.

1.	stand up	27.	girl
2.	sit down	28.	floor
3.	fast	29.	ceiling
4.	slow	30.	eat
5.	walk	31.	fish
6.	jump	32.	write
7.	stop	33.	draw
8.	lift/raise	34.	ear
9.	lower, put down	35.	knee
10.	turn around	36.	car
11.	hand	37.	throw the ball
12.	leg	38.	catch
13.	yell/scream	39.	cut (with scissors)
14.	look at	40.	to the left
15.	soft	41.	to the right
16.	loud	42.	hair
17.	hard	43.	foot
18.	touch	44.	watch
19.	point to	45.	clock
20.	hit	46.	arm
21.	head	47.	listen
22.	mouth	48.	chest
23.	eyes	49.	shoulder
24.	table	50.	pencil
25.	nose	51.	pen
26.	boy	52.	face

53.	take	89.	goes towards
54.	newspaper	90.	happy
55.	on top of/over	91.	another bad boy
56.	magazine	92.	another bad girl
57.	run	93.	sleep
58.	up	94.	in the street
59.	paper	95.	a little
60.	book	96.	see
61.	put	97.	corner
62.	once	98.	in front of
63.	twice	99.	between
64.	smile	100.	down
65.	under/below	101.	socks
66.	glass of water	102.	shirt
67.	around	103.	pile of money
68.	orange juice	104.	suit
69.	kiss	105.	skirt
70.	hug	106.	banana
71.	push	107.	spoon
72.	gift	108.	knife
73.	towel	109.	fork
74.	bowl	110.	gets broken
75.	tells him	111.	man
76.	tells her	112.	moon
77.	talk	113.	lettuce
78.	need	114.	ketchup
79.	cry	115.	takes a shower
80.	escape	116.	underwear
81.	big	117.	opens the door
82.	little	118.	skinny/thin
83.	house	119.	short
84.	trip	120.	honks at him/her
85.	fall	121.	seated
86.	laugh	122.	through
87.	cat	123.	pick up
88.	runs towards	124.	grab

100 Most Frequent Words

The following list is adapted from *A Frequency Dictionary of Spanish* (Davies, 2006). A few changes were made in the English translation. Only the infinitive form of verbs is given.

1.	el, la	the	25.	hacer	to do, make
2.	de	of, from	26.	o	or
3.	que	that, which	27.	poder	to be able to; can
4.	y	and			
5.	a	to, at	28.	decir	to tell, say
6.	en	in, on	29.	este	this
7.	un, una	a, an	30.	ir	to go
8.	ser	to be	31.	otro	other, another
9.	se	(3rd-person reflexive marker)	32.	ese	that
			33.	la	it, her
			34.	si	if, whether
10.	no	no, not	35.	me	me
11.	haber	to have (+ p.p.); (for) there to be	36.	ya	already, still
			37.	ver	to see
			38.	porque	because
12.	por	by, for, through	39.	dar	to give
			40.	cuando	when
13.	con	with	41.	él (ellos)	he, him, it (they, them)
14.	su	his/her/ their/your	42.	muy	very, really
15.	para	for, to, in order to	43.	sin	without
			44.	vez	time
16.	como	like, as	45.	mucho	much, many, a lot
17.	estar	to be			
18.	tener	to have	46.	saber	to know, find out
19.	le	(3rd-person indirect object pronoun)	47.	qué	what?, which?, how? (+ adj.)
20.	lo	the (+ adj.)	48.	sobre	on top of, over, about
21.	lo	it, him			
22.	todo	all, every, whole	49.	mi	my
			50.	alguno	some
23.	pero	but, yet	51.	mismo	same
24.	más	more	52.	yo	I

53.	también	also, too
54.	hasta	until, up to, even
55.	año	year
56.	dos	two
57.	querer	to want, love
58.	entre	between, among
59.	así	like that
60.	primero	first
61.	desde	from, since
62.	grande	large, great, big
63.	eso	that
64.	ni	not even, neither, nor
65.	nos	us, ourselves
66.	llegar	to arrive, get to
67.	pasar	to pass, spend
68.	tiempo	time, weather
69.	ella	(ellas) she, her, it (they, them)
70.	sí	yes
71.	día	day
72.	uno	one
73.	bien	well
74.	poco	little, few, a little bit
75.	deber	should, ought to; to owe
76.	entonces	so, then
77.	poner	to put; get, become (+ adj.)
78.	cosa	thing
79.	tanto	so much, so many
80.	hombre	man, mankind
81.	parecer	to seem, look like
82.	nuestro	our
83.	tan	as, too, so
84.	donde	where
85.	ahora	now
86.	parte	part, portion
87.	después	after, afterwards, later
88.	vida	life
89.	quedar	to remain, stay
90.	siempre	always, forever
91.	creer	to believe, think
92.	hablar	to speak, talk
93.	llevar	to take, carry
94.	dejar	to let, leave
95.	nada	nothing, (not) at all
96.	cada	each, every
97.	seguir	to follow, keep on, continue
98.	menos	less, fewer
99.	nuevo	new
100.	encontrar	to find

Appendix E

The Grammar Covered in Three Years in the Look, I Can Talk! Series

The three-year summary below was prepared by Joe Neilson of Salpointe Catholic High School in Tucson. Most examples in both this summary and the list that follows it are in Spanish. Most of the grammatical features mentioned occur in all language versions that are available.

Year 1 Text: *Look, I Can Talk!*

The basic structure and syntax of the language as told from a third-person singular perspective, including some examples of:

    a. reflexive vs. objective pronouns

    b. infinitive uses (*quiere* ___ , *puede* ___ , etc.)

    c. verb/subject agreement (conjugations):

        i. third-person singular (the dominant form)

       ii. third-person plural

      iii. first-person singular. Conjugations are acquired through retelling stories from different points of view.

    d. adjective agreement

Year 2 Text: *Look, I Can Talk More!*

Continues the first year and emphasizes and *dovetails* the following grammatical structures:

    a. more verb/subject agreement (conjugations — telling stories from different points of view — all forms)

    b. adjective agreement

   c.   infinitive uses (*quiere* ___ , *tiene que* ___ ,
      empieza a ___ , *va a* ___ , *le gusta* ___ ,
      puede ___ , *trata de* ___ , etc.)

   d.   reflexive vs. objective pronouns

   e.   preterite vs. imperfect

Year 3 Text: *Look, I Can Really Talk!*

Continues the second year, adding the following:

   a.   the future and conditional

   b.   the perfect tenses

   c.   the imperative

   d.   the present and imperfect subjunctive

   e.   complex structures (*if* clauses, pluperfect subjunctive, etc.)

Below is a detailed chapter-by-chapter listing of grammar covered in the first-year book, *Look, I Can Talk!* This list was prepared by Karen Rowan of Colorado Springs School in Colorado Springs.

Chapter 1
- reflexive verbs (Spanish examples: calls *himself*, *laughs*, *gets in*)
- the verb *there is/there are*
- adjective position
- singular vs. plural
- present progressive (*is crying*)
- indirect object pronouns (*gives to him*)
- *ser* vs. *estar* (Spanish only)
- interrogatives
- sentence structure in a question
- 3S verbs
- 3P verbs (p. 8)

Chapter 2
- the verb *there is/there are*
- adjective position
- *ser* vs. *estar*
- masculine vs. feminine (German, French, Spanish)
- singular vs. plural
- present progressive (*is snoring*)
- indirect object pronouns (*throws to him*)
- reflexive verbs
- 3rd-person singular verbs
- 1st-person singular (*soy, am, suis, bin*)
- stem changing verbs (*encuentra*)
- object of a preposition (*ti*)
- direct object pronouns (*lo lleva*)
- feminine and masculine nouns and adjectives
- interrogatives
- *goes to*

Chapter 3
- the verb *there is/there are*
- direct object pronouns (*no lo encuentra, la abre*)
- direct object pronouns like this: *búscalo* and *tú* commands
- present progressive
- reflexive verbs (*se sienta*)
- indirect object pronouns (*le dice*)
- stem changing verbs (*o-ue* verbs: *encuentra*)
- 1P (p. 24, story #5, 10)
- negative words (*ningún*, p. 24)
- 1S (p. 24)
- past participle (*cerrado, closed*)
- interrogatives
- prepositions

Chapter 4
- 3P
- indirect object pronouns
- reflexive verbs
- articles (*unos, some*)
- verbs with infinitive (*I want to buy*)
- direct object pronouns (*la ayuda*)
- 3P (32)

- 1S (32)
- *ser* vs. *estar*
- 2S
- interrogatives

Chapter 5
- past participle (*called*)
- *o-ue* verbs (*encuentra*)
- direct object pronouns (*los lee*)
- possessives (*sus*, *tuyo*, *contigo*)
- Double object pronouns — *le* changes to *se* (*se lo da*)
- the verb *there is/there are*
- stem-changing verbs (*e-ie* verbs: *piensa*, *pierdo*)
- personal *a* (*a sus amigos*)
- indirect object pronouns (*le dice*, *le queda*)
- preterite — *yo* form (*gané*)
- *ser* vs. *estar*
- subjunctive (*Lo puedes gastar como quieras.*)
- interrogatives
- 1S, 3S, 3P
- negative words (*nada*)
- verb with infinitive (*puede quedarse*)

Chapter 6
- the verb *haber*
- direct object pronouns (*los pone*)
- negative construction (*ni ... ni*)
- reflexive verbs (*se embarra*)
- indirect object pronouns (*le lava*)
- *ser* vs. *estar* (*está limpio*)
- personal *a* (*levanta al bebé*)
- interrogatives
- present progressive (p. 48)
- *el bebé me ve*
- 1S, 2S, 1P, 3S, 3P

Chapter 7
- 1S, 2S, 1P, 3S, 3P
- *ser* vs. *estar*
- present progressive
- indirect object and direct object pronouns

- reflexive verbs
- verbs with gustar
- possessives
- personal *a*
- interrogatives

Chapter 8
- verbs with the infinitive
- *e-ie, o-ue* stem-changing verbs
- reflexive verbs
- indirect object and direct object pronouns
- past participle
- interrogatives
- *esto*
- *ser* vs. *estar*
- 1S, 2S, 3S, 3P, 1P

Chapter 9
- indirect object and direct object pronouns
- reflexive verbs
- interrogatives
- time
- stem changing verbs *e-ie*
- *ser* vs. *estar*
- present progressive
- double object pronouns
- *tú* commands (*llévame*)
- negative expressions
- interrogatives
- 1S, 2S, 3S, 3P, 1P

Chapter 10
- adjective position
- *ser* vs. *estar*
- verbs with infinitive
- indirect object and direct object reflexive verbs
- preterite (*compraste*)
- *acabar de…, to have just…*
- subjunctive (*cambiemos*)
- expressions with *gustar*
- negative expressions

- attaching verb to direct object pronoun (*manejarlos*)
- 1S, 2S, 3S, 3P, 1P
- interrogatives

Chapter 11
- expressions with the verb *tener*
- time
- past participle
- adjective position
- *ser* vs. *estar*
- preterite
- verb with direct object pronoun (*capturarlo*)
- indirect object and direct object pronouns
- reflexive verbs
- 1S, 2S, 3S, 3P, 1P
- interrogatives
- present perfect subjunctive (*no haya matado*)

Chapter 12
- past participle
- indirect object and direct object pronouns
- past progressive (*estaba robando, was robbing*)
- object of a preposition (*conmigo*)
- stem changing verbs
- irregular *tú* commands
- future tense (*pasaré*)
- interrogatives
- reflexive verbs
- 1S, 2S, 3S, 3P, 1P

Appendix F

Letters from Teachers

Date: Thu, 11 Sep 1997 00:04:42 -0400

On August 4 & 5 I reluctantly attended a TPR Storytelling workshop. This workshop was conducted by Shirley Ogle and Melinda Forward. The workshop took place in Ann Arbor, Michigan. I will never be able to thank these two people for enlightening me. Shirley Ogle knew that out of the 13 people who were attending this workshop that I was the most skeptical. I am a grammarian. I teach 9th grade grammar (ENGLISH). I taught French from the grammarian point of view UNTIL (yes, I am screaming) until my eyes were opened to this method. No one could have predicted that I would have changed my perspective concerning this method.

We had open house tonight. The parents had to follow their sons' or daughters' schedule. I can't tell you how many parents commented on how they have learned French these past two weeks. I have to insert that I also teach French III this year. This class has been taught by the grammarian method for two years. I told them that French would be spoken at all times during their class period. THEY HAD A FIT!! (Yes, again, I am screaming!) My French I has no problem speaking French to me.

Will I get through all the tenses that I am supposed to accomplish this year?? No, I won't. Do I care??? No, I don't. Why???? Because my students are excited about speaking the language. Do our universities here in Michigan test with grammarian standards??? Yes, but I don't care. I have seen the difference of teaching in this manner. I see kids, even lower level kids, succeed. I am excited. I have been teaching for 25 years. I have never seen anything like this. IF the universities would accept this new method, they would see a big difference in the way students view a language. In Michigan 70% of the universities' placement tests is grammar. This WAS how I was preparing my students. NO MORE!! No, I will not complete the 12 tenses of French by the end of third year. (I knew them by the end of 2 years of French in 1968). BUT could I have a conversation??? NO. The parents of my French I students tonight were astounded by what their sons or daughters were doing. My French III parents were asking why I was being so mean because I was asking their sons or daughters to speak French.

I only have five more years before I retire. I am having the BEST (yes, I am screaming) time I have ever had in all the years of my teaching. I didn't think I would make it through the next five years. Now I know I can. By the way, I had 95 per cent pass the WRITTEN (yes, I am screaming) vocabulary test today. I am so proud of them. I cannot wait until tomorrow when I can applaud THEM!!!

You have to go through the workshop in order to learn this method. I still remember the Norwegian story that I learned from TPR Storytelling on August 4 and 5. Thank you Shirley Ogle and Melinda Forward!!! I will be forever grateful!!!

Sincerely,
Sue Steele
Brighton, MI

[See also the excerpt from Sue Steele's letter of August 26, 1998, in Chapter 13.]

Date: Late March, 1998

Dear Carol,

I am a TPRS™ teacher. I am so committed to this teaching strategy because it WORKS! I am amazed at what my first year students know and are able to do with the language. They are communicating in the language and are having fun! To the person who had all the questions regarding TPRS — I think Carol answered them, but I would also stress the fourteen techniques that are used at all stages of TPRS in order to internalize the language. You could contact me off-list and I would gladly explain them to you. (e-mail address below) The other day I read mini-stories that these first year TPRS students wrote (based on only five vocabulary words that I gave them) to my Advanced level senior class. The Advanced class is not in TPRS. I then asked these advanced students to guess what level student wrote the stories — they all immediately responded that they must be third year students! They could not believe that first year students wrote those stories. This is just one confirmation that I know that this method works. My TPRS students speak with such ease and assurance — and they speak a lot! Just to give you an example: at the beginning of every class I wrote one word on the board and as part of the warm-up for the class, I ask them to create a sentence using that word. Of course it is a word that they've used before. It is absolutely amazing how they try to "one up" each other by trying to come up with the most creative sentence! And by the way — it usually is not just one sentence — they actually tell a mini-story based on that one word! All done off the tops of their heads! How many teachers out there have the toughest time in teaching indirect object pronouns? I was among them. I would try all kinds of creative ways to get them to remember that with certain verbs you need to have a "le" or "les" as the indirect object. My TPRS students always include indirect object pronouns when they speak — it sounds so beautiful! They do it because it "sounds right." It is also very interesting to note that TPRS happens to encompass many of the multiple intelligences. It's a perfect fit! Many of the teaching tools in MI theory are present when teaching TPRS: spatial, linguistic, logical, kinesthetic, interpersonal and intrapersonal — even music (the tapes are great, Gale!). If anyone would like to know more about how TPRS works in the classroom, please don't hesitate to contact me off-list at nciabotti@aol.com. I will gladly share with you what I have learned and experienced. I firmly believe that this is the way we need to teach languages. Carol, we are working on putting a seminar together for you this summer. We hope to see you!

Sincerely,

Nancy J. Ciabotti
Spanish Teacher
Newburyport High School
Newburyport, MA

nciabotti@aol.com
Date: Tue, 28 Apr 1998 20:13:31 EDT
From: Rockymtnbd <Rockymtnbd@aol.com>
Subject: Testimonial for any TPRS skeptics!

Hello all, I'm new to the list and a newly converted TPR Story-telling teacher after 8 years of teaching. Just a few quick words to share my experience. I, too, was skeptical yet intrigued when I kept hearing and reading about TPRS "changing teachers' lives." However, I had grown so discouraged trying to get our school's very un-motivated, non-academically oriented students engaged in learning a foreign language (it is required for them to graduate from our school), that I was ready to try anything. I attended one workshop, spent a day observing and conferencing with a veteran, talented TPRS teacher, and then read all the material I could get my hands on from Blaine Ray, James Asher, Ramiro García and CW Publishing [now called TPRS Publishing] (Valeri Marsh and Christine Anderson — I think those are the correct authors). I was so intrigued with this method that I threw out what I was doing in my curriculum and started TPRS in early April!

Granted, I have only been doing TPRS for 3 and a half weeks, but I can say with all honesty that it has totally changed my relationship to teaching. I have rediscovered the joy and creativity of teaching (which had been squeezed out of me by years of very negative and uninter-ested students who say that no matter what, they will never see the relevance of being able to speak a FL) and my classroom has come alive. I know this might sound exaggerated but I kid you not. This technique is so much fun both for me and the students, but the best part is that I have honestly seen a HUGE improvement in their ability to express themselves and take risks and be creative in Spanish in just 3 and a half weeks!! I, too, have given two unannounced vocabulary quizzes on which 90% of the students got all the responses correct.

A few people have mentioned skepticism at the teacher's (and class's) ability to keep up the energy required for this technique. I was worried about that, too. What I've found is that I have MORE energy now than I ever did before, and I KNOW it is because both the kids and I feel so much JOY in how much they are learning. I feed off their excitement at what they are able to do with the language.

The other thing I love about this method is that it addresses so many different learning styles-visual, kinesthetic, auditory, interpersonal, etc. I have never seen so many of my students engaged and participating.

Usually at this time of year I am ready to collapse from exhaustion. This year, thanks to TPRS, I can't wait to start again with them next fall!!

Give it a try!! I am totally convinced that this is THE way to teach foreign languages.

Beth Dorman
Rocky Mountain School of Expeditionary Learning
Denver, CO

Date: Friday, June 12, 1998 11:58 AM

Hey gang, I just returned from Quebec with 15 students on our Study Abroad Program. They receive credit for French III and IV. Thanks to all of you who helped me with TPRS. I was scared at first because it is hard to grasp without having attended a workshop. I watched that video 10 times and read the Fluency book umpteen times (I kept it by my bed in Quebec). I have to say that it was a BIG success. The kids enjoyed it and as others have said, they retell the stories on the busses, in the restaurants, in the museums.... They learn the vocab and have no trouble retelling the stories. I did evaluations on the last day and they all said that they loved the "new" method. It really works! I am fired up for the Fall semester when I will be a workshop graduate (New Orleans, Aug. 4th I hope). I have lots of questions now to pose to those workshop leaders!!!

Thanks to all.

Robert J. Raymond
Mississippi State University
rjr4@ra.msstate.edu

Date: Monday, May 13, 2002 9:28:19 AM

When I first heard about TPRS it intrigued me. I joined the TPRS list and, after reading about the experiences and successes of the other TPRS teachers, I realised it was a gold mine. As I started using it and saw the results in teaching Arabic, I was convinced it was the best technique for teaching a second language. We had been struggling trying to make head way teaching Arabic using the grammar-based method. I could see TPRS was a painless way to learn Arabic. TPRS will enable students to understand, remember and retrieve vocabulary and language patterns, thus ensuring fluency in Arabic speech. I am now trying to prepare TPRS material in Arabic. Blaine has sure come up with a simple but effective method to solve the 2nd language dilemma.

Shamima Rasoolhoy
Malaysia
infokid@pc.jaring.my

Date: Friday, May 2, 2003

Last week in the first college/adult class I have taught I was evaluated by the department chair who speaks Spanish. We had about 6 or 7 vocab we were working with and we did a bit of gestures, PQA and then I started a MINI-STORY. Well, the students took off with the MINI-STORY and it turned into a story about Antonio Banderas knocking at our door at 2 AM and my big mean handsome husband going to the door. Antonio got so scared he ran into a tree, etc. The students acted it out to perfection. They then did retells and then POV. During my debrief with the department chair he asked me: "So, how long have your students been working on that story?" I said, "What story?" He said, "The story about Antonio Banderas." I said, "We created that story on the spot. They had been working on it for about 5 minutes." He said, "But they were retelling the story using the preterite and the imperfect correctly as well as changing point of view." I said, "Yes, that's what we do every day." Come to find out he had asked two students this same question (with the same answer) and found it difficult to believe! I got a major kick out of it and it really pumped up my class!

Debbie Shipman

Quincy High School and Feather River College, Quincy, CA
mst@inreach.com

By Stephen Krashen, January 7, 2008

Since 2000, when I starting visiting Taiwan to give lectures and go to conferences, I have probably spent a total of at least a month in Taipei. Despite my interest in languages, this exposure did me no good in acquiring Mandarin. Until last summer, all I could say (and understand) was "I like ice cream" and a few more phrases I learned from a wonderful tape that my former student Lucy Tse made for me many years ago.

This is, of course understandable: The outside world does not provide comprehensible input for adult beginners, or does so very reluctantly. That's why we have foreign language classrooms. The role of the class is to provide the comprehensible input that the output world does not.

This was confirmed for me: I got far more comprehensible input in the first 20 minutes in the first session of the TPRS Mandarin class than I had during the entire time I had been in Taiwan. It was dramatic confirmation of the value of the language class.

My description of the class is a list of the things Linda Li did right. I would include what she did wrong, but she didn't do anything wrong. Of course I define right and wrong as follows:

RIGHT: Consistent with my current view of how language is acquired.

WRONG: Inconsistent with my current view of how language is acquired.

Comprehensible input

Everything was comprehensible. Everything. Input was not always comprehensible the first time I heard it, but eventually everything was. Linda made sure of this. She was never afraid to use every tool available to her to make input comprehensible, motions, pictures, and generous use of translation on the board. [Why not? The translation was not there as orders to memorize the words but as a resource. No time was lost with elaborate non-verbal means when it would have difficult, and the feeling of the class was very Mandarin.]

One of the most dramatic and important things Linda did was to tell the false beginners to calm down. This happened the first day, after about 30 minutes. The result was dramatic. I think this was because the real beginners stopped feeling that something was wrong with them. False beginners give real beginners the impression that other students are progressing much more rapidly.

Linda ignored the false beginners when providing input. I noticed that she did not base her rephrasing and repetitions on the reactions of those who understood the best; these were, usually, the false beginners. Instead, she was incredibly sensitive to where the real beginners were.

No forced speech

Speaking was gently encouraged, but never required. No student was called on, except for a very few occasions near the end of the course. When this happened, Linda knew who she was calling on and how much they could say.

Affect

Providing comprehensible input and not forcing speech does a great deal to keep anxieties low, but in addition to doing this, Linda Li did more than that. It was obvious that she liked us! She was happy to be there, and was "in the moment" at all times. She managed to make input interesting to students with no knowledge of a language that had no cognates with other languages they knew. This was amazing.

Back to Taiwan:

Of course eight hours of Mandarin wasn't enough to make me an intermediate, not enough to put me in a position where I could have conversations with native speakers, even very dedicated ones. It was just enough to get me in trouble, starting an exchange and understanding nothing of what the other person said in response. And sometimes, my attempts to communicate were met with a combination of astonishment and laughter. But it felt GOOD. My best conversational partners were my good friends Kwan and Sean, who treated my attempts to speak Mandarin with respect. (Kwan is seven years old, Sean is nine, the children of my colleague Syying Lee). My Mandarin is now good enough for me to start doing some narrow listening, making recordings of my friends and colleagues talking about topics of interest to me, and of course listening to Linda Li's CD, which seems to have been made just for me!

Appendix G

(former Chapter 2)

Beginning with TPR

We used to always begin with TPR in all beginning language classes. We have found that it is usually more effective and efficient to minimize its use or even to begin with storytelling in middle school and high school foreign language classes in which it is feasible to use translation. We still advocate beginning with TPR with young children (below grade 5 (age 10-11)), in teaching English as a Second Language (ESL) (in situations where the students speak two or more first languages) and with preliterate students. This appendix indicates how we would do this.

Classical TPR

TPR is used for words that can be modeled and easily understood without translation. In TPR we get a total physical response as compared to a gesture, which is not a total physical response but a symbol that represents a word or phrase and its meaning.

We start out using TPR because we can teach more words faster. We can teach 10 to 20 words in a normal class period. It would take a week using TPRS™ to teach an equivalent number of words.

We suggest you teach about 50 to 100 words using TPR before you begin to use TPRS. These would be high frequency words that are TPRable. In Appendix D there is a list of some suggested words.

On the first day you could teach:

- Stand up, sit down, fast, slowly
- walk, jump, stop
- raise/lift, lower, your hand, your leg
- turn around, scream/yell, look at

The First Day of Class

The first day tell your class something like this:

"This year you are going to be learning a new language with a special method. It will be easy on you. All you have to do is do what I do. First, I will give you commands and you will perform the commands along with me. Then I'll give you some commands and you perform them while I do nothing. Sometimes I'll give you a command and I'll perform the wrong action. Remember to always do what I say and not necessarily what I do, because sometimes I'll try to trick you. Before we start, I'm going to tell you the rules of the class.

"1.   Do not speak English (or whatever the students' first language may be). (Actually, they won't need to speak much at all in the first few weeks. Show them a hand gesture to indicate that they would like for you to repeat something without having to tell you in English. Students might move their index finger in a circle to show you that they want you to repeat the command. This rule applies to the students only, not the teacher, and there are exceptions to it. One of the ways of making quick assessments of whether the class or individual students have internalized specific vocabulary is to ask for quick translations. Also, students can raise their hand and ask permission to speak English if they desperately need to say something or find something out.)

"2.   Perform the commands that you are told to perform."

Once you have the ground rules established, it is important that you consistently follow through with the enforcement of them, particularly in a high school or middle school class. In Appendix I, there is a description of a system I developed for enforcing the rules.

Before you start the actual lesson, Asher suggests that you tell the class what they will learn during this first class and that you tell them they will understand everything at the end of class. You do this by reeling off at a normal pace several commands in which you use the vocabulary of the lesson. The class invariably is in disbelief that, just a little while later, they will be able to understand all of what you have said. At the end of class you give them the very same commands to demonstrate to them that they have indeed learned what you said they would.

The First Lesson

Then start with the first three words, first saying just one word (in teaching some languages, just one verbal phrase), then performing the action yourself:

- stand up (you stand up and motion for the class to stand up)
- walk (you walk and be sure everyone in the class is walking)
- sit down (you sit down and everyone else will sit down)

After practicing *stand up*, *walk* and *sit down* three or four times, say "stand up" again but this time don't stand up; *delay* doing the action yourself until the whole class has done it. It is through delaying your actions that you begin to find out if your students have really internalized the words. This is the first step in assessing your students' grasp of new material. From this point on you are doing simultaneous practice and assessment of the new material.

Continual Aural Comprehension Checking

The first step in becoming a great TPR teacher is getting the idea of continually checking for aural understanding in your mind. The reason this is so important is that it is essential that everyone understand almost everything in class — throughout every course. Those who don't will get lost, feel lost, drop out mentally and — as soon as they can — give up learning the language. Your general procedure is always:

1. TEACH
2. CHECK

When you see that the class is responding well, keep giving commands but now without modeling them (without doing the actions yourself). If a teacher models every utterance, students will blindly just do what the teacher is doing. By not modeling, the teacher also is able to see how quickly students respond to the commands.

Since students seem to be responding well and catching on quickly, the teacher is naturally tempted to present more new words and zip right along. S/he sees the students perform the appropriate actions for all of these words and thinks that they know them all. Some TPR teachers may even teach 19 words in five minutes and believe that the students know all of them (see "Pacing" at the end of Chapter 6). There is an illusion of simplicity here. When the teacher checks several students one at a time, s/he discovers exactly what they know and what they need to work on. In reality it takes a lot of practice and checking for the students to master the words.

So, after practicing the first three words for a short time with the whole class, you must do an aural check of some individuals. If you don't, some students will just do whatever everyone else is doing, and you won't be able to tell whether they have really learned the words or not. You must check some barometer students — some of your very slowest ones, not the quick ones. The quick ones will catch everything anyway.

Checking aural comprehension at this point is extremely important. It gives you a clearer picture of what the class as a whole has mastered and what — if anything — they need more exposure to. Whether you are checking the group or an individual, you take note of the yet-to-be-mastered items and you keep using them in commands to the class and to individuals until you are satisfied that nearly everyone has internalized them. Then you can stop checking for them, although you will still use them as part of the ever-growing repertoire of vocabulary that the class knows.

Some teachers have had problems in using TPR because they continue to practice just what the students know instead of moving on. To avoid this problem, keep on presenting new words as you continue to practice the marked unmastered words. You should always be going forward while always reviewing difficult words that some of the students still haven't internalized. There is no reason to continue to emphasize *stand up* and *sit down* if the class knows these words. Your students do not want to dwell on what they already know. Anyway, as you move along, you will be putting all the words you have introduced into a variety of new contexts.

As you have seen, there are several ways to check for understanding. Some give you a fuller picture than others of which items have been internalized and which haven't. When I check an individual, I normally check him/her on several items rapid-fire, one after another. I am always paying attention to response time, no matter which means of checking I use, since this is an indication of degree of mastery. I look for unhesitating responses. These are the types of comprehension checks that I use:

1. I give the command and I delay performing it myself until after the whole class or one student has performed it. This means of checking is used shortly after the presentation of each set of three new items.

2. I give the command. The class or the student performs it while I do nothing; I don't model the command.

3. I give the command and do something different while I observe the students' actions. This is explained more thoroughly below.

4. I say the item in the target language and have the class or the student give me a quick oral translation in their first language. For example, if I'm teaching Spanish to English-speaking students, I say "camina" and the response is "walk." This is the most reliable way to check comprehension. If you never do this, you never know whether some students might be assuming that *camina* means go instead of walk, for example. (It will also clarify meaning and reassure students that they do understand correctly, thereby lowering stress.) Usually I give just one-word items, I give them fast, and I expect fast responses. For instance, I say "levántate," and the student says "stand up" right away. I'm ready with "siéntate," and the student comes back with "sit down." Immediately I say "camina" and the student says "walk."

This means of checking is used generally later in the process of teaching a set of three items. It may be used at any time when there is reason to suspect misunderstanding on the part of any student. (See Chapter 15 for a discussion of first language use in the classroom.)

Beyond the First Three Words

Once you feel the class knows the first three words, move on to the next set of three words. Add *jump*, *fast* and *slowly*. (The reason for introducing *fast* and *slowly* at this point is that they make the learning process much more lively and fun. You can walk fast and walk slowly. You can do anything fast or slowly.) Notice that you teach *fast* and *slowly* in context, along with various verbs. It is far more effective and efficient to do so when you can. After you have practiced these three, you have six words to practice. Combine all six words into novel commands and vary the order of the commands:

> Stand up slowly.
>
> Jump fast.
>
> Walk fast.
>
> Sit down slowly.
>
> Stand up fast.
>
> etc.

After you have modeled the new words two or three times, intentionally make some mistakes in your modeling. Tell the students to touch their noses while you touch your mouth. When some of the students touch their mouths, say (in the target language), "No, I said to touch your nose." This teaches the students to do what you say instead of what you do. It adds a playful aspect to the class, because they never know whether you will model the command correctly or not.

It is important to not get into predictable patterns. Students will soon expect you to tell them to stand up when they are sitting down. It is important to keep the students off guard by telling them to stand up when they are already standing or to walk or jump when they are sitting. When the teacher says to the students to sit when they are sitting, often they will be confused and do nothing. Whenever students don't respond to a command, just model it. For example, they are all sitting. You tell them to sit. Just stand up a very little bit and sit back down. This will show the students the exact action you want them to do.

When you feel that the class knows the first six words, move on to three more new words and then practice all nine words. So, this is the general procedure:

1. Say and model three new words.

   a. Model each new word at least two or three times correctly.

   b. Then intentionally make some mistakes yourself in modeling.

   c. Next, start delaying your modeling.

   d. As soon as you think the students know the words, stop modeling them.

2. Practice the three words until the whole class can respond physically to them in any order without hesitation. As you are practicing:

   a. Always practice with the group and then go to the individual. When you feel that everyone in the group knows the words, give some commands to a few individuals — a quick check to see whether the class has internalized the words.

   b. Be careful not to check your best students. The reason you are checking is to find words the class has yet to master. Your low students need to set the pace of the class, so they are the ones that should be checked. They are the ones that will give you the information you need (i.e., the words they don't know) so that you can practice these words with the group.

   c. Watch for reaction time. How fast do your students respond to commands? If they don't respond right away, they need more practice.

3. Add these three words to all the previous words and practice all these words in various combinations. As you do so, remember to heed *a*, *b* and *c* in Step 2 above.

At the very beginning, you can't combine a new vocabulary item in commands with already familiar words. But, very soon you can, so use a variety of combinations with each new item. For example, when you introduce *run* and you have already practiced the other words in the following sentences, you can use:

> Run to the window.
>
> Run and cry.
>
> Run and catch the ball.
>
> Run on the ceiling.
>
> Run in a circle.
>
> Run to the left.
>
> and much more

Finding Out What Students Need to Practice

Remember that students can do most actions in pantomime. You want to stimulate their imaginations and keep them alert, never knowing what to expect next. You can also make statements for students to perform, for instance: "Your hand jumps. Your hand runs backwards." When you reach concrete nouns such as *hand*, *mouth*, *eye*, *nose* and *hair* or others like *door*, *tomato* or *juice*, notice that they are really the easiest items to teach through TPR, e.g.: "Walk to the door. Touch your mouth. Kiss your hand. Throw the tomato. Drink the juice."

In TPR and in TPRS you are trying to see where the students *break down*. That lets you know where to go with your practice. When you see a student can't perform any given command, you then go back to the class and practice. Breaking down (not being able to perform the command) can result from not knowing the vocabulary, from the language being spoken too fast or from not understanding the context of the language. It is very important that you notice when students are not

298

able to perform, because this is how you find out what they need to practice. *This is the most important thing you can do to use your class time wisely.* You need to practice what students don't know. After you have practiced something a student didn't know, you then go back to the same student to see if s/he has mastered the material s/he didn't know a few minutes earlier. This also sends a powerful message about the high expectations you have of your students. You expect them to learn. If they don't know something, then it will be expected that you will practice it and that you will go back to the same student to see if s/he got it.

Always practice with the whole group and check individuals. You can also check small groups to add variety to what you are doing. You do this by signaling to a row or half a row to respond to a command or a series of commands. Constantly vary the size of the group responding to the commands. This gives students a rest at times and it helps cement words some students aren't sure of. They see others respond to the words and progress by watching them respond physically.

Finding Breaking Points Is the Key to Good Teaching

To find a breaking point, you can "raise the bar". One way to do this is to alternate between single commands and chain commands (described below). Chain commands sound totally different to a student. By constantly switching back and forth between single commands and chain commands, the students will likely be challenged. Chain commands are much more challenging than single commands. Whenever students can't do chain commands, you always back up to the single commands.

Using Single-Sentence Commands to Both the Class and the Individual

A single-sentence command is just one sentence with a delay afterwards. Say the command and have the class or the individual perform it. If you are working with the entire class, say, "Touch your nose," and let the entire class do the action before moving on to the next command. If you have some "difficult" words marked on a word list, practice each of them. After doing this for a few minutes, you can then address an individual and say each of the following sentences one by one:

Stand up.

Grab a knife.

Put it on your nose.

Laugh at the door.

Put the knife on your elbow.

Put the knife on your bellybutton and cry.

You could then go on to another individual and pick out a few more of the difficult words and practice them in single commands. During this time it is not your intent to teach the words. You are only trying to practice the words in an interesting way. So you don't model any of these commands. It is only if there is no response at all or if the student makes the wrong physical response that you would give the meaning of the word away by modeling it to the student.

Chain Commands

Chain commands are commands given in groups of three or four. Before saying the commands, either tell the class or signal to them to wait until you have given all the commands. For example:

Stand up, jump twice, touch your nose and sit down.

Raise your right hand, put it down, lift your head and laugh.

Touch your nose and your hair and put your head on the desk.

TIPS:

- Tell your class to take pictures in their minds of the commands and perform what they see in the pictures. If students will focus on the visual, they will be much more successful in TPR. My first experience as a TPR student was at a workshop at Boise State University in 1986. I was learning French. I had a very difficult time doing what the teacher ordered until he told me to think in pictures. He actually acted like he was taking a picture. Once he did that, I could visualize the actions and perform the pictures that were in my mind. I didn't focus on the foreign language any more — just the pictures of the commands.[1]

- Alternate between giving chain commands to the entire class and to individuals.

- Have a signal that they can make to show you that they understand. For example, when you say, "Stand up, jump, walk forward and sit down," all those in the class that have understood will raise their hand. Any clear signal will work. Gene Lynch, a TPR high school German teacher in Lompoc, California, has his students make their right hand into a fist and put it on their left hand when they have understood a chain command. As soon as some students have given the signal that they understand, the teacher calls on one of them to act out the commands.

Novel Commands

Using novel commands is another way to find out where students break down. A novel command is a new command. It is a command they have never heard before.

You can get a novel command in two ways. You can combine two words from two known sentences into a new sentence. If your students already know the words in the sentences *Touch your nose* and *Raise your hand*, then *Touch your hand* and *Raise your nose* would be novel commands. These sentences are totally new sentences to the students yet they come from known words. In other words, the known words are recombined to make a new or novel command.

Some novel commands don't have to actually be performed. Your students can just act like they are doing them. You can have students touch the ceiling (reach up as if they were touching it) or have them take off their noses and throw them. This type of novel command is great fun for the students, and it keeps the class interesting while you're doing TPR.

It is often difficult to think on your feet. So it is helpful to write some notes to remind yourself of some novel commands. You can make up some 3" x 5" cards with novel commands for each lesson — one command to a card. Write down a command and leave a blank space to fill in orally with many possibilities during class. For example:

Put your elbow on the _____ . (desk, fish, window, table, orange juice, floor, magazine, house, clock, egg, dog, etc.)

Your hand runs on _____ . (your chair, my arm, the door, her foot, your mouth, the table, John's hair, etc.)

Your _____ jumps on your _____ . (mouth/stomach, belly button/leg, tongue/head, eye/book, etc. — be careful!)

(Notice that these last two "commands" aren't, strictly speaking, commands. Nonetheless they are treated as commands in that they are performed by the students immediately after the teacher utters them.[2])

Take your cards to class. Using the first card, fill in the blank(s) orally, with every word you can think of, as you give the commands to the class. Then go on to the next command, on the next card. The idea is to use a lot of novel commands with each new word. As you can see from the examples above and below, you can use a lot of *imagination* in your commands and *pantomime* on the part of the students is very useful.

You can use novel commands for most nouns. For example:

apple
Pick up the apple and put it on your head.
Throw the apple up and catch it. (The students pretend to have an apple.)
Put the apple on your nose and laugh.
The apple runs around your ear.

chair

Sit on the chair and cry.

The chair jumps quickly.

Touch the chair with your nose.

Put your left knee on the chair.

window

Look at the window.

Point to the window with your left hand and to the door with your right hand.

Grab a big elephant and throw it at the window.

ceiling

Touch the ceiling with the book.

Laugh at the ceiling.

Look at the ceiling and don't laugh.

Novel Commands to an Individual

Novel commands to an individual can add great interest to a class, which is one of our main objectives. Have students do unusual things. You might have a student push a pencil on the floor with her/his nose, walk like a cat or jump like Superman. I have my high school students sing to each other romantically. I have a boy stand up and walk to a girl and take her hand. He then pretends to give her a flower, looks into her eyes and sings her a song we have learned in class. Anything that is unusual or different will make the class interesting. Students will not fall asleep when there is such a variety of activities going on.

Vocabulary Test

When the class appears to know the words, I test them with a translation test. Students see the words in the target language and write the definitions in English.

How well they do on the first test is very important. It tells me whether or not my pacing is OK. I often get 90 percent of my students to get 90 percent or higher. A realistic goal would be to have 80 percent of the class get 80 percent or higher, or if this is your first time through, maybe 70 percent of the class getting 70 percent or higher would be acceptable. If the figures are lower than that, you probably should go back and re-teach the most commonly missed words on the test.

If your students are having trouble with certain words, give them associations or other ways to remember them and then focus your practice on those words.

The tests should be unannounced. You need to see whether your students know the words on a long-term basis. If they study the night before, you will only find out how well they studied. Giving unannounced tests is a key to good teaching and a must for TPR and TPRS teachers.

Looking at the words your students missed will let you know where you fell down as a teacher. You will then be aware of those words and teach them better next year. You should also recycle those words in your succeeding lessons so that students can learn them better on a long-term basis.

Some books and a video you might find useful for the classical TPR stage are Asher (1996), Forward and Ogle (1997a and 1997-2001), García (1988), Marsh and Anderson (1995c, 1995e, 1996a or 1997), Ray (1992, 1993 and 1995 (video)), Seely and Romijn (1998), Segal (1989) and Miller (2002 (video)).

Notes

1. Visualization along with exposure to language is extremely effective. Some people are not good at visualizing and suffer in several ways as a result. Those who improve their visualization skill also improve in some or all of the following areas: aural comprehension, reading comprehension, oral expression, written expression, following directions, sense of humor, critical thinking (which includes logical thinking, problem solving, predicting and the perception of cause and effect relationships). Nanci Bell's (1991: 8; see also ibid.: 11-33) experience and research have led her to believe that:

visualizing is an answer to *how* we process language and thought. *The brain "sees" in order to store and process information* [author's emphases]. Both thinking and language comprehension are founded in imagery. Individuals with good language comprehension visualize concepts and form imaged gestalts. Individuals with weak language comprehension do not visualize concepts and therefore don't easily connect to language.

Prominent linguist David Crystal (1992: 181-182) has commented:

concrete nouns … are highly imageable, whereas abstract nouns are not. In the context of language teaching, high imageability may be a desirable feature of sentences being presented to the learner, as there is some evidence that they are easier to remember.

We encourage students to visualize both vocabulary items and story lines. Besides often helping learners to remember language, this practice may help some individuals to better their ability to visualize and thereby help them improve in some of the above-mentioned ways.

2.   In Spanish, French and some other languages the familiar imperative form is, with some exceptions, pronounced the same as the 3rd-person singular. This is convenient for making the transition from the imperative to descriptions such as the above and to stories. However, some languages have consistently different pronunciations of these forms. In English, the difference is slight; only -*s* (pronounced [s] or [z], depending on what the preceding sound is) or -*es* is added to the imperative form (with the exceptions of *be* and *have*). If you are teaching a language in which the imperative form of many or most verbs is pronounced differently from the 3rd-person singular form, you can teach these 3rd-person forms through items such as the last two examples above. You can also use such items for the exceptions in languages such as French or Spanish. For a more thorough discussion of the question of what form to teach first, see Seely and Romijn (1995: 87-89).

Appendix H

Gestures and Kindergarten Day

We used to recommend gestures as the main way of pre-teaching vocabulary, but now we believe that occasional translation along with lots of questioning is probably a more effective and efficient means of doing this. Many teachers still use gestures to pre-teach before asking a story. We recommend that both gestures and associations be used only as long as they are helpful in establishing the meaning of any particular new grammatical feature or vocabulary item.

Teaching the Words Through Gestures (Hand TPR)

Put the guide words for the mini-story on the board or the overhead projector. Elaine Carey suggests having your class stand, at least often, when they are working with gestures. Tell the students "feliz" and show them the action for happy by smiling. Make sure you have a clear and distinct action for each word or phrase. Although we don't actually use a hand sign or gesture in this particular case, for most words we do, so we use the terms *gesture* and *hand TPR* to cover all of the signs that we use for teaching this way. In fact, we could use a hand sign for *feliz* or for any word or phrase. Preferably the action for a word is obviously related to its meaning. We accompany many gestures with mouth sounds such as slurping, buzzing, howling or motor noises. These increase the fun. If you can't think of an appropriate action for a word, you might ask your students to suggest one. If no one can come up with an obvious sign, use any sign arbitrarily, just so it's not taboo in the culture of any of your students.[1] (Carol Gaab of the Phoenix area points out that ESL teachers need to be particularly careful to notice reactions to signs that may be confusing or offensive to students from other cultures. A gesture which seems obvious and benign to Americans may be meaningless or obscene to someone else.[2]) Tell the students that *feliz* means happy (so they won't confuse it with *smile*) and give an association like "*Fleas* are happy." Students may help you come up with good associations.

Next, make a sad face and say the word "triste" (pronounced "treestay;" association: "*trees stay* sad"). Then point to a girl and point to a boy (*girl* and *boy* are words for which you probably won't need associations, since they're real people that are present). Now practice these four words, having the students carry out one of the actions which you just showed them immediately after you say each of the words one by one. You say a word. They perform the appropriate action. Then another word and the action and so on. Mix up the order of the words so the students won't know what's coming next. Remember to use the skills of working with the group and the individual.

For variety, use chain commands. Have the class pause while you say three words in quick succession. Then, immediately after you finish saying the third word, the students do the appropriate hand action for each one of the three in the order in which you gave them. For example:

> Boy, girl, give.
>
> Girl, give, boy.
>
> Boy, give, girl.

Also for variety whenever you're doing TPR, sometimes have your students stand. This will "keep them on their toes."

TIP:

> Have the class close their eyes often. That way they won't be looking at others. In other words, they have to remember the word and they won't have any visual clues.

You have now given the students the words and the associations and practiced the words through gestures both in single commands and chain commands. You have also practiced the words with the group as well as with individuals. You have checked the comprehension of the students by having them close their eyes to see if they can do all of the actions to the words you say. You have also checked some of the slower individuals to see if they know the words, and you have provided associations for words that students have had trouble identifying.

Kindergarten Day

Kindergarten Day is an innovation of Susan Gross, formerly of Cheyenne Mountain Jr. High School in Colorado Springs, Colorado. It is a reading activity which was inspired by the recommendation that teachers read stories to students. The teacher selects a children's book which has colorful pictures. S/he reads the story to her/his students, making sure to show them the pictures on each page, as is done in elementary school. S/he frequently asks questions about the pictures, imitating the behavior of kindergarten teachers with picture books. It is important that the teacher make the language comprehensible to the learners, just as kindergarten teachers do.

Gross says that, in her classroom, some students like to sit on the floor and she sits in an easy chair. Some students get stuffed animals to hold while listening to the story. Once in a while students ask to bring in a treat for the class to munch on for Kindergarten Day.

Some benefits of this activity are:

- interesting comprehensible input
- low affective filter (see "Only Comprehensible Input?" in Chapter 12)
- Students feel like they are being given a "mini-vacation".

Notes

1. A good source for signs is a sign language dictionary. For example, see Butterworth and Flodin (1991) or Sternberg (1987).

2. A book that can help avoid problems is *Bodytalk: The Meaning of Human Gestures* by Desmond Morris (1994). It shows and explains over 600 gestures from cultures around the world.

Appendix I
Classroom Management

APPENDIX CONTENTS   Page

Blaine's Classroom Management Rules   309

Scott Benedict's Págame System   311

Classroom Management (by Tawanna Billingsley)   312

Mildred (by Ben Slavic)   314

BLAINE'S CLASSROOM MANAGEMENT RULES

The first day tell your class something like this:

"1. Do not speak English (or whatever the students' first language may be). (Actually, they won't need to speak much at all in the first few weeks. Show them a hand gesture to indicate that they would like you to repeat something without having to tell you in English. Students might move their index finger in a circle to show you that they want you to repeat the command. This rule applies to the students only, not the teacher, and there are exceptions to it. One important way to make quick assessments of whether the class or individual students have internalized specific vocabulary is to ask for quick translations. Also, students can raise their hand and ask permission to speak English if they desperately need to say something or ask something.)

"2. Perform the commands that you are told to perform."

Once you have the ground rules established, it is important to consistently follow through with the enforcement of them, particularly in a high school or middle school class.

I have developed a system for enforcing the rules that works quite well. I call it the "pay-me" system, or "págame" in Spanish, "paye-moi" in French or "bezahl!" in German. They all start with a 100 percent participation grade. This is 25 percent of their overall grade. A student must look engaged and answer in the target language when we ask questions in that language. S/he may answer in English (or her/his first language) if we ask a question in English. Otherwise, when a student speaks English or doesn't stay engaged in the class, s/he gets a "pay-me"/"págame"/"paye-moi"/"bezahl!" This takes away five percent of her/his nine weeks' participation grade. I let students make these up in two ways:

a. They can get four "free" "pay-me's." They can give me a greeting card for two of them and a non-monetary gift (such as a handshake) for two. This takes care of most students.

b. After they have made up their four free ones, they can write a 100-word essay in the target language to make one up. They can make up a maximum of two per week.

It is easy to keep track of each infraction. If a student speaks her/his first language, just say "pay me" in the target language. Then put a check mark beside her/his name. When s/he has ten "pay-me's," you talk to the student. Tell her/him s/he needs to make up the points. This statement lets the student know s/he has to change. If a student ever talks back when getting a pay-me, just say, "Make it up." This is a pat answer that you always say. Then you immediately go back to your lesson. Emphasize making up the pay-me's. Tell the student later that you really want her/him to be successful in class. Let her/him know it is not hard to make up the points and that it will really help her/his grade. This will send a message to the student that you care about her/him. S/he will also get the message to participate and not talk English. Finally, if you feel the student just doesn't care about her/his grade and continues getting pay-me's, then call her/his parents or write counselor referrals. At the beginning of the year we would send out parental letters explaining how students would be graded in the language class. We had good parental support because of this.

SCOTT BENEDICT'S PÁGAME SYSTEM
from his website, www.teachforjune.com

For me, participation cannot be a graded item. What I mean by that is, that participation, effort, behavior, cannot be calculated into the letter grade of the student. At my school, like many, we have a citizenship grade, and that's where I believe participation, effort, and behavior grades should be placed.

For us, the citizenship grade is broken down into the following marks: O(utstanding), S(atisfactory), N(eeds improvement), and U(nsatisfactory). I believe that a student should earn a satisfactory mark, not be given one. I also believe that, not unlike a citizen of a country, a good classroom citizen not only follows the rules, but also contributes to the overall progress of the class. For that reason, my citizenship grade is broken down into five subcategories: participation, homework, behavior, unexcused absences, and unexcused tardies.

For the participation segment, each student starts with 70 points (needs improvement). They need to have a net balance of 80-89 points at the end of the quarter to receive a satisfactory mark, and 90 or more to receive an outstanding. Students earn points for asking good questions, answering questions, using the target language in and out of the classroom, as prizes for games, etc. I hand these points out in the form of various currencies from Hispanic countries cut out on little slips of paper. It's the student's responsibility to keep track of these and turn them in at the end of the quarter.

Students lose points for various activities that take away from their personal learning or the learning of the class as a whole. I start with minus 2 points for bathroom passes, 3 points for hall passes or talking, 5 points for behavior issues, absences, tardies, 10 points for repeated behavior issues, and 15 points if the student has to receive a referral for their behavior. All of these points can be made up by writing a 100-word essay in the target language using the current vocabulary. I give back 5 points for each essay.

At the end of the quarter, I enter how many points the students turn in into the gradebook. The gradebook then adds these to the 70 they automatically receive at the beginning of each quarter and subtracts any negative points the students received and gives a net total. That net total determines their participation grade, which is then averaged with the other 4 components of my citizenship grade to give an overall citizenship grade that appears on their report card.

I like this system because it puts the responsibility of being a good citizen in the hands of the students and it takes the subjectivity out of determining these very subjective grades. If ever questioned, I can tell the student/parents exactly how that grade was calculated and what the student can do to improve it for next time.

CLASSROOM MANAGEMENT
Tawanna Billingsley, the Academy of Communications and Technology Charter School, Chicago. Written in 2003.

My name is Tawanna Billingsley and I have taught in an inner city middle/high school setting for eleven years now (the duration of my teaching career). I have been teaching in a school for the past nine years in a neighborhood that at one point had the highest murder rate in the city and I use TPRS™. My kids get it. They love it. It suits them better than the traditional approach. As a matter of fact, when I taught language using the traditional method of verb conjugation and the such, over half of my students received an "F" in the class, and boy was retention and homework completion a problem. However, when I switched, mid-year (about seven years ago) to TPRS (after a one day workshop), boy did things take off. For the past seven years the lowest grade I have had to assign was a "C", using this method. My students love to act out the story and they love the story retells, because they get to show what they have learned. They even turn in the homework (story illustrations, story retells and/or translations to parents, original story compositions).

In regards to management, I always take the first two weeks to get to know my students. They get to know me, and we establish and practice procedures for almost everything. For example, there is a procedure for entering the classroom when one is tardy, there is a procedure for homework turn-in, there is a procedure for transitions between activities. We practice all of them, several times, as research indicates that it takes 21 times of doing something to form a habit. We also do an activity about what respect looks like, sounds like, and feels like. I use the language generated from this activity all year. When redirecting student behavior I often ask students, "What should respect sound like right now? What does respect look like right now?"

Be prepared for lots of redirection.

We discuss as a class what scholarly behavior looks like and I then use the language generated from this lesson for the rest of the year. I try to put the ownership of behavior onto the students. One way I redirect students is to walk over to the off-task student and say quietly, "Is that scholarly behavior? I thought your intention was to learn Spanish. What should you be doing? Thank you."

One powerful way to stay out of confrontations with students is to use the language of choice, thereby again putting the ownership of behavior on them. For example, if a student is being a distraction, I walk over to the student and quietly say, "You have two choices — you can either.....(desirable behavior) or you can.....(some consequence that the student does not want to do), which one do you choose?"

If the student chooses the desirable behavior, I say, "Thank you.", and I walk away. If a student does not respond, I say, "You have 10 seconds and then I will make the decision for you." I count from one to ten. Most of the time students choose the desirable behavior. I say, "Thank you," and continue teaching. If a student chooses the consequence (or forces you to choose it), be sure to follow through (depending on the consequence, you may have to follow through after class). Make sure that your consequences are something that you can follow through on.

The key is to disengage the student as soon as possible and get back to teaching.

Anywhooo, I have attended numerous workshops on classroom management and I have lots of tools in my belt. If you need other suggestions, I would be happy to share. Also please ask Ben Slavic. He has some awesome techniques that you use while continuing to use the target language.

Just know that they can learn via TPRS and that they want to learn.

MILDRED

Ben Slavic, Summit Ridge Middle School, Littleton, Colorado.
Written in about 2006, published in his book *PQA in a Wink!* in 2007

Mildred is the captain of the girl's basketball team. She is rough. She had to be rough because she was thrown around physically by her abusive parents in a double wide trailer growing up. One day I learn that one of the walls in Mildred's trailer has a gaping hole in it, covered with plastic.

I sense on this first day of class that that Mildred would probably have little chance in her life to leave that trailer and stay in a five star hotel in Paris on a vacation. Mildred may not even be sure what I teach.

I have a problem, because Mildred's swagger upon first entering my classroom is saying, "I am going to take over this class, and bring five of my friends with me, and that is the way it is going to be."

Mildred just doesn't go to her seat. She walks around a little, not unlike an animal staking out new territory by peeing on things. Mildred is peeing, but not in the way Susie Gross means.

Have you ever taught a Mildred? Isn't it fun?

If in this moment I say to myself, "I am going to really love Mildred", it is a futile act. Mildred has not experienced enough love growing up to know how to even respond to it. Instead, I need a technique, a process, for dealing with Mildred in a specific way. I have two possible scenarios from which to choose:

Scenario 1:

"Mildred, sit down now. We are going to start class."

She doesn't. What do I do? Wag my finger in her face? Raise my voice? The class senses my indecisiveness. Mildred finally sits down, but not after establishing a negative mood in my classroom on the first day of class.

That was her purpose, because Mildred is comfortable in a negative mood. She thinks confronting people is a normal activity. She sits down, having displayed her power. You teach poorly the rest of the period, because Mildred is passively controlling the classroom via her aggression. Mildred wins.

What happened in this scenario? I allowed Mildred to bring her Personality A into my classroom, the personality she uses in all her classes and the one which will eventually cause her to drop out of high school before she graduates because it simply won't work for her in schools.

Is there a Personality B that you can develop with Mildred so that this doesn't happen? Is it possible for teachers in all subjects to interact in such a way with their students that the Mildreds of the world want to stay in school instead of dropping out?

Scenario 2:

When I greet Mildred at the door and sense her game, even though I know nothing about her, I sense that she may be "the one" who needs to learn some discipline at this point in the year a lot more than she needs to learn some French.

So when the students begin filling out their questionnaires, I casually sit down next to her and say, "Hi Mildred! What sport (activity, etc.) do you do?"

The reason I ask about sports is because a large part of teenagers personalities are centered around sports. It is a good way for them to get a workable identity in school. I have found that well over 50% of the kids, in eighth grade at least, when I do PQA with them, tell me about their sports first. It's what they do.

If Mildred tells me that she doesn't play sports, I find out one thing she does. If needed, I stay with Mildred for the filling out of the questionnaire, just sitting close by engaging her in idle conversation every few minutes, visiting with other students if possible, but keeping my focus on her on this first day of class.

The class is seated alphabetically (in a big rectangle around the room) to prevent Mildred from establishing a "cell" with her friends.

When I collect the questionnaires, I first look at Mildred's questionnaire and bring her sport to the attention of the class. I turn this into a positive for both of us in the following way:

I start in English, "Mildred, you play basketball? That is so cool. I used to play basketball some but I wasn't very good."

Remember, this isn't about teaching French. It is about establishing firm discipline in the classroom, a prerequisite to success in any classroom, and doing so via personalization. Then I say in the target language: "Classe, Mildred joue au basket! / Class, Mildred plays basketball!"

The students understand "class" because it is a cognate, and "Mildred" because I say it in English, but not "joue" so I write down: joue au basket – plays basketball.

Now I stay there. I circle that expression really slowly using the question words, pausing and pointing, going slowly, not moving off the sentence until it comes to a natural stopping point. It is a simple sentence and everybody gets it because I am following the visual metaphor offered on page 108 of the Conclusions section of TPRS in a Year!

My focus is not on the target language now, it is on Mildred. I am neutralizing her by making her the center of attention. I whisper in English to her, "What position do you play?" She says point guard. This fact becomes a fact of supreme importance to me as I continue with this super-slow circling.

By now I have a basketball in my hand. I have created a kind of tension around the basketball. Will I hand it to her as I continue around the room circling? Mildred and the class sense that she will get that basketball if she keeps paying attention.

By my feigning a few handoffs to Mildred, but each time withdrawing the ball, the kids begin to understand that Mildred won't get the ball until she responds successfully with "yes" or "no" to me in French.

What have I done by this? By talking about Mildred in the target language, I have forced Mildred to pay attention to me because I am talking about her and because I am so impressed that she is the point guard on the basketball team.

People love to hear how great they are, and Mildred is no exception. I am beginning to own Mildred, the person who came into my classroom intending to own me.

And, in fact, Mildred buys into the whole thing. She has no idea that her Personality A is getting neutralized, and that her Personality B is being built. She gets the ball when the circling naturally dies down. I then interest myself in another student's sport or activity, but not before making strong and meaningful eye contact with Mildred when handing her the ball about who is in charge of this class.

What if Mildred decides to chuck the ball to a friend or toss it up and down? I simply take it and put it in the cabinet. When Mildred comes into class the next day, she goes straight to my cabinet where she gets "her" basketball. She is shocked when I allow her to do that, but she doesn't know that I am training her in her new personality. She also knows that the minute she disrupts class with the ball, it is gone.

I return often to Mildred these first few weeks, circling the simplest of sentences about her, keeping her involved, smiling, inviting her to accept this new Personality B – that of an important athlete in the school who pays attention in French class.

By the end of the week I have a naming ceremony using a small plastic sword from Wal-Mart, in which Mildred is dubbed in English (shoulder, other shoulder, top of head – that idea from Robyn Valdizon, thanks Robyn) "Best Point Guard in the History of Colorado High School Basketball," a name she will keep (spoken in English) all year.

I will use this name in all sorts of PQA and extended PQA activities, in stories, and in readings. The Best Point Guard in the History of Colorado High School Basketball needs to learn how to read French to know what great things she has done on the court as described in the readings I have created about her Personality B.

As long as I keep Mildred engaged and important, she doesn't relapse into Personality A.

By always returning the focus to this wonderful basketball star (the greatest in the history of Colorado high school basketball!) and this great French student, Mildred buys into whatever I do. I win.

Personality B sets in fully by the end of the second week. The problem is solved, not by my loving Mildred, but by my doing a specific, designed, activity directed right at her in the first few classes of the year.

Appendix J

Multi-level Classes, Raising Enrollment and Teaching Present & Past Together

APPENDIX CONTENTS   Page

Multi-level Classes

Multi-level Classes with TPRS™: Unexpected Gains   319
(by Blaine Ray)

Writing Rubric for Levels 1 and 2 (by Joe Neilson)   324

Raising Enrollment

Raising Enrollment at East High School in Denver   326
(by Blaine Ray and Diana Noonan)

Excerpt from the Masters Thesis by Mark A. Webster   328

Teaching Present and Past Tenses Simultaneously

The Athenian Study (by Von Ray)   329

Multi-level Classes

MULTI-LEVEL CLASSES WITH TPRS: UNEXPECTED GAINS

by Blaine Ray

originally published in *The International Journal of Foreign Language Teaching*, Summer 2005, pp. 27-29
(www.ijflt.com)

TPRS, Teaching Proficiency Through Reading and Storytelling, formerly known as Total Physical Response Storytelling, has changed the way many teach second languages. It continues to grow as teachers continue to experience great success. At a workshop in Denver in April,

319

2004 I suggested multi-level classes, based on the idea that in a TPRS class, input will be comprehensible to all students, regardless of level.

Meredith Richmond, a Spanish teacher and Department Chair at East High School in Denver, Colorado attended that workshop. Soon after, she approached her principal about the possibility of doing an experimental multi-level class. The plan was to have students from levels one, two, three and four all take Spanish in the same class. To the best of our knowledge, this was the first time such a class had been attempted.

East High School had already been using TPRS as their primary method of instruction for more than six years and they had experienced much higher enrollments in upper level classes, especially from minority students.

To do the experiment, Meredith wrote a letter detailing the class and the experiment to interested Spanish students in the school. A total of 85 students expressed interest. Based on student interest, permission was granted for the department to proceed.

Meredith and other East High teachers attended another workshop in Colorado at the end of September. One workshop participant asked about the "bored superstar" in the TPRS class, meaning the student at the top of the class who is bored by the thorough repetitiveness of TPRS. I turned to Meredith and had her answer the question. If there was ever an opportunity for the "superstars" to be bored, the multi- level class would have been it. In fact, the fourth year students should have been bored stiff because of the constant repetitions that TPRS demands. I was very interested in Meredith's response, but it shocked me.

She said, "I must admit my level four students have made the most progress in the language so far this year."

I thought that statement was amazing. I felt maybe we foreign language teachers had underestimated the necessity of repetitions in class. If students really are going to gain fluency, maybe they need many more repetitions of the basics than we had previously thought.

A short time later, Meredith faxed me an essay from one of the first year students. It was written with almost no errors. It was amazing a level one student could write with that much accuracy.

At semester Meredith took some ten minute writing samples from her students. All writers were given the same task: to write a story with a character/s who has or had a problem and to resolve it. The stories were graded both on the number of words and on accuracy.

She used a scale developed by Joe Neilson based on the AP test. His scale had scores ranging from 1 – 6, with 1 indicating a lack of competence in written expression and 6 indicating very good competence in written expression (See page 29 [click here])

Table 1:		
WRITING SCORES	Homogeneous	Multi-level
first year	1.1	2.25
second year	2.4	4
third year	3.6	4.3
fourth year	3.7	4.8

Students in the multi-level classes had accuracy scores of: first year, 2.25, second year, 4, third year, 4.3 and fourth year, 4.8. These scores were compared to a control group of students also taught using TPRS but at the same level in homogeneous groups. In these groups first year students had an accuracy level of 1.1. The second year students had an accuracy level of 2.4; third year students were at 3.6, while fourth year students were at 3.7.

It is interesting to note that the multi-level students were more accurate at every level than their homogeneous counterparts. Also the level one multi-level students were almost as accurate as the homogeneous level two students.

The results were equally impressive in comparing the number of words the multi-level students produced relative to the homogeneous classes. The multi-level students produced an average of 62.75, 84.5,

90.87 and 132.6. At the same time the homogeneous classes were able to produce an average of 28.5, 56.8, 64.29, and 101.

Table 2:		
FREEWRITING NUMBER OF WORDS	Homogeneous	Multi-level
first year	28.5	62.75
second year	56.8	84.5
third year	64.29	90.87
fourth year	101	132.6

At the end of the year Meredith received feedback from students in the class. It is apparent they were pleased with the class since they all signed up for multi-level class two. Their main complaint about the class was that it was too easy. That is an interesting comment since it would be expected that only the top (level four) students would view the class as too easy. Meredith got feedback from most students that indicated the class was too easy. Students couldn't explain why it seemed they learned more yet did it with little effort.

One student wrote, Nathan (level 3) "I came from Hamilton MS where we worked out of text books a lot. I remember a lot more of what I learn in this class."

Natasha (level 1) "In the beginning of the class I had no Spanish and felt very discouraged and frustrated by my lack of vocabulary.

However, the repetition and variety of complicated language is very helpful to me now. I think I learned more Spanish than those in regular Spanish 1 classes and I feel my growth was very substantial."

Adrienne (level 2) "I could see how much I learned when I was reading. At the beginning of the year I picked really easy books and couldn't read them. Now I read much more difficult books. The Spanish movies helped my pronunciation."

Kalif (level 2) "I learned a lot of stuff this year! Last year I couldn't say one sentence!"

Ananda (level 3) "I think the pop up grammar helped me. I look at words differently now. I can see what they mean better."

Sydney (level 2) "I knew more than I thought I did. I realized it when I gave my book talk."

Ali (level 4) "I thought it was too easy until I realized how much we recycled words from 3 years ago and how many I actually know. I learned little details this year."

Meredith reported that 17 of the 26 in attendance the day feedback was collected reported (by show of hands) that they felt a change in their abilities in Spanish. They felt they had really learned something.

Nine students weren't sure what kind of progress they'd really made.

She said, "From my perspective, I'd say that enduring the initial struggle, emotional and academic, on the part of the "ones" is the toughest hurdle, closely followed by the "fours"' anxiety that the class wasn't challenging enough. It was a constant state of worry vs. trust, which isn't the most comfortable teacher posture. I learned a great deal from the process however and look forward to next years' fine tuning."

She went on to say, "I am fascinated by the "disconnection" between success and the perception of success I mentioned earlier. Is it valuable if it's 'easy'? Is it still success? I am going to work on some strategies to help students see their own growth and then trust it. They are firmly rooted in the traditional paradigm which tells them that their growth isn't real or perhaps adequate without looking like a grammar translation model complete with book, vocabulary lists to memorize and some agonizing grammar lessons."

This is just a start. There are still many more questions than answers, but it does appear that there is a place for multi-level teaching in the second language classroom. While no system works well with unmotivated learners, this system seems to give the fours the repetitions they need while at the same time give enough input to the beginners to get great strides in their language skills. Hopefully we can learn in the future if this is a valuable way to teach using TPRS.

This is not a blanket recommendation for multi-level teaching or for "immersion submersion." In a non-TPRS class or a non-comprehensible input-based class, it is possible that students might be left in a "sink or swim" type of environment. The level one students may be hopelessly confused the majority of the time. This class appears to have been so successful because the multiple levels made guaranteeing comprehensible input the highest priority.

WRITING RUBRIC FOR LEVELS 1 and 2

by Joe Neilson, Salpointe High School, Tucson, AZ

Though students write stories all year long, I "formally" assess writing only in the 4th quarter, using the following scale:

"ADAPTED" AP SPANISH COMPOSITION RUBRICS*
(FOR LEVELS 1 & 2)

6   DEMONSTRATES VERY GOOD COMPETENCE IN WRITTEN EXPRESSION
Very good to excellent control of elementary grammatical structures* and common verb tenses. Vocabulary appropriate to level.
Occasional second language interference. May have some errors in orthography and other conventions of the written language.

5   DEMONSTRATES GOOD COMPETENCE IN WRITTEN EXPRESSION
Good control of elementary structures and common verb tenses. Some errors may occur in more complex structures.
Vocabulary appropriate to level. Occasional second language interference. May have some errors in orthography and other conventions of the written language.

4   SUGGESTS A BASIC COMPETENCE IN WRITTEN EXPRESSION
Adequate control of elementary structures and common verb tenses. Frequent errors may occur in more complex structures.
Vocabulary appropriate but limited. Occasional second language interference. May have frequent errors in orthography and other conventions of the written language.

3-2 SUGGESTS LACK OF COMPETENCE IN WRITTEN EX-
PRESSION
Numerous grammatical errors even in elementary structures.
There may be an occasional redeeming feature, such as correct
advanced structure. Limited vocabulary; significant second language interference; pervasive errors of orthography may be present.

1 DEMONSTRATES LACK OF COMPETENCE IN WRITTEN
EXPRESSION
Constant grammatical errors impede communication; insufficient
vocabulary; frequent second language interference; severe problems with orthography may interfere with written communication.

*The "elementary grammatical structures" include (but are not limited to):

- verb/subject agreement

- adjective agreement

- infinitive uses ("quiere___", "tiene que___", "empieza a ___",
"va a ___", "le gusta ___", "puede___", etc.)

- reflexive vs. objective pronouns

- flow of verb tenses: present vs. preterite vs. imperfect (only for
Level 2 students)

The following scale is based on the grading scale (excellent=A,
good=B, fair=C, poor=D, incompetent=F).

LEVEL 1:		LEVEL 2:	
quarter #4		quarter #4	
6	A+	6	A+
5.5	A	5.5	A-
5	A-	5	B+
4.5	B+	4.5	B
4	B	4	B-
3.5	C	3.5	C-
3	C-	3	D
2	D	2	F
1		1	
F		F	

- These rubrics are based on the College Board AP Rubrics.

Raising Enrollment

RAISING ENROLLMENT
AT EAST HIGH SCHOOL IN DENVER

by Blaine Ray and Diana Noonan

Fall, 2003

East High School, of Denver, Colorado, gradually adopted TPRS as their method of teaching. This process started in 1996 after a Blaine Ray workshop. Diana Noonan, the department chair at East, stated, "In 1998 all members made some commitment to using exclusively TPRS with the lower levels. I believe that was the year the Denver Public Schools adopted *Look, I Can Talk!* into the curriculum." She continued by saying, "In '99-'00 all members committed to using TPRS as the principal method of instruction and we got rid of our traditional text-books." All second language teachers at the school were TPRS-trained.

They started with a pilot class in the spring of 1997. They took all of their students who had already failed Spanish 1 and put them in a second-semester TPRS class. This was a class of over 20 students. This class was so successful that it was the starting point of the school to adopt TPRS. A measure of that success was that almost all of those students continued on to level 3. Previously all would have dropped because they had received a failing grade in the course.

During these years, they witnessed an amazing growth in their upper level language classes. These classes included levels 3 and 4, AP, reading and composition, and culture. Before TPRS, East High had 123 students enrolled in Spanish 3. This year they have 275 students. In level 4 they started with 54 and now have 150. Spanish AP enrollments went up over 300%. They started with 21 and now have 86.

The overall school enrollment in advanced classes increased from 286 in '96-'97 to 623 in '03-'04.

Noonan stated that enrollment in advanced classes in '96-'97 among minority students was almost non-existent. She stated, "Unfortunately we do not have these stats from the '96-'97 years, but those of us who were teachers at East *know* that our advanced classes look 'different' now." Although they don't have exact numbers, teachers stated it was less than 10% of the enrollment in advanced classes. These classes were mainly made up of white females at that time. By this year, minority enrollment in upper level classes had soared. In fact, now these language classes have a 40% minority enrollment.

In Spanish AP the numbers are even more amazing. From the year 2001-2002 the number of Caucasian students increased from 58 to 66 by the year 2003-2004. The number of minority students had increased from 8 to 44. This was a 450% increase.

Evidence continues to mount that students sign up for TPRS classes in higher numbers than non-TPRS classes. TPRS has shown to be an effective way to keep students enrolled in a language program.

A disturbing finding of a 1994 ACTFL survey (Draper and Hicks, 1996) was a high attrition rate among students enrolled in foreign language courses between grades 9 and 12. The study indicated that only 8% of students starting out in level 1 made it to level 4. In Spanish classes, for instance, the attrition rate between the first and second year of study (grades 9 and 10) was about 29 percent; between the second and third year, about 63 percent; and between the third and fourth year, another 67 percent. In other words, of the 869,271 students who took first-year Spanish in ninth grade, only 74,684 (8.6 percent) were still taking that language four years later. Similar attrition rates, although not quite as dramatic, are evident for other languages.

The following is an
EXCERPT FROM THE MASTERS THESIS
*"Research for Developing an In-service for World Language
Curriculum Within the Tenets of Second Language Acquisition and
Total Physical Response Storytelling"*
by Mark A. Webster, April, 2003:

Attrition and Retention in the Upper Levels

Traditionally across the country, there is an attrition that occurs between Level I and Level III. The majority of students satisfy college foreign language requirements with two years of foreign language study in high school. Many students decide not to study additional levels due to the intensive grammar study and because it just isn't fun anymore. In my experience, in the past we would to lose 30-60 additional 60% after Level III. This would total between two to four sections of classes or more, depending on the year. Annually, we had two sections of 20 students in Level III and between 8-15 students in one section of Level IV Spanish. This is after we began five to six full sections of Level I and four to five full sections of Level II.

With the implementation of SLA and TPR-S, I find that schools tend to maintain and increase enrollment numbers in programs coast to coast. At Spring Lake High School, the typical attrition between Levels II, III, and IV has been greatly reduced. Our school has a student population that fluctuates between 680-700 students and we now have two full-time Spanish teachers and one full-time French teacher. In addition, we have a Spanish teacher at the middle school that teaches between two and three sections of Level I each year. We now enjoy full sections of 25-30 students from Level I to Level IV. Our program added Advanced Placement Spanish in 2001, due to increased enrollment. The student totals in the AP level have grown from 12 in 2001 to two sections of 25 in 2002-2003. Next year, in 2003-2004 we will have two sections of 25 in AP Spanish, as well as two sections of Level IV Spanish. The same phenomenon is occurring in French. We retain our students. Students tend to say that the reason that they stay is that they enjoy the course immensely and that they are able to communicate. (Appendix 2.91)

TPRS teacher Michael Kundrat of Central Lake High School in Central Lake, Michigan "boasts an astounding retention rate of 40-50% between Levels I though IV, compared to the national average which is just under 9%" (TPRS Publishing, 2003, para. 4).

Fairfield Junior-Senior High School in Goshen, Indiana is also seeing their student numbers increase after implementing TPR-S and SLA. Andrea Ganger has stated that her enrollment in the upper levels has increased 200% over the last two years. Her numbers "have increased from a total of 25 German students during year 1 of TPRS, to 48 this year (year 2 of TPRS), to 72 next year" (Ganger, Apr. 2002 e-mail).

Teaching Present and Past Tenses Simultaneously

THE ATHENIAN STUDY

by Von Ray

Edited by: Susan Gross

The 2004 Athenian Study examines the effectiveness of teaching both present and past tenses simultaneously. At the onset of the experiment, my hypothesis was that teaching the two tenses at the same time would yield better acquisition and production of the two tenses. This study compares two groups of students from the Athenian Middle School of Danville, California. The control group consists of 32 7th graders who all took Spanish as 6th graders at our school. As 6th graders, they were taught by my colleague Diane Grieman, who uses TPRS, Teaching Proficiency through Reading and Stories. Throughout the course of the year they received roughly 100 hours of comprehensible input in the present tense by acting out stories, answering questions about those stories, and reading (translating) a number of novels and stories in Spanish. During their 7th grade year, they received another 100 hours of comprehensible input from me. The students acted out stories in the past tense on even days and read (translated) stories in the present tense and had class discussions in Spanish on odd days.

The experimental group consists of 13 6th graders, all of which were true beginners at the start of the year. I taught the 6th graders exactly like the 7th graders, acting out stories in the past tense and reading (translating) stories and discussing the material in the present tense. Therefore the only differences between the two groups were the total number of hours of instruction by year's end (200 hours to 100 hours) and the fact that the first 100 hours for the 7th graders were all in the present tense.

Throughout the year, both groups appeared to be acquiring both tenses well. However, I observed an interesting pattern among the 7th graders. From time to time, I would have the students give a 2-3 minute retell of the story at the end of a given class period. During these retells, I noticed that 7th graders would strongly favor the present tense in speech, even though they had heard and understood those same verbs in the past tense throughout the year. For example, when students were trying to say, "he said to her", they would often say (in Spanish), "he says to her". I saw this pattern among almost all of my 7th graders.

One on occasion, a boy was retelling a story and he said "le dice" (he says to her) 5 or 6 times in a row. I reminded him, "That means "he SAYS to her", how do you say "he SAID to her?" After a moment, the student said, "Oh yes! I meant to say le dijo." As he continued to retell the story, he said "le dice" many more times when he should have said "le dijo". I attribute this to their 100 hours of present tense input from the previous year. Because they heard "le dice" thousands of times as 6th graders, that's what they acquired. That's what had stuck. They had not only acquired "le dice", it had become ingrained. Even though they understood "le dijo", they reverted to "le dice" during retells because they hadn't acquired "le dijo" like they had "le dice."

My 6th graders, in contrast, were much more accurate in their production of past tense stories. They were able to say "le dijo" for "he said to her". The reason, I believe, is because they had not heard "le dice" exclusively. They learned simultaneously that "le dice" means "he SAYS to her" and that "le dijo" means "he SAID to her". On days that we acted stories in the past tense, the 6th graders were hearing "le dijo" and understanding "he said to her" and on days that we read stories they read "le dice" and understood "he says to her". As a result, they seemed to have a better feeling for the two tenses because they were acquiring them at the same time. They were much more likely to say "le dijo" for "he said to her" than the 7th graders.

At the end of the academic year, I gave both groups a short paragraph to verbally translate into English. They had never seen the paragraph before, but they had learned all of the words throughout the year. I made a video recording of each student translating the paragraph. I gave each student roughly 30-45 seconds to first read the passage to him/herself before recording. I did not answer any of their questions if they asked. The objective was to assess which group was more accurate in production. Here's the passage I gave them:

There is a sad boy. He is sad because he had an elephant but now he doesn't have it. The boy was walking in the park when a girl saw the boy and his elephant. She said to him, "I want to play soccer with the elephant." The girl grabbed the elephant. Now the girl is playing soccer with the elephant. How sad!

The paragraph contains five verbs or combination of verbs in the present: *there is, is sad, doesn't have, I want to play, and is playing.* It also contains five verbs in the past: *had, was walking, saw, said to him, grabbed.* In grading the students, I only graded them on whether they got the sense of present versus past correct. Because I was not grading for any other grammatical accuracy other than correct tense, I gave students credit for saying "es juega", "es triste", "quiero juega", etc. They didn't have to produce it 100% correctly in order to get a point for accuracy. If they needed to use the present and they used the present, then I gave them a point. If they needed to use the past and they used the past but missed something else, then I gave it to them. I also did not mark them wrong if they did not distinguish between the preterite and imperfect tenses. Some of my students said "caminó" instead of "caminaba" or "andaba." A few said "veía" instead of "vio". I counted it right because my interest was in discovering their awareness of present versus past. This study was not about whether they could distinguish between the preterite and imperfect tenses; it was about whether they could distinguish between the past and the present. With that in mind, here are the results of the video assessment:

Numbers are listed for both the whole group and the top half. The percentages are given for overall accuracy (their accuracy out of the 10 verbs), present tense accuracy (their accuracy for just the 5 present tense verbs), and past tense accuracy (their accuracy for just the 5 past tense verbs).

7th Grade (32 students) (After 200 hours)	6th Grade (13 students) (After 100 hours)
Oral Accuracy	
Overall ALL = 58% Overall TOP HALF = 71%	Overall ALL = 67% Overall TOP HALF = 74%
Present Tense Accuracy	
Present tense ALL = 89% Present tense TOP HALF = 100%	Present tense ALL = 84% Present tense TOP HALF = 89%
Past Tense Accuracy	
Past tense ALL = 27% Past tense TOP HALF = 48%	Past tense ALL = 49% Past tense TOP HALF = 68%

The following week, I had the students translate the story in writing. Here are the results of their writings:

7th Grade (32 students)	6th Grade (13 students)
Written Accuracy	
Overall ALL = 65% Overall TOP HALF = 80%	Overall ALL = 79% Overall TOP HALF = 88%

Present Tense Accuracy	
Present tense ALL = 92% Present tense TOP HALF = 100%	Present tense ALL = 83% Present tense TOP HALF = 99%

Past Tense Accuracy	
Past Tense ALL = 39%	Past Tense ALL = 72%
Past Tense TOP HALF = 63%	Past Tense TOP HALF = 86%

I have a few conclusions from this data. My first conclusion is that the present tense is more easily acquired than the past tense. Maybe it's the more complex verb endings of the past tense, maybe the idea of "past tense" is more abstract for 6th and 7th graders. The 6th graders received more repetitions of the past tense verbs throughout the year because there is more input on days that we act stories than on days that we read stories. However, they were significantly more accurate in the present than the past in both writing and speech.

The most important conclusion is that the tenses are optimally acquired when they are taught simultaneously. The current model suggests that we start with the present tense, teach it for a year, and then move on to past tense and other tenses. Based on this data, I believe that the past and present (as well as other tenses) should be taught simultaneously starting with Level 1. Interestingly, this approach mirrors first language acquisition. We all acquired our first language by hearing the tenses mixed. What would happen if we spoke to babies only in the present tense for the first 3 years of their lives, the next 2 in the past tense, and the next 2 review the present and past and then add other tenses? I believe that we would not acquire the tenses nearly as well than when they're naturally mixed. This study suggests that second language acquisition should mirror first language acquisition.

Lastly, by observing both groups produce language throughout the year and in this assessment, I believe that the 100 hours of present tense comprehensible input that the 7th graders received as 6th graders resulted in a less than optimal acquisition rate of the two tenses. By teaching the two tenses simultaneously, I believe that the 6th graders acquired the two tenses at a more efficient rate than the 7th graders.

Appendix K

TPR Storytelling Materials
and
Other Helpful Resources for the TPRS Classroom

This list is based on one prepared by Amy Catania in December, 2007, and a list in the book *TPRS in a Year* by Ben Slavic.

www.benslavic.com:

TPRS in a Year! by Ben Slavic

Excellent TPRS™ how-to manual, describing 49 TPRS skills. Includes in-depth sample stories describing how to construct stories using TPRS.

PQA in a Wink! by Ben Slavic

Addresses personalization and personalized questions and answers, providing specific suggestions about PQA and classroom discipline that are easy to blend into any curriculum.

TPRS in the Realm! by Ben Slavic

How to build episodes into a megastory that lasts all year and how to build a virtual community with TPRS.

Bucky va à Paris / Bucky va a México by Ben Slavic – level: 1, 2 (French, Spanish)

14 humorous episodes teach (via TPRS circling) conversational French or Spanish and travel terms as Bucky the monkey travels abroad. A 128-page book with six CDs. For individual language learners.

www.bethskelton.com:

Putting It Together / Todo junto by Elizabeth Skelton and Denise Milligan – level: 1-2 adult, HS, MS (English, Spanish)

Teacher's guide with lesson plans and personalized mini-stories, illustrated student books for English and Spanish.

Putting It Together Teacher-training DVD by Elizabeth Skelton

42-minute DVD showing four classrooms in action — elementary, secondary and adult — with English language learners in content areas.

www.blaineraytprs.com:

Look I Can Talk! Series by Blaine Ray et al. – level: 1, 2, 3 (English, French, German, Spanish)

A comprehensive high school curriculum. Includes teacher guide, student text, mini-stories, accelerated mini-stories, extended readings, vocabulary lists, tests, overheads, accompanying novels (see Chapter 10, "Reading" for titles).

Japanese in Action by May and Kimura – level: 1 (Japanese)

A student book and teacher manual containing mini-stories and other related TPR and TPRS activities, including picture cards for teaching vocabulary.

www.goodteachingstuff.com:

Cuentos Fantásticos by Amy Catania – level: 1, 2 / Elem, HS (English, Spanish, French)

Two easy-to-use volumes each with 40 illustrated short and long stories with supporting personalized mini-stories. Units are based on a humorous character or setting and a vocabulary theme.

www.sabineundmichael.com:

Sabine und Michael by Michael Miller – level: 1, 2 (German)

TPRS curriculum in German. Items available for both levels: a teacher's book, blackline masters, student workbook, a CD of songs, instructional DVD, and a reader.

www.teachersdiscovery.com:

Contes historiques by Michele Threlkeld – level: 3 (French)
A collection of 15 illustrated stories for teaching French history. Also available is a resource book for "La Marseillaise," with history, culture, vocabulary and activities.

www.TPRSofNJ.com:

Mis libritos by Piedad Gutiérrez – level: 1, 2 (Spanish)
Simple and funny mini-stories for beginner readers practicing one word or a few structures, rich in cultural elements.

Mis Cartillas by Piedad Gutiérrez – level: K-6 (Spanish)
Thematic units for beginner and intermediate levels following the TPRS steps: vocabulary and structures, mini-stories, and complementary readings.

www.tprstorytelling.com:

Hi Kids! by Carol Gaab – level: K-3rd grade (French, Spanish, English)
An introductory TPRS curriculum with ancillary materials based on high-frequency structures: greetings, numbers, family, colors, descriptions, feelings, etc.

Tell Me by Valeri Marsh and Christine Anderson – level: 4th-6th grade (French, Spanish)
Introductory level.

Tell Me More Classic by Valeri Marsh and Christine Anderson – level: MS (French, Spanish, English)
Introductory level with ancillary materials: teacher's manual, test materials, overheads, daily readings, Spanish songs by Gale Mackey. *Tell Me More! Japanese Adaptation* also available.

NEW Tell Me More Spanish by Carol Gaab and Kristy Placido, French by Carol Gaab, Kristy Placido and Loïc André – level: HS, adults

Level 1 curriculum. Includes comprehensive teacher's manual, games and activities, daily readings, interactive language CD and PowerPoint stories on CD.

Tell Me Even More by Carol Gaab and Kristy Placido – level: HS, adults (French, Spanish)

Level 2 curriculum with ancillary materials: comprehensive teacher's manual and daily readings, tests and PowerPoint stories.

¡Cuánto me cuentas! by Carol Gaab and Teri Abelaira – level: HS, adults

Level 3 Spanish curriculum with ancillary materials: comprehensive teacher's manual, daily readings, tests and PowerPoint stories. French version forthcoming.

Several novellas have been published by TPRS Publishing. See their website.

www.tpr-world.com:

TPR Storytelling by Todd McKay – level: 1-3 elem, MS (English, French, Spanish)

A 3-year curriculum. Illustrated stories revolve around one family. Includes cultural topics, games, student books and teacher manual, testing packet, video demo, TPR cards.

www.waltmania.com:

Complete Lesson Plans for TPRS by Jalen Waltman – levels: 1A, 1B (English, Spanish)

A guide to setting up a TPRS classroom with step-by-step lesson plans and supplemental materials. Each book contains 30 lessons for one semester.

superchickcomics@hotmail.com:

Three different *Superpollo Comics* by Rita Barrett with TPRS support material – level: 1 elem, MS (Spanish)

Other Helpful Resources for the TPRS Classroom

www.blaineraytprs.com (Blaine Ray and Von Ray, Utah)

Blaine Ray Workshops. Lots of information about TPRS — practical and theoretical. Many TPRS materials for teachers and students and for teacher training. Many links. Workshops by several top-notch TPRS presenters.

www.comprehensibleinput.com (Jason Fritze, California)

Find out more about comprehensible input and TPRS. Access many comprehensible input links, resources and useful files. Find out about Jason's workshops.

www.cpli.net (Contee Seely, California)

TPR in context — books (*Live Action* series of commands in six languages, *Recurrent Action Grammar* and *TPR Is More Than Commands—At All Levels*) and interactive software in Spanish and English. TPR materials by Berty Segal Cook. Co-publisher of TPRS novellas and *Fluency Through TPR Storytelling* with Blaine Ray Workshops. Co-publisher with Fluency Fast of novellas by Karen Rowan. Publisher of other innovative effective materials such as *Cuéntame: 286 Spanish Conversation Cards*, *QuestionWord Posters*, *ConverseMore Posters*, etc. Books by leading second language acquisition theorist Stephen Krashen, including *Foreign Language the Easy Way*.

www.educatorinservice.com (Janice Holter Kittok, Minnesota)

Download free teaching tips. Sign up for a TPRS workshop and experience TPRS firsthand as a learner of Swedish.

www.fluencyfast.com

Fluency Fast Language Classes, adult language classes taught nationwide using a comprehension-based approach. DVDs of previous classes available in Spanish and French.

www.ijflt.com

The International Journal of Foreign Language Teaching: a free quarterly online journal containing current research, articles and helpful resources for foreign language teachers.

www.ritornello.com (Judi Mazziotti, New York)

Foreign Language Magic 101: a DVD showing how to use magic tricks to provide comprehensible input in your second language classroom. Props also available.

www.kristyplacido.com (Kristy Placido, Michigan)

The co-author of some of the materials in the *Tell Me* Series provides many links to Spanish language TPRS materials and other Spanish language websites, including a link to the music resource *Sing, Dance, Laugh, and Eat Quiche/Tacos* by Barbara MacArthur.

www.sdkrashen.com (Dr. Stephen Krashen, California)

Access Dr. Krashen's books and articles on language acquisition. Learn about comprehensible input, free voluntary reading and more.

www.storyask.com

A wiki where you can freely define the verb *to storyask*. By learning to ask good questions and to listen well to the answers, we can make more meaningful stories that really connect with language learners.

www.susangrosstprs.com (Susan Gross, Colorado)

Find out more about TPRS and language acquisition, get free materials and sign up for Susie's acclaimed TPRS workshops.

www.teachforjune.com (Scott Benedict, Nevada)

"Teach for June" isn't a slogan to get through the school year, but a new attitude towards foreign language teaching. This site is full of useful resources and articles about TPRS.

www.tprstories.com (Karen Rowan, Colorado)

Find out more about TPRS from Karen Rowan, the author of the TPRS supplements to the *Paso a Paso* and *Realidades* textbooks, coordinator of the National TPRS Conference and workshop presenter.

www.tpr-world.com (Sky Oaks Productions, Dr. James Asher, California)

Learn more about Total Physical Response from the psychology professor who researched this approach and made it world-famous. Order TPR books and TPR teaching materials such as Dr. Asher's *Learning Another Language Through Actions* and Ramiro Garcia's *Instructor's Notebook: How to Apply TPR for Best Results*.

http://groups.yahoo.com/group/moretprs/join

Join the Yahoo listserv group MoreTPRS, an invaluable place to share with experienced TPRS teachers.

Bibliography

Please note: this bibliography has been updated.

REFERENCES

Asher, James J. 1977. *Learning Another Language Through Actions: The Complete Teacher's Guidebook.* 1st ed. Los Gatos, CA: Sky Oaks.

Asher, James J. 1988. *Brainswitching.* Los Gatos, CA: Sky Oaks.

Asher, James J. 1994. *The Super School.* Los Gatos, CA: Sky Oaks.

Asher, James J. 1996. *Learning Another Language Through Actions: The Complete Teacher's Guidebook.* 5th ed. Los Gatos, CA: Sky Oaks.

Babbitt, Natalie. 1985. *Tuck Everlasting.* New York: Farrar, Straus and Giroux.

Babbitt, Natalie. 1993. *Tuck para siempre: Tuck Everlasting.* Trans. by Narcís Fradera. New York: Farrar, Straus and Giroux.

bar-Lev, Zev. 1993. Sheltered initiation language learning. *Applied Language Learning*, 4, 1 and 2: 95-130.

Bell, Nanci. 1991. *Visualizing and Verbalizing For Language Comprehension and Thinking*, revised ed. Paso Robles, CA: Academy of Reading Publications.

Breen, Maureen and David White. 1996. The philosophy of French Funetics: An essay in applied gifted intelligence. *Roeper Review*, 19, 1: 44-50.

Breen, Maureen and David White. 1998. *French Through Funetics: Language Learning Through Logos.* Berkeley, CA: Command Performance.

Bridwell, Norman. 1963. *Clifford, the Big Red Dog.* New York: Scholastic.

Bridwell, Norman. 1987. French translation by Lucie Duchesne. *L'anniversaire de Bertrand.* Ontario: Scholastic.

Bridwell, Norman. 1989. *La familia de Clifford.* Spanish translation by Argentina Palacios. New York: Scholastic.

Brown, J. Marvin and Adrian S. Palmer. 1988. *The Listening Approach: Methods and Materials for Applying Krashen's Input Hypothesis.* White Plains, NY: Longman.

Burling, Robbins 1982. *Sounding Right.* Rowley, Mass.: Newbury House.

Butterworth, Rod and Mickey Flodin. 1991. *The Perigree Visual Dictionary of Signing.* New York: Putnam. Over 1,250 signs of American Sign Language.

Carnegie, Dale. 1981. *How to Win Friends and Influence People.* Rev. ed. New York: Simon and Schuster.

Crystal, David. 1994. *An Encyclopedic Dictionary of Language and Languages.* London: Penguin.

Chomsky, Noam. 1965. *Aspects of the Theory of Syntax.* Cambridge, MA: MIT Press.

Danziger, Paula. 1975. *The Cat Ate My Gymsuit.* New York: Dell.

Davies, Mark. 2006. *A Frequency Dictionary of Spanish.* New York and London: Routledge.

Draper, Jamie B. and June H. Hicks. 1996. Foreign Language Enrollments in Public Secondary Schools, Fall 1994. *Foreign Language Annals*, 29 (3), 303-06.

Draper, Jamie B. and June H. Hicks. 2002. "Foreign Language Enrollments in Public Secondary Schools, Fall, 2000." American Council on the Teaching of Foreign Languages (www.actfl.org).

Ellis, Nick C. (ed.). 1994. *Implicit and Explicit Learning of Languages*. London: Academic Press.

Felix and Theo. 1991a. *Das Gold der alten Dame*. Berlin and Munich: Langenscheidt.

Felix and Theo. 1991b. *Ein Mann zu viel*. Berlin and Munich: Langenscheidt.

Felix and Theo. 1991c. *Oh, Maria*. Berlin and Munich: Langenscheidt.

Felix and Theo. 1998. *Einer singt falsch*. Berlin and Munich: Langenscheidt.

Felix and Theo. 1999. *Elvis in Köln*. Berlin and Munich: Langenscheidt.

Felix and Theo. 2002. *Oktoberfest*. Berlin and Munich: Langenscheidt.

Forward, Melinda and Shirley Ogle. 1997a. *Beginning TPR Storytelling*. Available from the authors; see Appendix B.

Forward, Melinda and Shirley Ogle. 1997b. *Organizing and Managing a TPR Storytelling Classroom*. Available from the authors; see Appendix B.

Forward, Melinda and Shirley Ogle. 1997-2001. *Passing on the Power*. First-year secondary-level materials. Five 6-week chapters — Hello!, At the Supermarket, At the Cafe, Seasons and Activities, Family and Animals — with supplementary materials. Versions in French, Spanish and English. Available from the authors; see Appendix B.

Gaab, Carol. 1999. *¡Hola Niños!* Chandler, AZ: TPRS Publishing.

Gaab, Carol. 2000. *Salut les enfants!* French adaptation by Joe Hodgson. Chandler, AZ: TPRS Publishing.

Gaab, Carol. 2002. *Hi Kids!* Chandler, AZ: TPRS Publishing.

Gaab, Carol and Kristy Placido. 2003. *Tell Me Even More!* (in Spanish and French; French adaptation by Joe Hodgson.) Chandler, AZ: TPRS Publishing.

García, Ramiro. 1988. *Instructor's Notebook: How to Apply TPR for Best Results*. 2nd ed. Los Gatos, CA: Sky Oaks.

Heyne, Isolde. 1994 and 1996. *Yildiz heißt Stern*. Würzburg: Arena; Berlin and Munich: Langenscheidt.

Hurwitz, Johanna. 1987. *Class Clown*. New York: Scholastic.

Hurwitz, Johanna. 1994. *El payaso de la clase*. Trans. New York: Scholastic.

Hurwitz, Johanna. 1990. *Class President*. New York: Scholastic.

Hurwitz, Johanna. 1993. *El presidente de la clase*. Trans. New York: Scholastic.

Johnstone, Keith. 1981. *Impro: Improvisation and the Theatre*. New York: Routledge.

Kanter, Abby. 1994. *Gran aventura de Alejandro*. Trans. of *The Adventures of Alejandro*. New York: Amsco.

Krashen, Stephen D. 1977. Some issues relating to the Monitor Model. In Brown, H. et al (eds.)

Krashen, Stephen D. 1983. The din in the head, input, and the language acquisition device. In Oller, John W., Jr., and Patricia A. Richard-Amato (eds.). *Methods That Work*. 1st ed. Rowley, MA: Newbury House.

Krashen, Stephen D. 1989. We acquire vocabulary and spelling by reading: Additional evidence for the input hypothesis. *Modern Language Journal*, 73: 440-464.

Krashen, Stephen D. 1991. Sheltered subject matter teaching. *Cross Currents*, 18: 183-186.

Krashen, Stephen D. 1992. Under what circumstances, if any, should formal grammar instruction take place? *TESOL Quarterly*, 26, 409-411.

Krashen, Stephen D. 1993a. *The Power of Reading.* Englewood, Colorado: Libraries Unlimited.

Krashen, Stephen D. 1993b. The effect of formal grammar teaching: Still peripheral. *TESOL Quarterly*, 27, 722-725.

Krashen, Stephen D. 1994. The input hypothesis and its rivals. In N. C. Ellis (ed.), 45-77.

Krashen, Stephen D. 1997. *Foreign Language Education The Easy Way.* Culver City, CA: Language Education Associates.

Krashen, Stephen D. 1998. TPR: Still a very good idea. *novELTy* (A Journal of English Language Teaching and Cultural Studies in Hungary) 5(4): 82-85. Also at http://www.languageimpact.com/articles/other/krashentpr.htm.

Krashen, Stephen D. and Tracy D. Terrell. 1983. *The Natural Approach: Language Acquisition in the Classroom.* Hayward, CA: Alemany Press. Currently available from Tappan, NJ: Prentice Hall Regents.

MacGowan-Gilhooly, Adele. 1993a. *Achieving Fluency in English.* 2nd ed. Dubuque, IA: Kendall/Hunt.

MacGowan-Gilhooly, Adele. 1993b. *Fluency First in ESL.* Audio tape of "TeleTE-SOL" session on June 22, 1993, and handout. Alexandria, VA: Teachers of English to Speakers of Other Languages.

MacGowan-Gilhooly, Adele. 1995. *Achieving Clarity in English.* 2nd ed. Dubuque, Iowa: Kendall/Hunt.

Mackey, Gale. 1996. *¡Mírame, puedo cantar más!* Audio CD. Also lyrics and exercise book (with Contee Seely, 1997). Berkeley, CA: Command Performance.

Mackey, Gale. 1997a. *¡Mírame, puedo cantar!—Nivel 1.* Berkeley, CA: Command Performance.

Mackey, Gale. 1997b. *Spanish Grammar Songs.* Bakersfield, CA: Blaine Ray Workshops.

Mackey, Gale. 2000. *¡Mírame, puedo cantar!—Nivel 1* y *¡Mírame, puedo cantar más!* Audio CD. Berkeley, CA: Command Performance.

Maroscher, Gerhard. 2007. *Short Stories: German 2.1 Reader.* www.germanreaders.com

Marsh, Valeri. 1997. Total Physical Response Storytelling: A Communicative Approach to Language Learning. *Foreign Language Notes, Foreign Language Educators of New Jersey*, Xxix, 2, 4-7.

Marsh, Valeri and Christine Anderson. 1995a. *¡Cuéntame!: TPR Storytelling.* Introductory Spanish course for elementary school students, especially for grades 3 to 5. 2nd ed. Chandler, AZ: TPRS Publishing.

Marsh, Valeri and Christine Anderson. 1995b. *¡Cuéntame más!: TPR Storytelling.* Beginning Spanish course for grades 7 and up. 3rd ed. Chandler, AZ: TPRS Publishing.

Marsh, Valeri and Christine Anderson. 1995c. *¡Cuéntame más!: TPR Storytelling.* Teacher's manual. 2nd ed. Chandler, AZ: TPRS Publishing.

Marsh, Valeri and Christine Anderson. 1995d. *Raconte-moi!: TPR Storytelling.* Beginning French course for elementary school students, especially for grades 3 to 5. 2nd ed. Chandler, AZ: TPRS Publishing.

Marsh, Valeri and Christine Anderson. 1995e. *Raconte-moi encore!: TPR Storytelling.* Teacher's manual. Chandler, AZ: TPRS Publishing.

Marsh, Valeri and Christine Anderson. 1996a. *¡Cuéntame!: TPR Storytelling.* Teacher's manual. Chandler, AZ: TPRS Publishing.

Marsh, Valeri and Christine Anderson. 1996b. *Raconte-moi encore!: TPR Storytelling.* Beginning French course, especially for grades 6 to 8. Student manual. 2nd ed. Chandler, AZ: TPRS Publishing.

Marsh, Valeri and Christine Anderson. 1997. *Raconte-moi!: TPR Storytelling.* Teacher's manual. Chandler, AZ: TPRS Publishing.

Marsh, Valeri and Christine Anderson. 1998. *Tell Me More.* Introductory ESL course for middle and elementary school students, especially grades 6 to 8. Chandler, AZ: TPRS Publishing.

Marsh, Valeri and Christine Anderson. 1999. *Tell Me More! Japanese Adaptation.* Beginning course, especially for grades 7 and up. Chandler, AZ: TPRS Publishing. (adaptation by Sandra García)

Marsh, Valeri and Christine Anderson. Forthcoming. *Tell Me a Story.* Chandler, AZ: TPRS Publishing.

May, Laurie and Kaoru Kimura. 1998. *Japanese in Action.* Student book, teacher's manual and picture card textbook (8 1/2" x 11" illustrations). Baltimore, Maryland: Mayworks.

McKay, Todd. 2000. *TPR Storytelling, Especially for Children in Elementary and Middle School.* Student books, transparencies, testing packets (years 1, 2 and 3; available in Spanish, French and English) and teacher's guidebook (with James J. Asher). Los Gatos, CA: Sky Oaks.

Miller, Michael. 1999. *Sabine und Michael.* Level 1 Teacher's Book, Blackline Masters, Student Workbook, song CD. Materials for German in 5th to 10th grades. Colorado Springs, CO: Sabina und Michael.

Miller, Michael. 2000. *Sabine und Michael.* Level 2 Teacher's Book, Blackline Masters, Student Workbook, song CD. Materials for German in 6th to 10th grades. Colorado Springs, CO: Sabina und Michael.

Miller, Michael. 2002a. *Hilde und Günter.* Level 1 German reader for 5th to 10th grades. Colorado Springs, CO: Sabina und Michael.

Miller, Michael. 2002b. *TPRS Training Video.* Narration in English, classroom footage in German. Colorado Springs, CO: Sabina und Michael.

Morris, Desmond. 1994. *Bodytalk: The Meaning of Human Gestures.* New York: Crown Trade Paperbacks.

Moscoso, Verónica. 2005. *Los ojos de Carmen.* Bakersfield, CA: Blaine Ray Workshops and Berkeley, CA: Command Performance.

Moscoso, Verónica. 2006. *Les Yeux de Carmen.* Bakersfield, CA: Blaine Ray Workshops and Berkeley, CA: Command Performance.

Moscoso, Verónica. 2007. *The Eyes of Carmen.* Pismo Beach, CA: Blaine Ray Workshops and Berkeley, CA: Command Performance.

Myers, Walter Dean. 1993. *Somewhere in the Darkness.* New York: Scholastic.

Myers, Walter Dean. 1994. *Un lugar en las sombras: Somewhere in the Darkness.* Trans. New York: Scholastic.

Neilson, Joe and Blaine Ray. 1996. *Mini-stories for **Look, I Can Talk!*** Bakersfield, CA: Blaine Ray Workshops. (available in English, Spanish, French (version by Brigitte Ballard, 1997) and German (version by Kimberly Watts, 1999))

Neilson, Joe and Blaine Ray. 2005a. *¡Mírame, puedo hablar muchísimo!* Bakersfield, CA: Blaine Ray Workshops.

Neilson, Joe and Blaine Ray. 2005b. *Look, I'm Really Talking !: French.* Bakersfield, CA: Blaine Ray Workshops.

Nikolov, Marianne and Krashen, Stephen D. 1997. Need we sacrifice accuracy for fluency? System 25: 197-201.

Nöstlinger, Christine. *Die Ilse ist weg.* 1993. Berlin and Munich: Langenscheidt.

Oller, John W., Jr. and Patricia A. Richard-Amato, eds. *Methods That Work.* 1983. Rowley, Massachusetts: Newbury House.

Pressler, Mirjam. *Bitterschokolade.* 1986. Stuttgart: Beltz; Berlin and Munich: Langenscheidt.

Ray, Blaine. 1990. *Look, I Can Talk!* Los Gatos, CA: Sky Oaks. (available in English, Spanish, French, German)

Ray, Blaine. 1992. *Look, I Can Talk! Teacher's Guidebook.* 2nd ed. (for Spanish, French, German and English) Los Gatos, CA: Sky Oaks.

Ray, Blaine. 1993. *Teaching Grammar Communicatively.* New York and Roanoke, VA: Gessler Publishing. (out of print)

Ray, Blaine. 1996a. *Mini-stories for **Look, I Can Talk More!*** Bakersfield, CA: Blaine Ray Workshops. (available in English, Spanish (1998), French (version by Brigitte Ballard, 2000) and German (version by Lee Chambers, 2000))

Ray, Blaine. 1996b. *Mini-stories for **Look, I Can Really Talk!*** Bakersfield, CA: Blaine Ray Workshops. (available in English, Spanish (1997) and French (version by Brigitte Ballard, 1997))

Ray, Blaine. 1999. *Pobre Ana.* Bakersfield, CA: Blaine Ray Workshops and Berkeley, CA: Command Performance. (also available: audio CD read by native speakers (2002), movie on video (2002) and CD of songs from the movie (2002))

Ray, Blaine. 2000a. *Pauvre Anne.* Bakersfield, CA: Blaine Ray Workshops and Berkeley, CA: Command Performance. (adapted to French by Janet Gee)

Ray, Blaine. 2001a. *Arme Anna.* Bakersfield, CA: Blaine Ray Workshops and Berkeley, CA: Command Performance. (adapted to German by Helen Small)

Ray, Blaine. 2001b. *Patricia va a California.* Bakersfield, CA: Blaine Ray Workshops and Berkeley, CA: Command Performance. (also available: audio CD read by native speakers (2002) and movie on video (2002))

Ray, Blaine. 2002a. *Extended Readings for **Look, I Can Talk!*** Bakersfield, CA: Blaine Ray Workshops.

Ray, Blaine. 2002b. *Fama va en Californie.* Bakersfield, CA: Blaine Ray Workshops and Berkeley, CA: Command Performance. (adapted to French by Victoria Reynolds and Gloria Simpson)

Ray, Blaine. 2003b. *Petra reist nach Kalifornien.* Bakersfield, CA: Blaine Ray Workshops and Berkeley, CA: Command Performance. (adapted to German by Andrea Kistler)

Ray, Blaine. 2004. *Mini-stories for **Look, I Can Talk!**: with an Extended Reading for Each Mini-story.* 2nd ed. Bakersfield, CA: Blaine Ray Workshops. (available in Spanish, French (2004, 1st ed.), German (2005, 1st ed.) and English (with Joe Neilson, 2005, 1st ed.))

Ray, Blaine. 2007. *Introduction to TPR Storytelling.* Video. Arroyo Grande, CA: Blaine Ray Workshops.

Ray, Blaine and Susan Gross. 1999. *TPRS Gestures and Mini-stories*. 2nd ed. Bakersfield, CA: Blaine Ray Workshops. OUT-OF-PRINT

Ray, Blaine and Joe Neilson. 1994a. *Look, I Can Really Talk!* 2nd ed. Bakersfield, CA: Blaine Ray Workshops and Berkeley, CA: Command Performance. (formerly available in English, Spanish, French and German)

Ray, Blaine and Joe Neilson. 1994b. *Look, I'm Still Talking!: English.* Bakersfield, CA: Blaine Ray Workshops.

Ray, Blaine and Joe Neilson. 1994c. *Look, I'm Still Talking!: German.* Bakersfield, CA: Blaine Ray Workshops.

Ray, Blaine and Joe Neilson. 1998, 1999. *TPRS Mini-Cuentos Video.* Parts 1-4. Bakersfield, CA: Blaine Ray Workshops.

Ray, Blaine and Joe Neilson. 2005 (Spanish and French), 2006 (English). *Mini-stories and Extended Readings for* **Look, I'm Really Talking!** (Spanish title: *Mini-stories and Extended Readings for* **¡Mírame, puedo hablar muchísimo!**) Bakersfield, CA: Blaine Ray Workshops.

Ray, Blaine, Joe Neilson, Dave Cline and Carole Stevens. 1992. *Look, I Can Talk More!* Los Gatos, CA: Sky Oaks. (available in English, Spanish and French)

Ray, Blaine, Joe Neilson, Dave Cline and Carole Stevens. 1997. *Look, I Can Talk More!* German version. Bakersfield, CA: Blaine Ray Workshops.

Ray, Blaine, Von Ray and Michael Thompson. 2002. *Accelerated Mini-Stories for* **Look, I Can Talk!** Spanish, English and French versions. Bakersfield, CA: Blaine Ray Workshops. (adapted to French by Monique Gregory) OUT-OF-PRINT

Ray, Blaine and Karen Rowan. 2000. *TPRS Gestures and Personalized Mini-stories for* **Look, I Can Talk More!** Bakersfield, CA: Blaine Ray Workshops.

Ray, Blaine, Michael Thompson and Carmen Andrews-Sánchez. 2003 (Spanish), 2004 (French and German), 2005 (English). *Mini-stories and Extended Readings for* **Look, I Can Talk More!** Bakersfield, CA: Blaine Ray Workshops.

Romijn, Elizabeth Kuizenga. 2008. *Recurrent Action Grammar.* Berkeley, CA: Command Performance.

Rorschach, Elizabeth. 1991. Methods to use in whole language classrooms. In *Fluency First in ESL*, MacGowan-Gilhooly, 1993b, handout, 9-10.

Rowan, Karen. 2000. *TPR Stories for Paso a paso 1.* Upper Saddle River, NJ: Prentice Hall.

Rowan, Karen. 2002. *TPR Stories for Paso a paso 2.* Upper Saddle River, NJ: Prentice Hall.

Rowan, Karen. 2004. *TPR Stories for Realidades 1.* Upper Saddle River, NJ: Prentice Hall.

Rowan, Karen. 2008. *TPR Stories for Realidades 2.* Upper Saddle River, NJ: Prentice Hall.

Seely, Contee and Elizabeth Romijn. 1998. *TPR Is More Than Commands—At All Levels.* 2nd ed. Berkeley, CA: Command Performance.

Segal, Bertha. 1992. *Teaching English Through Action.* 5th ed. Brea, CA: Berty Segal, Inc. (also available in Spanish, French, German, Japanese, Russian, Secwepemc, Iñupiak and St´at'imcets versions)

Selden, George. 1960. *The Cricket in Times Square.* Illustrated by Garth Williams. New York: Farrar, Straus and Giroux.

Selden, George. 1992. *Un grillo en Times Square* (Translation of *The Cricket in Times Square*). Translated by Robin Longshaw. Illustrated by Garth Williams. Madrid: Rialp. (distributed in the U.S. by New York: Farrar, Straus and Giroux)

Spada, N. 1986. The interaction between type of contact and type of instruction: Some effects of the L2 proficiency of adult learners. Studies in Second Language Acquisition, 8, 181-199.

Spada, N. 1987. Relationships between instructional differences and learning outcomes: A process-product study of communicative language teaching. *Applied Linguistics*, 8, 137-155.

Steig, William. 1984. *Dominic*. New York: Farrar, Straus and Giroux.

Steig, William. 1994. *Dominico*. Trans. New York: Farrar, Straus and Giroux.

Stine, R.L. 1992. *Monster Blood*. New York: Scholastic.

Stine, R.L. 1995. *Sangre de monstruo*. Spanish trans. New York: Scholastic.

Sternberg, Martin L.A. 1987. *American Sign Language Dictionary*. New York: Harper and Row.

Terrell, Tracy D. 1977. A natural approach to second language acquisition and learning. *Modern Language Journal*, 61: 325-336.

Terrell, Tracy D. 1982. The Natural Approach to Language Teaching: An Update, *Modern Language Journal*, 66 (2): 121-132. In Oller, John W., Jr. and Patricia A. Richard-Amato, eds. *Methods That Work*. 1983. Rowley, Massachusetts: Newbury House.

Terrell, Tracy D., Magdalena Andrade, Jeanne Egasse and Elías Miguel Muñoz. 1986. *Dos mundos*. New York: McGraw-Hill.

Terrell, Tracy D., Mary B. Rogers, Betsy K. Barnes and Marguerite Wolff-Hessini. 1988. *Deux mondes*. New York: McGraw-Hill.

Turner, Lisa Ray and Blaine Ray. 1998. *Casi se muere*. Bakersfield, CA: Blaine Ray Workshops and Berkeley, CA: Command Performance.

Turner, Lisa Ray and Blaine Ray. 2000a. *El viaje de su vida*. Bakersfield, CA: Blaine Ray Workshops and Berkeley, CA: Command Performance.

Turner, Lisa Ray and Blaine Ray. 2000b. *¡Viva el toro!* Bakersfield, CA: Blaine Ray Workshops and Berkeley, CA: Command Performance.

Turner, Lisa Ray and Blaine Ray. 2001a. *El viaje perdido*. Bakersfield, CA: Blaine Ray Workshops and Berkeley, CA: Command Performance.

Turner, Lisa Ray and Blaine Ray. 2001b. *Le voyage de sa vie*. Bakersfield, CA: Blaine Ray Workshops and Berkeley, CA: Command Performance. (adapted to French by Geneviève Poucel)

Turner, Lisa Ray and Blaine Ray. 2002a. *¿Dónde está Eduardo?* Bakersfield, CA: Blaine Ray Workshops and Berkeley, CA: Command Performance.

Turner, Lisa Ray and Blaine Ray. 2002b. *Le voyage perdu*. Bakersfield, CA: Blaine Ray Workshops and Berkeley, CA: Command Performance. (adapted to French by Marie-Cécile "Missy" Fleurant-Freeman)

Turner, Lisa Ray and Blaine Ray. 2002c. *Presque mort*. Bakersfield, CA: Blaine Ray Workshops and Berkeley, CA: Command Performance. (adapted to French by Marie-Cécile "Missy" Fleurant-Freeman)

Turner, Lisa Ray and Blaine Ray. 2002d. *Vive le taureau!* Bakersfield, CA: Blaine Ray Workshops and Berkeley, CA: Command Performance. (adapted to French by Marie-Curtis Briggs and Alison DeHart)

Turner, Lisa Ray and Blaine Ray. 2003a. *Die Reise seines Lebens.* Bakersfield, CA: Blaine Ray Workshops and Berkeley, CA: Command Performance. (adapted to German by Helen Small)

Turner, Lisa Ray and Blaine Ray. 2003b. *Fast stirbt er.* Bakersfield, CA: Blaine Ray Workshops and Berkeley, CA: Command Performance. (adapted to German by Andrea Kistler)

Turner, Lisa Ray and Blaine Ray. 2003c. *Mi propio auto* Bakersfield, CA: Blaine Ray Workshops and Berkeley, CA: Command Performance.

Verano de Varela, Patricia and José Luis Lopetegui. 2000. *TPR Songs.* Audio CD of 10 songs in English. Buenos Aires: English and More.

Verano de Varela, Patricia and María Rosa Sallaberry. 2000. *TPR Songs Workbooks.* Buenos Aires: English and More.

Webster, Mark A. 2003. "Research for Developing an In-service for World Language Curriculum Within the Tenets of Second Language Acquisition And Total Physical Response Storytelling," unpublished M.Ed. thesis, Grand Valley State University, Holland, MI.

West, Brana Rish. 1997. *Talk Your Head Off (...and Write, Too!)* Upper Saddle River, NJ: Prentice Hall Regents.

Wright, Betty Ren. 1991. *Ghost in the House.* New York: Scholastic.

Wright, Betty Ren. 1993. *Un fantasma en la casa.* Trans. New York: Scholastic.

Zelman, Nancy Ellen. 1996. *Conversation Inspirations: Over Two Thousand Conversation Topics.* 2nd ed. Brattleboro, VT: Pro Lingua.

ADDITIONAL WORKS OF INTEREST

Blanton, Priscilla, Lynda Cortez, Pam Pate. *TPR Storytelling Presentation.* Video. Austin, TX: Holt, Rinehart and Winston.

Gross, Susan and Joe Neilson. 2006. *Advanced TPR Storytelling DVD.* Bakersfield, CA: Blaine Ray Workshops.

THE AUTHORS

Blaine Ray was born October 24, 1951, and grew up in Boise, Idaho. In 1971-73 he was in Chile on an LDS mission. He graduated from Brigham Young University in 1975 with a degree in Spanish Education. He received his MA in Curriculum and Instruction from Boise State University in 1984. Blaine taught Spanish for 25 years in Idaho, Oregon and California. While experimenting with Total Physical Response in Oregon in about 1987, he began to develop TPR Storytelling®. He has authored or co-authored three levels of books in the *Look, I Can Talk!* series, as well as three books of mini-stories for the same series and the Spanish novellas *Pobre Ana, Patricia va a California, Casi se muere, El viaje de su vida, Pobre Ana bailó tango, Mi propio auto, ¿Dónde está Eduardo?, El viaje perdido* and *¡Viva el toro!* (Eight of the nine are also available in French versions, five in German, three in English and one in Russian.) He has given workshops in all 50 states in the U.S. and in 15 other countries around the world. For 35 years he has been married to his wife Christy. They have four children — Tami, Von, Shelli and Jana — as well as four grandchildren, and they reside in Arroyo Grande, California, or as of March, 2009, in Eagle Mountain, Utah.

Contee Seely is publisher at the Command Performance Language Institute in Berkeley, California. He was born in Asheville, North Carolina, in 1939 and grew up in Washington, DC. In 1961 he graduated from Princeton University. He taught English to adult speakers of other languages in Ecuador, Peru, Chile and the San Francisco Bay Area and taught Spanish in high school and to adults (including Peace Corps trainees) and at Vista College (now called Berkeley City College) in the Bay Area. He is the author of *¡Español con impacto!* (out of print). With Elizabeth Kuizenga Romijn he is co-author of *TPR Is More Than Commands—At All Levels* and of the *Live Action* series of books in English, French, Spanish, German, Italian and (also with Kazue Fukuda and Mary Sisk Noguchi) Japanese. With Elizabeth Kuizenga Romijn, Larry Statan, Elizabeth Hanson-Smith and Robert Wachman, he created the CD-ROMs *Live Action English Interactive* and *Live Action Spanish Interactive*. In 1989 he received the Excellence in Teaching Award presented by the California Council for Adult Education. Contee and his wife of 40 years, Maggie, live in Berkeley and have a son, Michael, and a daughter, Christina.

The Three Steps of TPR Storytelling

Step 1 Establish Meaning

Write the meaning in English (students' first language) on the board.

Gesture (especially for younger students).

Personalize the vocabulary:

Ask questions using the new words.
Ex: If the word is a noun, ask if a student likes it. If the word is a verb, ask if s/he does it.

Show interest by asking follow-up questions.

Ask the entire group about the first student.

Invite reactions by entire group.

Ask similar questions of another student.

Compare and contrast students.

Always look for confusion (hesitation or no response) and use translation to clear it up.

Make sure that every student knows all of the new vocabulary words.

Show interest and enthusiasm.

Capitalize on the comparison between students to make a little story about them.

Permission granted to reproduce this chart

Step 2 Story

Get actors to dramatize the story. The actor performs after each statement.

Spend plenty of time on the story (do NOT hurry).

Follow each statement with many questions. **Use a variety of questions:** translation, low-level, open-ended and creative.

Use translation to clarify grammar and structure. (Use pop-ups frequently throughout the story.)

Creative questions (that have no answer yet) invite unexpected or personalized details.

Students must answer all questions. They respond to statements with "Oh!" and "Ahh!"

Use the information that you learned about students (in step 1) to personalize the story.

Recycle parts of the story many times.

Retell the story without actors (but with more questions and embellishments) if you need to.

Teach to the eyes! Look at the audience, not at the actors.

Enjoy the sparkle students.

Step 3 Reading

Give students a printed story.

Students **translate** the story (as a group or one at a time).

Make sure that students understand everything in each paragraph.

Use translation to explain grammar so that grammar is tied to meaning, not to a grammar rule.

Discuss the reading in the language:

- Relate the situation, characters and plot to students' lives.
- Ask if they have ever been in such a situation.
- Capitalize on the cultural information in the story.
- Use the story to teach life lessons.
- Give a short quiz on the reading.
- Act out a scene from a novel.
- Discuss character development, choices and values.

Repeat step 3 for as many readings as you have. Extended readings and novels should be translated in this manner.

Based on a chart by Susan Gross

It is the teacher's job to show enthusiasm and to be supportive at every step of every lesson.

DISTRIBUTORS
of Command Performance Language Institute Products

Entry Publishing & Consulting P.O. Box 20277 New York, NY 10025 (212) 662-9703 Toll Free (888) 601-9860 Fax: (212) 662-0549 lyngla@rcn.com	*Midwest European* *Publications* 8124 North Ridgeway Ave. Skokie, IL 60076 (847) 676-1596 fax (888) 266-5713 fax (847) 676-1195 info@mep-eli.com www.mep-eli.com	*World of Reading, Ltd.* P.O. Box 13092 Atlanta, GA 30324-0092 (404) 233-4042 (800) 729-3703 Fax (404) 237-5511 polyglot@wor.com www.wor.com
Applause Learning Resources 85 Fernwood Lane Roslyn, NY 11576-1431 (516) 365-1259 (800) APPLAUSE Toll Free Fax (877) 365-7484 applauselearning@aol.com www.applauselearning.com	*Carlex* P.O. Box 81786 Rochester, MI 48308-1786 (800) 526-3768 Fax (248) 852-7142 www.carlexonline.com	*Delta Systems, Inc.* 1400 Miller Parkway McHenry, IL 60050 (815) 36-delta (800) 323-8270 fax (800) 909-9901 custsvc@delta-systems.com www.delta-systems.com
Taalleermethoden.nl Ermelo, THE NETHERLANDS (31) 0341-551998 Taalleermethoden.nl	*TPRS Nederland vof* *Broek in Waterland* THE NETHERLANDS (31) 0612-329694 www.tprsnederland.com	*Adams Book Company* 537 Sackett Street Brooklyn, NY 11217 800-221-0909 fax 800-329-2326 orders@adamsbook.com www.adamsbook.com
TPRS Publishing, Inc. P.O. Box 11624 Chandler, AZ 85248 (800) TPR IS FUN = 877-4738 Fax: (480) 963-3463 TPRISFUN@aol.com www.tprstorytelling.com	*Continental Book Co.* 6425 Washington St. #7 Denver, CO 80229 (303) 289-1761 Fax (800) 279-1764 cbc@continentalbook.com www.continentalbook.com	*MBS Textbook Exchange* 2711 West Ash Columbia, MO 65203 (573) 445-2243 (800)325-0530 www.mbsbooks.com
Sosnowski Language Resources 13774 Drake Ct. Pine, CO 80470 (303) 838-0921 (800) 437-7161 Fax (303) 816-0634 orders@SosnowskiBooks.com www.sosnowskibooks.com	*Follett Educational Services* Woodridge, Illinois (800) 621-4272 www.fes.follett.com	*Tempo Bookstore* 4905 Wisconsin Ave., N.W. Washington, DC 20016 (202) 363-6683 Fax (202) 363-6686 Tempobookstore@usa.net
International Book Centre 2391 Auburn Rd. Shelby Township, MI 48317 (810) 879-8436 Fax (810) 254-7230 ibcbooks@ibcbooks.com www.ibcbooks.com	*EverydayELL.com/Cutting Edge Education* Salt Lake City Utah (866) 697-7592 www.everydayell.com www.cuttingedgeeducation.com	*Teacher's Discovery* 2741 Paldan Dr. Auburn Hills, MI 48326 (800) TEACHER (248) 340-7210 Fax (248) 340-7212 www.teachersdiscovery.com
Canadian Resources for ESL 15 Ravina Crescent Toronto, Ontario CANADA M4J 3L9 (416) 466-7875 Fax (416) 466-4383 thane.ladner@sympatico.ca www.eslresources.com	*BookLink* 465 Broad Ave. Leonia, NJ 07605 (201) 947-3471 Fax (201) 947-6321 booklink@intac.com www.intac.com/~booklink	*Spring Book Center* 491 Czerny St. Tracy, CA 95376 Toll free: (866) 431-1199 (209) 830-4455 Fax (209) 830 4400 info@springesl.com www.springesl.com
Encomium Publications 1124 Fuller Street, Suite 2 Cincinnati, OH 45202 (800) 234-4831 (513) 871-4377 Fax (513) 871-4312 info@encomium.com www.encomium.com	*Sky Oaks Productions* P.O. Box 1102 Los Gatos, CA 95031 (408) 395-7600 fax (408) 395-8440 TPRWorld@aol.com www.tpr-world.com	*Independent Publishers* *International (IPI)* Sunbridge Bldg. 2F 1-26-6 Yanagibashi, Taito-ku, Tokyo, JAPAN 111-0052 Tel: +81-(0)3-5825-3490 Fax: +81-(0)3-5825-3491 contact@indepub.com www.indepub.com